# How to Recruit, Motivate, and Manage a Winning Staff

## A MEDICAL PRACTICE HOW-TO GUIDEBOOK

### Laura Sachs Hills

With a Foreword by Nancy Collins

GREENBRANCH
PUBLISHING

Phoenix, Maryland

**PUBLISHER**
Nancy Collins

**BOOK DESIGNER**
Laura Carter
Carter Design Studio

**PHOTOGRAPHER**
Betsy Bell
Priceless Designs
Photography

**INDEX**
Deborah K. Tourtlotte

**EDITORIAL ASSISTANT**
Jennifer Weiss

**How to Recruit, Motivate, and Manage a Winning Staff**
A Medical Practice How-To Guidebook

Copyright © 2004 by Greenbranch Publishing, LLC
ISBN 0-9700469-7-9

Published by
**Greenbranch Publishing, LLC**
PO Box 208
Phoenix, MD 21131
Phone: (800) 933-3711
Fax: (410) 329-1510
Email: info@greenbranch.com
Website: www.mpmnetwork.com

This publication is designed to provide general medical practice management information and is sold with the understanding that neither the author nor the publisher is engaged in rendering legal, accounting, ethical, or clinical advice. If legal or other expert advice is required, the services of a competent professional person should be sought.

**Other Books By Laura Sachs Hills**
*The Professional Practice Problem Solver*
*Do-It-Yourself Marketing for the Professional Practice*

Printed in the United States of America by United Book Press, Inc.
www.unitedbookpress.com

*This book is lovingly dedicated to my husband*
*Cornell Dexter Hills*

# Table of Contents

## PART 1
## Recruiting a Winning Staff:
## Finding the Best and Brightest for Your Practice

## PART 2
## Motivating a Winning Staff:
## Boosting Morale and Improving Communication

# Table of Contents

# Table of Contents

## APPENDIX 2
## Sample Letters that Enhance Staff Recruitment, Motivation and Management

## Appendix 3: Tools for Staff Training

Included in the book is a CD-ROM which includes the following:

Appendix 1: A-Z Treasury of Quick-Reference Staff Management Checklists in Adobe PDF format.

Appendix 2: Sample Letters that Enhance Staff Recruitment, Motivation and Management in MS Word document format.

Appendix 3: Tools for Staff Training in Adobe PDF format.

# Acknowledgments

Many people have provided special knowledge, encouragement, inspiration, ideas, and/or assistance with this project. Particularly, I wish to thank Nancy Collins, Marjory Spraycar, Rebecca Roberson, and Dr. Marcel Frenkel for their extremely valuable help in editing this manuscript. I also wish to thank Bob Crawford for introducing me to the field of practice management and giving me my first break nearly 25 years ago. As well, I thank the many private practice professionals and their staffs who so generously shared their experiences, joys, heartaches, horror stories, and fabulous ideas with me.

To my daughters, Meredith, Alicia, and Victoria, I thank you for your support and encouragement throughout the many years I devoted to this project. I am so proud of each of you and I love you. Thank you to my father, David Kirschenbaum, who taught me to strive for excellence. Thanks, too, to my mother, Janice Kirschenbaum, who I know would have been very proud of this accomplishment. I wish she could have been here to see it. To Bob Sachs, I thank you for your support, friendship, and confidence in me as I developed many of the ideas that ended upin this book.

And finally, to my husband, Cornell Hills, I thank you for loving me unconditionally and for your encouragement, understanding, comfort, devotion, and appreciation. You have been my rock, sounding board, personal cheering squad, and best friend. You are always there for me through my worst moments and my best. I don't even want to think about how I would have done this without you. I love you and always will.

# About the Author

**Laura Sachs Hills** is a management, communications, and marketing consultant for professionals in private practice. She consults with practitioners throughout the country to develop effective staff management, practice building, communications, and practice management programs.

Ms. Hills is well-known for her no-nonsense, how-to-do-it staff management articles that appear regularly in *The Journal of Medical Practice Management.* As well, Ms. Hills is a popular public speaker for professional associations and conducts lectures, seminars, workshops, and teleconferences on a variety of staff, practice management, and marketing topics. She is the author of *The Professional Practice Problem Solver* and *Do-It-Yourself Marketing for the Professional Practice,* both published by Prentice-Hall. As well, Ms. Hills is the former editor of *Physician Manager, Doctor's Tax Report, Procom Update,* and *Professional Marketing and Management,* all monthly subscription newsletters.

Ms. Hills holds a Master of Arts degree in English from George Mason University where she is currently a doctoral student. She holds a Bachelor of Arts degree with honors from Rutgers College and is a member of *Phi Beta Kappa.* She resides in Fairfax, Virginia, a Washington, D.C. suburb, with her husband, Cornell Hills, and their daughters, Meredith Sachs, Alicia Hills, and Victoria Sachs. Ms. Hills is also an accomplished pianist and enjoys conducting music appreciation programs for seniors each week at a nearby assisted living facility.

# Foreword

As competent as you may be at what you do and as personable and people-oriented as you may be, your *staff* can make or break your professional practice. Every person who works in your practice has an important impact on the quality of care your patients receive, on your own enjoyment of your work, and on your bottom line. Your staff affects every aspect of your practice management, including your patient relationships, professional image, referrals, efficiency, and even the very growth and profitability of your practice.

Unfortunately, many medical practitioners and office managers lack the background, training, and management know-how to develop a first-rate professional staff. They deal with the tasks of recruiting, managing, and motivating their employees by using largely seat-of-the-pants guesswork, intuition, and trial and error. In the process, their practices are often plagued by interpersonal conflicts and in-fighting, poor morale, low productivity, needless errors and misunderstandings, employee turnover, embezzlement, malpractice, and the enormous amount of stress that comes from having to deal with such problems on a daily basis.

With this book, Laura Sachs Hills has put together a very readable and enjoyable step-by-step approach to personnel management specifically designed for a medical practice. You'll learn the very best ways to recruit, hire, motivate, evaluate, and when necessary, fire employees. You'll discover how to handle an array of problem employees, establish excellent office policies, conduct productive staff meetings, prevent or deflect staff conflicts, deal with tardiness, and absenteeism, become a better delegator, and much, much more.

Much of what has been written in the past on these subjects is very theoretical or is not geared to the specific needs of a 21st century medical practice. What Laura Sachs Hills has done so well with this book is that she has transposed important and time-tested staff management concepts into a simple and easy-to-follow program for comprehensive personnel management.

I am thrilled to have been part of bringing this excellent volume to publication. I hope you will read and use this book right away to develop a first-rate professional staff for your practice.

Nancy Collins
*President, Greenbranch Publishing LLC*
*Publisher, JMPM*

In this book, you will learn how to recruit, motivate, and manage the best people for your staff. As you read, you may be struck by the amount of time, effort, and money necessary to follow my advice. You may wonder whether it is really necessary to go through so much simply to have people work for you.

Every staff management mistake you make will cost you dearly, not only in terms of your own aggravation, staff morale, and patient dissatisfaction, but also in terms of money. A mediocre or poor employee will slow you down and cut your production, cause your patients to leave your practice, and discourage referrals. A dishonest employee can rob you blind. A vindictive employee can sabotage your best efforts. And, whenever an employee leaves your employment for whatever reason, he or she will reach deep into your pockets. It can cost you as much as one-third of the first year's salary to replace a non-supervisory member of your staff, when considering recruitment costs and lost production. Higher-level employees typically cost a practice even more.

Putting maximum effort into your staff is a good investment in your practice. In fact, I believe it is the very best investment you could ever make. That's why I wrote this book.

A top-notch, super-charged staff will bring you many rewards, financial and otherwise. Don't settle for anything less. I look forward to including your successful staff management techniques in one of my future journal articles or books.

Laura Sachs Hills
Fairfax, Virginia

# What This Book Will Do For You

*"What's your biggest practice management problem?"*

When Laura Sachs Hills asks this question at her seminars, nine times out of ten the answer has something to do with staff, no matter where she is speaking or to which professional associations. Finding, hiring, motivating, managing, evaluating, and keeping good employees seems to be nearly every private practice professional's biggest problem.

This book contains Laura Sachs Hills' very best staff management strategies for use in your medical practice, ranging from the very elementary to the very advanced. It provides practical, step-by-step advice and all the complete, how-to-do-it instructions you will need to implement them in your practice. In addition, this book is supported with field-tested examples, sample dialogues, action checklists, hands-on self-quizzes, and well over 150 tips, separated from the text, all based upon what has worked for others in your situation.

The advice in this book is outlined in a 1-2-3 bulleted fashion for your easy use, making it very easy to adopt any of these techniques for your own. The ideas are practical and realistic, and they work regardless of the size of your staff or the focus of your practice. And, Laura Sachs Hills has tailored the material to fit exactly with your needs and resources, no matter where you practice, your specialization, or your experience managing others.

*How to Recruit, Motivate, and Manage and Winning Staff* offers a dazzling array of special features that will help you manage your staff to its fullest potential. Notably, it:

- Presents scores of practical ideas that have worked for others. The table of contents should whet any practitioner's appetite for the extensive menu of staff management techniques that follow. In all, literally hundreds of great ideas are at your fingertips.
- Provides all the how-to-do-it, step-by-step instruction you will need to take any technique from theory to reality. Laura Sachs Hills has overflowed this book with the "this is how you do it" instruction you desperately need but that you won't find in other resources. It cuts through the theory and gets right to the heart of what you'll need to know, whether it is about placing help-wanted classified ads, interviewing prospective employees, motivating a lethargic staff, establishing incentives, dealing with troubled employees, taking steps for legal protection, setting and introducing new personnel policies, conducting performance and salary reviews, firing an employee—the list goes on and on. When you're done reading this book, you'll have no doubt about what to do or how to do it.

- Gives numerous examples and samples. When you're about to implement a new staff management strategy, it is invaluable to see successful examples and illustrations of how you might do it. Laura Sachs Hills has laced this book with scores of successful applications, sample dialogues, tables, and checklists. In addition, Appendix 2 offers a variety of prototype letters you can use or adapt to enhance your staff motivation and management efforts.
- Alerts you to potential problems and errors. This book will save you a great deal of time, money, and aggravation by pointing out the mistakes others have made in their staff management efforts. Use this book to put Laura Sachs Hills' expertise and the experiences of others to work for you.
- Helps you analyze your current situation. Every professional practice needs a clear and accurate assessment of its personnel needs and problems to develop a successful staff management strategy. This book will help you assess your current staff and your management shortcomings. Laura Sachs Hills uses clear exposition and self-evaluation exercises to teach you how to evaluate your situation, build upon your strengths, and tackle your weaknesses.
- Uses a no-nonsense, down-to-earth, concise style. Much of the instruction in this book has been boiled down to easy-to-follow checklists. Laura Sachs Hills purposely uses simple, clean, everyday language and writes in her extremely tight "newsletter" style, for which she is well known. You won't waste time or effort trying to decipher garbled instructions or convoluted ideas.
- Organizes the material in logical, easy-to-follow sequence for quick reference. Each chapter unfolds logically and is supported with many descriptive subheadings. As well, Appendix 1 offers 26 time-saving checklists to help you address some of the most perplexing staff management problems.
- *How to Recruit, Motivate, and Manage and Winning Staff* will be an invaluable tool for any managing practitioner, lay administrator, or office manager in a medical practice. It takes the mystery out of a complex, often bewildering subject and can guide you to a more productive, motivated, and trouble-free staff. Take the time now to skim the table of contents so that you will become familiar with the many staff management problems and opportunities addressed in this book. Then, refer to these pages throughout your career as you apply your staff management skills.

In your hands you have one of the best reference guides and time-saving tools you will ever find. Use *How to Recruit, Motivate, and Manage and Winning Staff* again and again to help you develop a motivated, caring, and productive staff.

## PART 1

# Recruiting a Winning Staff: Finding the Best and Brightest for Your Practice

# Creating Job Descriptions and a Job Applicant Wish List

*How can you recognize the best job applicant for an open position in your practice when he or she shows up at your door? The up-to-date, comprehensive job description will be your best guide. This chapter suggests what information should be included in job descriptions, who should write job descriptions for your practice, and when and how to determine appropriate salary and benefits for each job description. In addition, this chapter offers an important disclaimer for job descriptions that will protect you legally and that every employee in your practice should sign.*

A current job description should list tasks of the job as well as the skills, education, and experience of the ideal candidate.

Before you can recruit for an open staff position, you must have a very good idea of the kind of individual you should be looking for. Otherwise, how will you know what to look for or when you've found the right person for the job?

Ideally, every position in your office should have a current job description at all times that lists the tasks of the job as well as the skills, education, and experience of the ideal candidate. However, if your job descriptions are outdated, or if they don't yet exist, your first step should be to write one for the open position. Only then will you be able to write a meaningful recruitment ad, screen job applicants intelligently, and ask appropriate interview questions.

## WHAT GOES INTO A JOB DESCRIPTION?

The more detailed your job description, the better. At the very least, each job description should include the following basic information:

- Name of the position;
- Required skills, attributes, experience, credentials, and level of education;
- Preferred skills, attributes, experience, credentials, and level of education;
- Specific tasks and responsibilities of the job, divided into primary and secondary tasks;
- The person to whom the individual will report; and
- The salary and benefits you are willing to offer, for the position, perhaps expressed as a range from minimum to maximum salary.

## HOW TO DETERMINE THE SALARY AND BENEFITS

When recruiting for your staff, you will generally attract the caliber of employee you are willing to pay for. Therefore, to attract the best person for the job, you will want to offer a competitive salary that is at least a little above average for the position.

To begin to figure out what that is, try to find out what other practices in your area are paying their staff members in similar or equal positions. A good place to look for this information is in your newspaper's classified ads. Make it a habit to clip, save, and study recruitment ads from other practices.

If your job description is for a position that doesn't require professional experience or training, you may be competing for the best applicants with non-professional employers such as businesses, schools, or local government. For example, an individual who might apply for an entry-level receptionist, bookkeeping, or business assistant position in your medical practice might easily be employed outside a medical practice.

**Clip, save, and study recruitment ads from other practices.**

If so, skim the classified ads placed by local companies and other employers to find out what they pay for similar positions in their offices. Or, if you're comfortable doing so, call a few companies directly and speak to their personnel managers. Or, seek help from your local professional association, business association, or your local Chamber of Commerce.

> **TIP:** *Flexibility of hours, more time off, and unusual fringe benefits (including free or reduced-fee professional services) may help you attract excellent applicants. When you simply can't offer a very competitive salary, you may have to rely upon these to lure the best applicants to your practice. In addition, the small size of many medical practices can be a draw for some applicants, who dislike the impersonal nature of large companies. Include these as benefits as well as the more traditional ones in your job descriptions.*

## HAVE STAFF WRITE THEIR OWN JOB DESCRIPTIONS

The best person to write a job description for a position in your practice is the person already in that position. Your current staff will know all of the details of their own jobs first-hand and will be likely to remember things about their jobs that you won't.

If you don't have a current job description for a job opening and the person currently holding the position is leaving on good terms, ask him or her to draft the description for you before leaving. Of course, this is easiest when you know the person is leaving with ample notice. However, it is possible to ask even a former employee to draft a job description if you are willing to pay him or her for the time the task will take.

Your staff members may also be very helpful to you when you need to draft a job description for a new position. They will be keenly aware of the needs of your office and can be given the task of writing the description, provided that you explain clearly what you're looking for. Assign one person to be in charge of the project but ask him or her to draw upon input from co-workers. A staff meeting may be the best way to launch this sort of project.

Ideally, you should not wait until you have a staff opening to write job descriptions. Every person on your staff should have an up-to-date job description whether or not he or she is leaving your practice. Too often, however, a job description once written never changes and becomes outdated when the staff member's duties change and/or expand. Outdated job descriptions have no value. In addition, they can encourage resentment by improperly suggesting to staff that they are being asked to do much more than they should be.

> Include standard and non-standard benefits in your job description.

Every person on your staff should have an up-to-date job description whether or not he or she is leaving your practice.

---

### Who Is Your Ideal Job Candidate?

Your job description should indicate the skills, training, and experience of your ideal job candidate. However, beyond these requirements, you will also want an individual who is honest, hardworking, caring, and who will fit in well with your practice. While there are of course exceptions, the best medical practice employees generally fill all of your job description requirements but also have these traits in common:

- They put family first before work.
- While money is important, job satisfaction is their top concern.
- They have a good self-image. They dress and groom appropriately.
- They have a lot of energy that can be directed positively.
- They are emotionally mature. They show concern for others and have sound financial judgment.
- They are enthusiastic but are not rebels ready to jump on any bandwagon.
- They value a boss they can respect.
- They consider attendance, accuracy and diligence important responsibilities of any job.
- They have a need to finish a task once it's started.
- They take pride in what they do.

---

The most useful job descriptions are living, breathing documents that are routinely updated. Therefore, a few days before your scheduled performance reviews, give each member a copy of his or her job description and ask him or her to update it. You should do the same, because your perceptions of the job may be different. Then compare your revisions at the performance review and agree on a new, fully updated description. This way, you will have a new, up-to-date job description for every position after every performance review.

> **TIP:** *This exercise usually serves as an excellent springboard for discussing job performance in general. Revising and updating the job description may help you assess whether the staff member's job duties are appropriate and reasonable or whether he or she is the best person in your practice to handle each of the duties.*

## LEGAL PROTECTION FOR JOB DESCRIPTIONS

After you prepare written job descriptions for your employees, it is a wise precaution to have each of them sign and date a statement that accompanies his or her description, such as this:

- This job description is not intended to be all-inclusive. The employee will also perform other reasonably related duties as assigned by the doctor, practice administrator, or other office management.
- The doctor, practice administrator, or other office management reserves the right to change job duties and hours as needed.
- This document is not intended to suggest a written or implied contract of employment. ▲

The most useful job descriptions are living, breathing documents that are routinely updated.

# Finding Suitable Applicants for a Staff Opening

*Many medical practices run classified ads to seek applicant for job openings and do little else. Several effective recruitment strategies, however, can be used in addition to or instead of classified advertising.*

*This chapter suggests strategies for working both inside and outside the practice to draw in top-notch job applicants. It describes how local schools, employment agencies, and temporary agencies can help fill positions in medical practices and how such arrangements typically work.*

*This chapter also suggests ways to bring excellent former employees back to the fold. Finally, it offers practical tips for protecting yourself financially when hiring a new employee through an agency and paying a placement fee.*

When it's time to look for applicants for a job opening in your medical practice, you may think that all you need to do is place a help-wanted ad in your newspaper's classified section. Certainly, good classified advertising can be an effective recruitment strategy. In addition to placing carefully developed and well-timed classified ads (or even instead of placing them), however, you will want to consider several other excellent recruitment methods.

## SPREAD THE WORD INSIDE YOUR PRACTICE

The first recruitment strategy you might try is to tell your existing staff about any job openings in your practice. Your staff will probably

> Your staff will appreciate hearing about staff openings directly from you.

Motivated local students are usually ideally suited to part-time and summer work.

appreciate hearing about the openings directly from you. For one thing, they may wish to apply for the job themselves (if they are qualified). For another, they may be able to recommend someone they know for the position.

In my experience, new employees referred by a practice's present employees tend to perform better than those who become aware of the position through other means, such as newspaper ads. Successful employees often use informal methods such as the grapevine for getting a job. Your own employee may know someone who would be ideal for the job in your practice but who is not actively looking for a job change. Perhaps your employee can lure that stellar applicant to your practice, even though he or she would never respond to a newspaper classified ad or come to you through an employment agency.

Even in the smallest practice, it's best to hold a brief staff meeting to announce and describe the job opening, the requirements for the job, and the experience, certification, and/or educational credentials you are seeking in an applicant. That way, everyone who works in your practice will hear the information in the same way and at the same time.

---

### Financial Protection When Hiring Through an Agency

An employer often pays the employment agency's entire fee, which is typically one to one-and-one-half times the new employee's first month's earnings. This leaves you very little guarantee, since you can't recover the fee if the employee quits or is fired after the period guaranteed by the agency (usually 30 days). Therefore, many employers establish a shared employment-fee agreement. In so doing, they improve the chances that the employee will stay and make a greater effort to succeed. Here's how it works:

1. Pay half of the agency placement fee and have the employee pay for the other half.

2. Agree that if you are mutually satisfied and the employee stays with you for an established probationary period, your practice will reimburse the employee's half of the fee. For example, you might offer to pay the entire half of the fee in a lump sum after six months. Or, you might agree to spread your reimbursement throughout the employee's first year of employment, paying one-fourth every three months.

3. Pay your reimbursement to the employee separately, not in the regular paycheck, to make it more memorable and special.

Beyond your staff, you might also tell your local professional association, friends, family, and other area professionals you know about your job opening. These people may very well know qualified applicants who would be interested in your job vacancy.

> **TIP:** *Patients might be interested in your job or may have a friend or family member who would be. You must be very careful, however, that you don't lose, disappoint, or anger patients by rejecting them or their family or friends. For this reason, it is generally best not to publicize the opening broadly to your patients using means such as a bulletin board or your patient newsletter.*

## SEEK STUDENTS FOR APPROPRIATE PART-TIME WORK

If you have a part-time or summer opening that would be suitable for a student, you might want to list it with the job placement or counseling office of local high schools, trade schools, community colleges, or universities. Motivated local students are usually ideally suited to part-time work and summer work; they are very happy and even grateful to have good job experience. Generally, students are willing to take minimum wage or close to it.

Many high schools and colleges have cooperative education or internship programs that help match employers with appropriate student workers. To participate, you usually have to agree to:

- Pay minimum wage
- Guarantee a minimum number of work hours per week
- Complete two or more written evaluations during the term of employment

Most programs provide a director or guidance counselor who serves as your contact person. These programs usually have a mechanism for immediate termination if you encounter serious problems with the student.

Some tips for participating in a cooperative education or internship program include:

- Finding a student who has at least one full year of school remaining before graduation. That way, it will be possible to have the same student continue with you for a year or two.
- Hiring a student who might be interested in working full-time for you after graduation.
- Finding a student who is willing and able to work part-time after school during the school year and full-time during summer and

It is generally best not to publicize staff openings broadly to your patients.

school breaks. Many practices find it helpful to have the extra help in the summer when full-time staff members take their annual vacations.

> **TIP:** *A school's job placement or counseling office may also be a good place to recruit for a full-time opening. If so, remember that you must be willing to hire a fresh graduate who probably has little or no job experience.*

## TEMPORARY AGENCIES MAY OFFER PERMANENT EMPLOYEES

If you ever employ a temporary workers whom you'd like to hire permanently, call the temporary employment agency that placed them to see if they are available. In general, your temporary employment contract will require you to hire any person placed by the agency *through* that agency. That means that you'll have to pay the agency's buy-out fee or commit to a long-term temporary assignment.

## CHECK WITH FORMER EMPLOYEES

By the same token, if you had a wonderful employee who left your practice but is still living in your area, you might contact him or her and see if there's any interest in coming back to work in your practice. You can sometimes hire back an employee who left for personal reasons such as to have a baby or to retire. The circumstances may have changed for the former employee, who may now wish to come back to work, perhaps on a part-time basis. Or, you may have some luck if the employee left to take another job that didn't work out as well as he or she had hoped.

Obviously, in order to hire back a former employee, you must both have been satisfied, and the door must have been left open when the employee left. For this reason, it is a good idea to keep in regular contact with your best former employees, perhaps with a holiday card or subscription to your practice newsletter.

> **TIP:** *One practitioner invites former employee (whom he calls his practice "alumni") to his annual holiday parties. He finds this to be an effective and easy way to keep the door open for future employment possibilities. He also reports that happy former employees continue to be strong referral sources for his practice.*

## USE AN EMPLOYMENT SERVICE

If you wish to work with employment agencies, seek a recommendation. Ask your colleagues to describe the various

> You can sometimes hire back an employee who left for personal reasons.

agencies they have used and determine which ones have been the most successful. Then select two or three agencies and take the time to visit each one personally.

To begin your evaluation, meet the counselor with whom you'll be working. Give the counselor your complete job description, the qualities and qualifications you are looking for in the prospective employee, and the type of individual you wish to have working for you. Make it clear that you expect the agency to earn its fee by screening applicants for you and sending only those prospects that best fit your job description and needs.

> TIP: *Many employment agencies specialize in medical practice placements. Such agencies can prove to be useful when you need to find qualified applicants for hard-to-fill positions. Ask your professional association if it has a job-placement service or if it knows of any agencies that cater to medical practices (and specifically, to your area of specialization).* ▲

If you wish to work with employment agencies, seek a recommendation.

# Writing Classified Ads That Attract Top-Notch Applicants

*Advertising in the help-wanted pages of local newspapers and magazines can be an excellent way to attract job applicants to your practice. However, you will need to run a great ad to attract great job applicants.*

*This chapter describes step-by-step how to write great ads and is laced with examples of both good and bad ad copy. It shows the reader how to create an attention-getting headline, how to use a subhead to define the position, and how to elaborate on the job opening in the body of the ad, all for the purpose of attracting top-notch applicants. This chapter also shows ways to avoid discrimination in advertising copy, discusses the use of blind-box ads, reveals the best and worst times to place help-wanted ads, and suggests ways to evaluate ad effectiveness. Finally, this chapter includes a list of great words to use in ads, as well as examples of complete ads that readers may use as a resource for writing their own ads.*

You will need to run a great ad to attract great job applicants.

**Sell the benefits of the job and your practice by making your ad attractive and competitive.**

I magine for a moment that you are an excellent candidate for a job in a medical practice. Would this help-wanted ad catch your eye?

> Medical Office
> Full time, experience preferred.
> Send resume to: G-11, JOURNAL.

My guess is that you would NOT be attracted to this ad unless you were committed to working in a medical office and this was the only ad for such a position in the paper. Although this is typical of the ads placed in papers every day, this ad is vague, impersonal, and lacking in basic information about salary, job benefits, and the employer's location. Also, as you'll see in this chapter, this ad violates just about every rule of effective advertising.

## WHY IT PAYS TO WRITE THE BEST AD YOU CAN

In depressed employment markets, a poorly composed ad like the one above would still draw a slew of applicants. Even so, good recruitment advertising should help you locate applicants of *quality*, not *quantity*. It is much better to run a good ad that attracts two or three well-qualified individuals than a poorly written one that draws a hundred mediocre or poor respondents.

Recruitment specialists indicate that often the most highly qualified individuals already have jobs and are not actively seeking a change. Nevertheless, as many as 35% of these "cold prospects" read the want ads at least once a week. A well-written ad can lure these ad "skimmers."

There's another reason to abandon the brand of dull, uninspired ads shown above. Many people now take for granted standard employee benefits such as insurance, paid vacations, and holidays. Instead, they base their decision to apply for a job on whether it offers out-of-the-ordinary benefits, convenient hours and location, and whether it will be personally rewarding.

To get the best applicants, you must not merely offer your position and blandly state the essential facts. Instead, you must sell the benefits of the job and your practice by making your ad attractive and competitive.

## THE HEADLINE: YOUR ATTENTION-GETTER

The conventional rule of thumb in classified ads is that five times more people read only the headline than the rest of the ad. In fact, a catchy headline can compensate for an otherwise dull ad and draw a strong response on its own merits.

Think of your headline as the bait with which to draw in your catch. It must demand attention, perhaps even tease a bit, and make the reader

## Zingy Verbs for Recruitment Ads

| | | |
|---|---|---|
| Acquire | Demonstrate | Maintain |
| Adjust | Design | Manage |
| Administer | Determine | Modify |
| Advise | Develop | Monitor |
| Analyze | Devise | Plan |
| Apply | Direct | Prepare |
| Appraise | Draft | Present |
| Arrange | Drive | Process |
| Assess | Edit | Program |
| Assist | Enlist | Prohibit |
| Assure | Ensure | Project |
| Brief | Establish | Purchase |
| Bring | Estimate | Qualify |
| Budget | Evaluate | Rate |
| Buy | Expand | Recommend |
| Catalog | Expedite | Relate |
| Chair | Explain | Report |
| Change | Finance | Research |
| Classify | Forecast | Review |
| Close | Formulate | Revise |
| Communicate | Gather | Seek |
| Compare | Grade | Select |
| Complete | Guide | Set |
| Conceive | Implement | Solve |
| Conclude | Improve | Specify |
| Conduct | Initiate | Study |
| Contact | Inspect | Suggest |
| Continue | Instruct | Summarize |
| Control | Interpret | Target |
| Correct | Interview | Teach |
| Counsel | Introduce | Test |
| Critique | Investigate | Train |
| Deal | Join | Treat |
| Decide | Keep | Type |
| Define | Lead | Use |
| Delegate | License | Verify |
| Deliver | List | Write |

**Five times more people read the headline than the rest of the ad.**

want to read on and learn more about the position and the practice. Startling statements and thought-provoking questions usually make good headlines. For example:

- Do You Like to Help People?
- Here's the Cure for Boredom
- Come Help Others—And Help Yourself
- Shirley's Leaving!!! Can You Fill Her Shoes?

Be creative and put yourself in the reader's place. Ask members of your staff for suggestions. They are apt to know what might appeal to applicants like themselves.

Next, help your catchy headline leap off the page by giving it bold graphic treatment. Set it in large, bold type, larger than the ad copy, and surround it with generous white space. This will cost a little more than the typical classified ad, but it is worth the few extra dollars to catch the right reader's eye.

Finally, try to write a subhead for your ad to define the position further and screen out inappropriate applicants. Subheads can be short and to the point. For example:

- Medical Office/Part-Time
- Registered Nurse
- Downtown/Free Parking
- Office Manager
- Pediatric Practice
- Modern Office Building

## DESCRIBE THE JOB IN MORE DETAIL

Now that your headline and subhead have captured your audience's attention, sustain the interest with fresh and descriptive ad copy about the job and your practice. First, review your job description for the available position. Then, on scratch paper, list the job duties, skills, and qualifications that you absolutely require. Next, list those you'd prefer that your applicants have, but that aren't essential. For example, some of the skills and qualifications you would look for in a front-desk receptionist may be found in Table 1.

Next, reword your top requirements and preferences in as interesting a style as possible. For example:

> *We're looking for someone with a pleasant telephone voice, good people skills, and the ability to handle a busy patient load while maintaining a sense of humor. Some typing and computer experience a plus.*

Don't try to convey every aspect of the job, but only the most important, attractive, and interesting. Remember, your goals are to pique curiosity,

> Help your headline leap off the page by giving it bold graphic treatment.

### TABLE 1.

| Required skills | Preferred skills |
| --- | --- |
| Good telephone voice | Medical office experience |
| Neat appearance | Typing/word processing |
| Good with people | Business school training |
| Good spelling and grammar | Computer training/experience |
| Attention to detail | Bilingual |
| Neat, legible handwriting | Insurance processing experience |

| TABLE 2. | |
|---|---|
| Formal, impersonal | Informal, personalized with pronouns |
| Receptionist; much patient contact | As our receptionist, you will be the first contact many new patients have with our busy office. |
| Must have proven ability to function well | We're looking for someone with good organizational skills who can handle high-stress office situations with grace and a smile. |

generate enthusiasm, provoke response, and eliminate unsuitable candidates. Don't try to tell everything in the ad.

When possible, personalize your ad copy by using pronouns, such as "you," "we," and "our." Use relatively informal language. For instance, use simple words and contractions as you would in speaking. This makes your office seem like a more desirable place to work. Through your language, communicate that you are a group of caring human beings, not a large, faceless machine. Compare the examples in Table 2.

## ACCENTUATE THE POSITIVE

As you write your ad copy, try to answer every reader's unspoken desire to know, "What's in it for me?" by playing up the benefits of the job. Describe in as upbeat a tone as possible all the "goodies" that come with the position.

For example, if you have unusually good fringe benefits such as well days (as opposed to "sick days"), health club membership, floating holidays, a uniform allowance, or childcare credit, say so in your ad. Do you offer especially pleasant surroundings? A newly remodeled or expanded office? An incentive bonus plan? Continuing education? Then put that right at the top. For example:

> We enjoy a fully-equipped staff lounge, 12 paid holidays each year, and convenient downtown location one block from the King Street Metro station.

It's also beneficial to describe yourself a little. Do you run a general practice, or specialize? How many doctors are in your office? Do you keep evening or weekend hours, and would the applicant be expected to work them? For example:

> We're a three-doctor, very progressive orthopedic practice specializing in pediatrics, and we're open on Saturdays.

## SHOULD YOU LIST THE SALARY?

Most experts believe that you *should* indicate the salary, or salary range, in the ad. Omitting the salary leads to time-consuming contact with applicants interested in salaries that exceed what you will pay. In general, fewer people respond to ads that omit salary.

Most experts believe that you should indicate the salary, or salary range, in the ad.

> It is worth a few extra dollars to catch the right reader's eye.

# SAMPLE CLASSIFIED ADS

Here are three excellent recruitment ads for positions in medical practices. Feel free to use all or part of them when writing your own classified ads.

### HERE'S THE CURE FOR BOREDOM
OB-GYN Office Receptionist—Full-Time

As our receptionist, you will be the first contact that many new patients have in the obstetrics portion of our busy, five-doctor OB-GYN practice. We're looking for a vivacious, sensitive individual with a pleasant telephone voice, good people skills, and the ability to handle a busy patient load while maintaining a calm disposition. Some typing and computer experience will be a plus. Come join our growing practice and enjoy a fully-equipped staff lounge, 11 paid holidays each year, and the chance to help bring healthy babies into the world. Salary: $26,000/year or more, depending upon experience and qualifications. Call Susan Rigby at 555-1234 between 9:00 and 12:00 for more information or to apply, or send a letter of interest stating experience and background to: Dr. Milton Kaplan, 1234 Avenue J, Brooklyn, NY 11234.

### DO YOU LOVE KIDS?
Pediatric Nurse Practitioner—Part-Time

Here's a great opportunity for a caring nurse practitioner who is crazy about kids and who enjoys a busy, fast-paced day, especially during cold and flu season. We are a growing, four-doctor pediatric practice located in a modern, bright office on Madison's progressive West side, and we seek a hard working nurse practitioner to help manage a steady flow of patients three days a week. Salary: Up to $35/hour, depending on experience and qualifications. To apply, stop by our office between 9:00 and 12:00 this week to meet Myra and to fill out an application form. Children's Medical Associates, 3500 Odana Road, Madison, WI 53711.

### SHIRLEY'S LEAVING—CAN YOU FILL HER SHOES?
X-Ray Technician, Orthopedics—Full-Time

Shirley's husband was transferred suddenly, so we have an immediate opening for a meticulous X-ray technician in our Bellefonte office. If you fit that description and would like to work in a restored Victorian mansion in the historical district, read on. We're a progressive, two-doctor orthopedic practice and offer our staff many unusual benefits, such as a bonus plan, uniform allowance, childcare allowance, and membership to AAA and the Racquet Club. We also provide excellent medical insurance and many opportunities for continuing education, Salary: $28,000–$38,000/year, depending on experience and qualifications. If you think you'd like to join our team, please call Carol Sturz, our office manager at 555-1234, or come see our beautiful office in person any afternoon this week. Dr. Ilyse Silver, 1234 Curtin Street, Bellefonte, PA 16842.

Salary is usually described in one of the following ways:

1. Flat dollar figure: $10/hour.
2. Amount to ceiling: Up to $15/hour, depending on experience.
3. Low-to-high range: 10 to $15/hour, depending on experience.
4. Base pay: $10/hour or more, depending on experience.

When possible, keep the dollar figures somewhat flexible by avoiding the flat dollar figure (*i.e.*, $10/hour). The most highly qualified applicants will expect to be paid more and should feel that there is a chance for that pay in your pay range.

## HOW TO GET THE READER TO APPLY

End your ad with a call to action. Tell the reader how to apply and make the process as simple as possible. Don't insist on a resume. Doing so deters unprepared cold prospects from applying. The best method is to ask the applicant to call or send a letter of interest to a specific person named in the ad.

> **TIP:** *When the position is particularly hard to fill, ask for the applicant to call so that response is easy and you can do some preliminary screening. For example:*
>
> *Call Norma Sletson at 555-1234 between 9:00 and 12:00 for more information, or to apply.*

Once the applicant calls, screen him or her to see if he or she is suitable for the position. If he or she is suitable, explain specifically what he or she is to do next: answer a short questionnaire, complete the employment application by mail or in person, or schedule an interview.

> **TIP:** *To manage the flood of incoming phone calls, try setting specific hours during which applicants should call. This will free up some of your receptionist's time, so he or she won't have to answer applicants' calls during peak busy hours. A better alternative is to list a number that applicants can call after normal working hours or on Sunday. This leaves your office phone free and helps you get quality people to apply who are employed full time and who may not be able to call during regular business hours.*

## TO BLIND BOX OR NOT TO BLIND BOX?

Glance again at the poorly written ad at the beginning of this article. Notice that it directs inquiries to G-11, JOURNAL. This is known as a *blind box*.

The best and most well-written classified ads will go to waste if no one sees them.

**Classified ads can be a subtle way to market your practice.**

Many employers use blind box ads to hide their identity, and in doing so, keep applicants from pestering them with phone calls or visits. A blind box ad can also hide the fact that the employer is seeking applicants for a position from the staff. However, a blind box ad is usually not a good recruitment strategy, especially for hard-to-fill positions.

Blind box ads discourage respondents. They have a lower response rate than ads that reveal the name of the employer. In fact, even if an ad is described as a "dream job," recruitment experts say that fewer than half of ad readers would answer a blind box ad. Many may be afraid that such an ad could be from their own employer, or that the employer would be unsuitable.

Also remember that classified ads can be a subtle way to market your practice. Many people read the help-wanted ads—up to 35% of the general population every week, 60% every month! If that many people see your practice name and associate it with a progressive, positive image, it's likely that some of them will think kindly of you the next time they need the professional services you offer, or are referred to your office.

## DOES YOUR AD DISCRIMINATE?

Once your ad is written, review it for any non-discriminatory requirements or discriminatory wording. For examples see Table 3.

| TABLE 3. | |
|---|---|
| Do say: | Don't say: |
| The position requires experience and maturity. | We're looking for an older applicant. |
| This is a beginning position—no experience necessary | We're looking for a young person. |
| We're looking for an individual who . . . | We're looking for a woman who . . . |
| We're looking for a bilingual, Spanish-speaking individual. | We're looking for an Hispanic applicant. |

When you have the slightest doubt about the wording, have your attorney check your ad.

## HOW LARGE AN AD SHOULD YOU RUN?

The best and most well-written classified ads will go to waste if no one sees them. Often, an ad can get lost among the pages of ads that appear in larger newspapers. For this reason, invest in a bold-face, large-type headline with white space around it. Run a relatively long ad, so that you have room to sell the job.

When the position is particularly hard to fill, investigate the cost of running a two-column or display ad. Such ads facilitate the use of more white space and graphics to draw attention to your message.

TIP: *An investment of 2% of the position's annual salary in advertising will repay itself many times over, if it helps you attract and hire a competent, highly motivated applicant.*

## WHEN AND HOW LONG TO RUN YOUR AD

Sunday is by far the best day to advertise a job opening in most seven-day-a-week newspapers. Also, Sunday-Monday is an effective two-day combination because applicants may read about the position on Sunday but be unable to call your office until Monday.

Advertising only during the week in a daily paper is usually not worthwhile. However, weekday advertising can support your Sunday efforts and is usually cheaper than prime Sunday rates. Ask your newspaper to explain any deals it has for buying ad space in multi-day blocks.

Some newspapers designate certain days during which they focus on employment. These could be especially effective times to advertise. Suburban weekly newspapers and small local magazines can also be a good source for classified advertising media because they remain in the home a week or longer. Homeowners' association newsletters that take classified ads can also be effective and very inexpensive.

Many newspapers recommend running classified ads for a long period, usually one full week or longer. However, you should run your ad only as long as you need to. In general, you will be able to tell if you have ample applicants after only a few days, especially if you ask them to call rather than write. Therefore, don't commit to running an ad for more than two weekends or one week unless you can put a stop to it and get a refund.

The worst times to advertise for job openings are just before and during holidays and on Fridays and Saturdays. Also, December traditionally is a slow time for classified ad recruiting.

## EVALUATING YOUR ADS

Keep a file of all the classified ads you ever run. Cut out each ad and paste it to a form that looks like Figure 1.

> An investment of 2% of the position's annual salary in advertising will repay itself many times over.

PASTE AD HERE

Where ad was run: _____

Dates ad was run: _____

Cost of ad: _____

Initial response: (How many calls/letters?) _____

How many people interviewed: _____

Who was hired: _____

Did this person apply because of ad?

Yes     No

Comments about ad effectiveness: _____

_____

_____

Figure 1.

Try to figure out what worked in your ad and what didn't, and what you can do better next time.

Review your classified ad file each time you create a new ad or revise an old one. Try to figure out what worked and what didn't, and what you can do better next time. In short, try to learn from past mistakes and successes.

> **TIP:** *Also begin to save classified ads run by your competitors and especially appealing ones for other types of jobs. Use these not only to learn what kinds of salary and benefits competitors offer, but also how to make your ads more competitive in the future.* ▲

# Preliminary Screening of Job Applicants in Five Steps

Advertising for a staff opening is a lot like fishing.

*If you receive a gargantuan response to your next help-wanted ad, take heart. Having too many job applicants need not be a problem if you take a little time to do some preliminary screening. This chapter suggests a five-step screening technique that will help you identify the best applicants from a large pool.*

*Specifically, this chapter explains how to eliminate unsuitable candidates and offers practical guidelines for ranking qualified applicants. It also offers advice about verifying job eligibility and using skill tests in the application process.*

*Finally, this chapter offers seven specific characteristics to look for when conducting brief telephone screening interviews with job candidates, as well as additional tips for making your screening process most effective.*

Advertising for a staff opening is a lot like fishing. You put your classified ad in the paper and wait. Sometimes you just won't get a nibble. Other times, the "fish" will be jumping like crazy.

Medical practices are often surprised when they find themselves inundated with job applicants' phone calls, resumés, letters, faxes, e-mails, and in-office visits. Advertising response rates are traditionally highest when help-wanted ads are well written, well timed, and enticing; when practices are located in tight or economically depressed job markets; and when medical practices advertise entry-level positions that do not require clinical credentials or prior medical practice experience.

If you receive a larger response to your classified ad than you had bargained for, don't despair. A large job applicant pool is usually more desirable than a small one. It is always good to be in the position of having a choice of applicants. Keep in mind, however, that you will not be able to interview every applicant in a large pool, nor should you want to. Conducting too many job interviews wastes your time and can actually be counterproductive. Meeting too many applicants will wear you down and may make it nearly impossible for you to keep applicants straight.

When you have more job applicants than you can interview, you will need a strategy for paring down your applicant list to a reasonable number. I recommend that medical practices interview no more than the top five job candidates, using the following five-step technique:

**Step 1—Start by eliminating the unsuitables.** Your first step in the screening process is to identify applicants who are clearly unsuitable for the position. Review your job description and eliminate any applicant who does not meet your minimum requirements for skills, training, attributes, credentials, or level of education.

For example, if you require the applicant to be a good writer, eliminate any applicant who submits a sloppy resume or letters with typographical and grammatical errors. If you require the applicant to be an R.N., college graduate, etc., eliminate applicants who lack these credentials. Also eliminate applicants who lack the level of experience and proficiency in specific skills that you require.

> **TIP:** *If you're not sure about an applicant's suitability, don't eliminate him or her without further checking. Doing so is unfair and may cost you a great employee. Also, eliminating qualified applicants because of incorrect assumptions on your part could be deemed a form of employment discrimination.*

**Step 2—Rank the remaining applicants.** With the unsuitable job applicants out of the way, turn your attention to the remaining applicants in your pool. Investigate each one *briefly* and then rank them as A, B, C, or D.

To begin, review your job description again, this time noting your *required* skills, training, etc., as well as the credentials you prefer for the job. Then read the completed application forms and sort applicants into one of four categories:

> A large job applicant pool is usually more desirable.

| Ranking | Attributes |
|---------|-----------|
| A | Applicants who have all of your required skills and all of your preferred skills. |
| B | Applicants who have all of your required skills and most of your preferred skills. |
| C | Applicants who have all of your required skills and a few of your preferred skills. |
| D | Applicants who have all of your required skills and none of your preferred skills. |

**TIP:** *When you're in doubt about an applicant's skills, give him or her the higher ranking. If you have an unusually large applicant pool, use pluses and minuses (B+ or C–) to differentiate further between job applicants.*

**Step 3—Screen the applicants by phone.** Your next step will depend upon the number of job applicants you have in each category. If you have only three or four applicants with either an A or B ranking, you will need to do no further preliminary screening. You can interview all of those applicants. If you have more A candidates than you can reasonably interview, however, conduct further screening.

A short telephone conversation is the most practical method for screening job applicants quickly. You have two choices here:

- First, you can choose to incorporate telephone screening into your application process. To do so, require all job applicants to call your office (or someone *outside* of your office who can handle the influx of calls) to respond to your ad. If you want to use this strategy, prepare a short questionnaire and use it with every applicant. Use this initial phone screening to eliminate applicants who are clearly unsuitable. Then ask only the qualified applicants to apply.
- The second telephone screening strategy takes place only with the most promising candidates, after you've had a chance to review all application forms and give them a preliminary ranking. You might call your 10 or 15 most highly rated candidates to try to determine which five you should invite to your office for an in-depth interview. Before you pick up the phone, prepare for the conversation by jotting down specific thoughts or questions you have about the candidate from his or her application, resumé, or letter. Prepare one or two thought-provoking questions to ask all applicants so you can compare their answers side by side. (See accompanying sidebar for a list of possible questions/concerns for telephone screenings.)

**Step 4—Choose applicants to interview.** Your goal in screening will be to invite the five highest-ranked applicants to your office for an in-person interview. In the ideal case, you will choose five candidates with a very strong ranking.

If you have more A candidates than you can reasonably interview, conduct further screening.

Incorporate telephone screening into your application process.

## What to Look for When Screening Applicants by Phone

When screening job applicants with a brief phone interview, you might take note of the following characteristics:

1. **Salary expectations (ballpark figure):** It makes no sense to interview applicants who feel that they must make more money than you can reasonably pay. Ask all applicants to describe their salary goals.

2. **Transportation:** Describe where your practice is and ask if commuting to and from your office will be a problem.

3. **Hours:** Describe the hours the applicant would be expected to work and ask if they will be a problem.

4. **Long-term view:** Is the applicant looking for a job with great opportunity for advancement? Discuss long-term career goals, as well as the applicant's plans for staying in your geographic area.

5. **First impression:** Listen to the applicant's voice when he or she answers the phone before you tell who is calling. If the applicant seems to answer with a smile, that's a great sign. If the applicant's voice picks up a bit when he or she learns who you are, that's still very encouraging.

6. **Professionalism:** Listen for grammatical errors, inappropriate use of slang, undue awkwardness, etc.

7. **Poise:** Ask one or two questions that will help you assess how the candidate might respond when put on the spot. Don't be confrontational. Rather, keep your questions friendly, open-ended, and easy. For example, you might ask what made the applicant apply for the job. Or, simply ask the applicant to tell you a little bit about himself or herself.

Rank the applicant numerically when you hang up. If you feel he or she made your day, give that person a 10. If you wish you hadn't called, rank the applicant a 1.

For harder-to-fill positions, you may need to revise your expectations and interview candidates in your B, C, or even D categories. A candidate with the right personality and abilities can usually acquire the specific skills or training that he or she lacks. It is smarter in the long run to hire an employee with a C or D ranking who has the potential to become an A than one who is a B but will never improve.

**TIP:** *If an applicant strikes your fancy but has a lower ranking than other candidates, take a chance and interview him or her* *anyway. Instinct is usually right in these cases. The applicant may turn out to be a diamond in the rough and just the person you've been looking for.*

**Step 5—Verify the applicant's work eligibility.** Before you invest time and effort in the applicant with an interview, take a moment to verify that he or she is eligible to work in your practice. All employers must verify work eligibility. There are no exceptions, no matter where you practice or how many people you employ. The penalty if you don't verify work eligibility is a stiff fine by the U.S. Immigration and Naturalization Service.

While you're screening on the phone or on your application form, ask the job applicant whether he or she is a U.S. citizen or eligible to work as an employee in your office. If so and you have ranked him or her highly, conduct your interview. Before you hire the applicant, however, you must still establish identity and work eligibility. Contact your attorney or the local Immigration and Naturalization Service Office if you have any questions about the procedure for establishing an applicant's work eligibility.

## ADDITIONAL TIPS FOR IMPLEMENTING THE FIVE-STEP SCREENING TECHNIQUE

Here are several tips when you screen a large pool of job applicants for a staff opening:

1. **Choose the best person or people to do your screening.** The person should have good instincts about people and be able to make good decisions. The screener should not be averse to

> **All employers must verify work eligibility.**

---

### Use Applicant Skills Testing with Care

Administering a test to assess a job applicant's skill level is legal. For example, many employers issue typing tests or other skills tests. Three factors are extremely important when issuing skills tests to job applicants:

1. The skill must be required for the job.
2. The test must accurately assess the applicant's skill level.
3. The test must be nondiscriminatory and issued to all job applicants in a consistent, nondiscriminatory fashion.

For legal protection, have your attorney review all screening tests you intend to use to determine whether they do or might discriminate unfairly. Avoid any test that leaves you vulnerable to the charge of unfair hiring practices.

Turn no applicant away until you have filled the position.

conducting the screening and should not feel desperate to fill the vacant position. Busy practices or those with urgent needs to fill an opening may wish to hire out the screening process.

2. **Have one person do all of your screening.** Or, if several people will take part in the screening process, have them all review all of the applications. Do not divide the screening task. Screen every applicant with the same eyes and ears so you can be consistent.

3. If your classified ad draws in a large number of unsuita le applicants, review your ad copy critically. Look for ways to revise your ad next time so you can eliminate the need to screen unsuitable applicants. Did you leave out essential job requirements? Is your office in a remote location that is undesirable to typical applicants? Did you omit the fact that you require unusual hours?

4. **When conducting telephone screening, make notes about each applicant before making the next call.** It can become very hard to remember who said what or what your impressions were of each person if you call them rapid-fire and don't take notes as you go.

5. Turn no applicant away until you have filled the position. ▲

# Interviewing Job Applicants for a Staff Opening

*It can be very challenging to identify a potentially strong employee for your practice based upon a resume or written application alone. That is why a well-structured and carefully prepared interview is such an important part of the recruitment process. However, many interviewers have vague interview goals or do not know how to make their limited time with the applicant count.*

*This chapter describes the key ingredients for a successful interview and offers practical tips for interview preparation. Sample interview questions, legal considerations, and interview follow-up tips are offered, as well as practical advice about involving members of your staff in the interview process.*

It's sometimes hard to tell who is more nervous during an employment interview: the job candidate or the interviewer. However, preparing thoroughly for and carefully choreographing employment interviews will go a long way to putting the interviewer at ease and making the interview more productive and worthwhile, both for the interviewer and the interviewee.

It is very important to be selective about the candidates you will select to interview. Interviews are time-consuming and require a great deal of your focus and attention. It is in no one's interest to waste time interviewing applicants who are unsuitable for the job. Therefore, I strongly suggest that interviewers avoid interviewing dozens of applicants. Rather, it is much more effective to screen the qualifications of job applicants for a staff opening and select the top three, four, or five candidates for in-person interviews.

> It's sometimes hard to tell who is more nervous during an employment interview: the job candidate or the interviewer.

To be able to evaluate all job candidates on a level playing field, have each one complete your practice's application form, even if he or she has submitted a resume. Read each application very carefully and critically to spot discrepancies, gaps, ambiguities, or other concerns. Then aggressively seek answers to make-or-break questions through a telephone (not in-person) screening with the applicant. Then, if the applicant is still in the running, invite him or her to your office for a face-to-face meeting.

## BASIC LOGISTICS FOR EFFECTIVE INTERVIEWS

You'll need no more than 30 minutes for most interviews. In some cases, you'll need no more than 5 to 10 minutes. However, schedule interviews 30 to 45 minutes apart so you'll have the time you need both for the interview and for recording your thoughts immediately afterwards.

Choose a private, non-threatening environment for your interview. A private office is the ideal place provided that it is neat and orderly. If possible, plan to sit next to the applicant, not behind a foreboding desk, either in front of the desk or at a conference table. As well, plan to have your phone calls held during the interview.

> **TIP:** *Many interviewers find that it is least disruptive to their schedules to hold interviews before or after office hours or during lunch hour. However, if you would like to do this, be sure to have at least one other person from your staff present. Don't allow yourself to be alone in your office with a job applicant at any time, especially one who is of the opposite gender. Doing so risks physical harm and false accusations.*

## HOW TO PREPARE FOR EACH INTERVIEW

Because the job application is filed in advance and you'll have conducted a preliminary telephone screening to straighten out ambiguities, there should be no need to waste time during the interview to cover simple background information. Before the applicant arrives, read his or her application again and underline in red any items that continue to concern you such as missing information, frequent changes in employment, misspellings, conflicting information, or sloppiness. Then use a blue marker to underline the applicant's particular strengths.

On a separate sheet of paper, note the questions you'd like to ask about the application. As well, note general questions you'd like to ask all applicants. (See sample on next page.)

**Aggressively seek answers to make-or-break questions through a telephone screening.**

## 30 Excellent Interview Questions

1. Now that you've told me a little about yourself, why do you think you'd like to work here as our receptionist?
2. Why is a position in this office important to you?
3. Tell me some of the things that happened in other jobs that were particularly satisfying to you.
4. What would you most like me to know about you?
5. What did you think of your previous employer?
6. What would you like me to tell you about the position?
7. If you could have made any changes in our last job, what would they have been?
8. What did you like most and least about your last job?
9. What was your most interesting job or project?
10. Describe the best person you ever worked with.
11. How would working in our practice benefit you?
12. Which three characteristics best describe you? Why?
13. Why did you leave your past jobs?
14. When you and your former employer had a disagreement, how did you resolve the conflict?
15. What were your responsibilities in your last job?
16. Describe the best boss you ever had. The worst.
17. What are your greatest strengths? Weaknesses?
18. If you had the experience, training, talent, etc. to do any job, what would you do?
19. What are your five-year goals? Ten-year?
20. What do you expect from the office that hires you?
21. What would you do if your boss made a decision with which you strongly disagree?
22. Is there any reason you don't expect to perform this job for at least the next three years?
23. Do you have the legal right to work in the United States?
24. May I contact your present employer?
25. Can your vacation schedule be arranged around the schedule of our office?
26. Do you have any physical or mental conditions that may limit your ability to perform this job?
27. How many days of work do you feel you've missed in the last two years? Why?
28. What do you think constitutes a good attendance record? What do you consider to be good reasons for missing work?
29. Is there any reason that you can't be bonded?
30. What do you think each of your references would say about you, positive and negative?

Choose a private, non-threatening environment for your interview.

## GREETING THE APPLICANT

When the applicant arrives, your receptionist should greet him or her as he/she would greet any guest. Specifically, your receptionist should:

- Introduce himself or herself, smile, and give a warm welcome.
- Explain where the applicant can hand his/her coat, put a wet umbrella, etc.
- Suggest that the applicant take a seat, relax, read a magazine, etc.
- Explain how long you'll be before you see the applicant.

Just as it is important that the applicant make a good first impression on you, it is equally important that you and your staff make a good first impression on the applicant, particularly if you must compete with other practices for top-notch employees. You'll want the applicant to take the job—enthusiastically—if it turns out that you offer it to him or her.

## HOW TO BEGIN THE INTERVIEW

The applicant is bound to be at least a little nervous. This is not necessarily bad. You'll probably find it quite helpful to see how the individual reacts in a tense situation. However, you should do all you can to put the applicant at ease. Certainly, you should not purposely make him or her any more nervous than he or she already is.

Have your receptionist escort the applicant to your office and introduce you. Something short and sweet is in order, for example: "Dr. Tyson, this is Theresa Bowman. Ms. Bowman, this is Dr. Tyson." Stand when the applicant walks in, smile, shake hands, and say hello. Then offer the applicant a seat and sit beside him or her. At this point, note to yourself your first impression. Did the applicant seem poised? Awkward? Sloppy? Neat? Dressed appropriately? Inappropriately? Does he or she seem to have a definite presence? Or does this applicant fade into the woodwork?

Start off with a little pleasant small talk. A good neutral subject is your office and its location. For example, you might ask, "Did you have any problem finding our office? A parking place? How was the traffic this evening?"

Next, briefly describe the position for which the applicant has applied. As well, tell a little bit about your practice and yourself. Explain any important requirements for the job, for example, the starting date, the hours to be worked, certifications, required skills, etc.

Next, ask an easy question that lets the applicant talk. The best question to ask is usually something like, "Will you tell me a little about yourself?" If the applicant hesitates, lead him or her further with questions like, "What is your past working experience?" or "What job did you like best, and why?" The idea in all of this is not so much to gather information but

> Don't allow yourself to be alone in your office with a job applicant at any time.

rather to establish rapport with the applicant and put him or her at ease. At the same time, you should be trying to assess the applicant's poise and self-confidence.

> **TIP:** *You may be tempted to make a snap judgment about the applicant based upon these first few moments. Don't. Although first impressions are important, some people need a few moments to warm up. Others may come on like gangbusters but lack the deep qualities you are seeking.*

## HOW TO USE YOUR LIST OF PREPARED QUESTIONS

By this time, the applicant should be ready for some of your tougher questions. As you ask them, avoid questions that will elicit a simple *yes* or *no* response or that seem as though you're conducting your own Spanish Inquisition. A few thoughtful, open-ended questions will reveal much more about the applicant than a rapid-fire interrogation. Refer to your notes to be sure you ask all the questions you want to ask.

Of course, the specific questions you ask will depend upon the position you're trying to fill, the applicant, your own personal style, and how much time you have. For inspiration and to help you get started, see the Sidebar, "30 Excellent Interview Questions." To stay within the law, remember that there are certain questions you can't ask applicants, such as those about the applicant's age, marital status, children or child care arrangements, spouse's occupation, type of transportation, stability of marriage, ethnic background, religion, criminal record, pregnancy, family plans, and physical handicap. However, there are several subtleties of the law that you may not know. To learn about some of these, review the Sidebar, "What You Can and Can't Ask Job Applicants." In addition, if you are at all in doubt about the questions you plan to ask during an employment interview, consult your attorney.

Finally, be mindful of your own presence and demeanor during the interview. Many interviewers talk too much. Although your goal is to put the applicant at ease and ask questions, you must do so by allowing the applicant to do the majority of the talking. Remember that you already know what you sound like. You're there to find out what the applicant is all about.

## DISCUSSING REFERENCE CHECKS, AMBIGUITIES, AND RED FLAGS

At this point in the interview, you can tie up any loose ends that continue to exist. For example:

- Tell the applicant that you may or will be checking references. Be sure you know all other names the applicant was using while earning

> Second interviews will enable you to make a more informed choice.

Be mindful of your own presence and demeanor during the interview.

## What You Can and Can't Ask Job Applicants

Legally, you can't ask a job applicant questions about marital status, pregnancy, physical handicaps, etc. Still, there are ways to gather needed information without violating any laws. Consider these examples:

### Questions to Avoid

- Inquiries about the applicant's name that would indicate his/her lineage, ancestry, or national origin.
- Inquiries about preferred title (Miss, Ms., or Mrs.)
- Name and address of relative to be notified in case of accident or emergency
- Applicant's marital status
- Number and ages of children
- Information on child care arrangements
- Any questions concerning family planning or pregnancy, even if the applicant brings up the subject
- Specific inquiry into a foreign address that would indicate national origin.
- Names and relationships of persons with whom the applicant resides
- Whether applicant owns or rents his/her home
- Suggestion that a candidate is not suited for a job because of a physical disability or his/her age

### Permissible Questions

- Inquiries about name changes necessary to perform a check on the applicant's work and educational record
- Name and address of person to be notified in case of accident or emergency
- Whether the applicant can meet specified work schedules or has commitments that may hinder work attendance.
- Inquiries about duration of stay on job or anticipated absences, directed to men and women alike.
- Applicant's address
- How long at current and previous addresses?
- How long a resident of this state or city?
- Inquiries about whether the applicant feels that he/she is capable of all the job duties you have described to him/her
- Inquiries about whether the applicant is aware of any conditions that may interfere with his/her ability to perform the job duties described

degrees or certifications or working elsewhere Double check that you have the names, addresses, and phone numbers of six or more job references as well as the *applicant's written permission to contact references*, former employers, schools, etc.

- Clear up any lingering doubts about the applicant by seeking more definitive answers about ambiguous credentials, dates, awards, or honors. If anything the applicant says seems vague or evasive, say so, and ask your questions again.
- Tell the applicant that you'll be interviewing other candidates for the position and when he or she may expect to hear from you next.
- Ask whether he or she has any questions about the position, your practice, or if there is anything else he or she would like to tell you.
- Finally, escort the applicant back to your reception area, shake hands, thank him or her, and say goodbye.

## TAKING NOTES ABOUT EACH APPLICANT

When interviewing five or more candidates in a row, it can be extremely difficult to remember your impression of each one, or for that matter, who was who. Therefore, note taking during the interview process is very important.

As each applicant speaks to you, take brief notes of those things that strike you most forcefully. List questions you want to ask as well as interesting impressions you get of the applicant. In so doing:

- Don't let the applicant see what you're writing.
- Don't allow note taking to interfere with listening to the applicant.
- Write in telegraphic style using only key words and phrases to capture your ideas.

Immediately after the applicant leaves and before you interview the next applicant, flesh out your notes and add further thoughts, either on paper, at the computer keyboard, or dictated into a tape recorder. Of particular importance, note special qualities that set this applicant apart. Answers to questions like those below will help refresh your memory later when you're trying to make a decision between several applicants:

- Do I like the applicant?
- Was I reasonably comfortable with him or her?
- Did I have doubts about anything he or she said or implied?
- Am I "on the fence" about this applicant?
- Do I find myself trying to rationalize on the applicant's behalf?

> **TIP:** *To simplify and expedite note taking, many interviewers find it helpful to prepare a short questionnaire to be completed immediately after each interview. On it, you might give yourself a chance to answer questions by rating applicants on a scale (see Sidebar for sample)*

> If anything the applicant says seems vague or evasive, say so, and ask your question again.

### Sample Post-Interview Questionnaire

Applicant's Name: _____

Interview Date: _____

| | Strongly Agree | Agree | Undecided | Disagree | Strongly Disagree |
|---|---|---|---|---|---|
| 1. This applicant seemed to be confident. | | | | | |
| 2. He/she was dressed appropriately. | | | | | |
| 3. I liked this applicant. | | | | | |
| 4. He/she was attentive to my questions. | | | | | |
| 5. He/she seemed to be enthusiastic about the job. | | | | | |
| 6. I would like to work with this applicant. | | | | | |
| 7. Our patients would like this applicant. | | | | | |
| 8. This applicant has the preferred skills for the job. | | | | | |
| 9. This applicant has the required skills for the job. | | | | | |
| 10. I believe this applicant would do a good job. | | | | | |

Additional Comments:

---

*Second interviews are important for several reasons.*

## CONDUCTING A SECOND INTERVIEW

Once you've completed your interviews and checked references for your top applicants, you'll be ready to narrow in on a decision. Occasionally, you may encounter an applicant who was so good that your choice will appear to be extremely easy. But even when that's the case, it's usually best to put off your final decision until you've had a chance for a second interview.

Second interviews are important for several reasons. For one thing, they will either confirm or change your initial impression, enabling you to make a more informed choice. For another, under the usual procedure of interviewing several applicants and then making a decision, the person hired is often the one who stands out from the crowd, not necessarily the best person for the given practice. Often, too, it's hard to keep applicants straight in the midst of several back-to-back interviews.

The second interview gives you the time you need with your top candidates. When conducting second interviews:

- Schedule another half-hour interview with your top two or three choices.
- Reverse the order in which you see the applicants for the second interview.

Recruitment experts warn that the order in which you see applicants can influence your opinion of them. Conventional wisdom among recruiters is that the first person interviewed for a job is three times as likely *not* to get the job as the last person.

- Review each candidate's application form and your notes from your first interview. Write down any questions you'd like to ask the applicant either about his references, information you didn't get at the first interview, or subjects you'd like to cover more fully.
- At the second interview, describe more fully what the applicant's daily job duties might be.
- If time permits, provide a complete tour of your office and introduce the applicant to members of your staff.
- Ask each applicant to skim your office policy and procedures manual and ask questions regarding job duties and office policies.

## INVOLVING STAFF IN THE INTERVIEWS

Who in your practice should do the interviewing? And who should have a say in the hiring decision? The answers will not be the same for every practice or for that matter, for every position you're trying to fill:

- Sometimes, the physician(s) will want the office manger, key members of the staff, or the departing employee to attend and participate in first interviews, second interviews, and the hiring decision.
- Sometimes, the physician(s) will want the lay administrator or staff to do the screening and first interviews and participate only in the second interviews and/or the decision.
- Sometimes, the practice manager or administrator or the staff can do the interviews and make the hiring decision without physician input.
- Sometimes, the physician(s) will prefer to do all of the interviews and make the decision alone.

Deciding whom to include and not include in your interviewing and hiring process is very important. Consider:

- **The position.** If you don't understand the details of the job as well as someone else in your practice, it usually makes sense to get help. You might also seek input from individuals who will work very closely with or supervise the new employee.
- **Your own management style and preferences.** It does little good to get input from others if you don't feel you want to or if you must make the decision alone.

> The order in which you see applicants can influence your opinion of them.

At the second interview, describe more fully what the applicant's daily job duties might be.

- **Time constraints.** Screening and interviewing takes a considerable amount of time. You may not have the hours you need to do a good job of it without delegating some tasks to others.
- **Staff availability.** An over-committed staff will probably not have the time or desire to participate in interviews.

> **TIP:** *Some management consultants suggest that the staff will be most receptive to and accepting of a new employee if they've had a hand in choosing. The flip side is that they may resent a new employee they didn't want. Therefore, while you will want to involve relevant members of your staff when you can, don't do so unless you plan to consider their opinions and preferences seriously.* ▲

# Verifying a Job Applicant's Factual Credentials

*Nearly one-third of all job applicants may make unjustified claims, exaggerate, omit important information, or lie in their resumes, employment applications, or interviews. Checking credentials before you hire is the best way to protect your staff and patients and to save time, money, and effort.*

*This chapter identifies the most common job application lies and pinpoints the three most common resume/application red flags. In addition, this chapter suggests specific information that the applicant should supply in the application to help the employer get to the truth. It offers practical advice for verifying academic credentials, employment history, and awards and honors. Finally, this chapter provides useful suggestions for avoiding discrimination suits in hiring practices and techniques for coping with employees who have lied to you.*

Checking credentials before you hire is the best way to protect your staff and patients.

Unfortunately, for employers, deception by job applicants is quite common, and today's medical practices need to be on the lookout. As many as 30% of all applicants for all types of jobs make unjustified claims or over-exaggerate or omit important information on resumes or applications.

The next time you hire, don't automatically assume that credentials the applicant claims are true. The only way you can be sure is to verify the facts yourself or to hire someone reliable and thorough to do the checking for you.

## THE MOST COMMON LIES

Applicants who lie are usually trying to hide, exaggerate, or sometimes falsify information about their past. Although the lies may be about anything, the most common ones are about:

- employment history
- former job responsibilities
- periods of unemployment
- former job title(s)
- personality traits, and
- former salary

In addition, applicants frequently lie about their academic credentials. In fact, as many as one-third of all college degrees investigated may turn out to be either faked, inflated, or at least modestly misrepresented by job applicants.

## WHY BOTHER TO CHECK?

Misrepresentation by job applicants is a real problem with potentially serious consequences. For one thing, candidates who don't get a job are victims when a less-qualified individual lies. More frightening, perhaps, is the possibility that employees and patients who come in contact with underqualified employees will be open to potential harm.

Hiring an applicant who has lied will also be extremely costly when you must later fire him or her. In all, staff turnover for each position in your practice takes up a great deal of time and thousands of dollars when you tally your efforts and expenses, including those for recruiting, screening, lost production, and training.

Checking references and credentials *before* you hire is the best way to protect your staff and patients and to save time, money, and effort. If you have no time to do the job yourself, you can delegate it to a staff member, partner, or associate who does have the time. Another option is to consider hiring an outside firm or individual to do the checking for you.

As many as 30% of all applicants for all types of jobs make unjustified claims, over-exaggerate, or omit important information on resumes or applications.

Reference checking can be assigned on a freelance basis to a spouse, former employee, or other trusted individual who is not working in your practice. Simply:

- Tell the freelancer what you need to know and where to look for the information.
- Agree on a fair hourly wage.
- Have the individual submit a written report and a bill for time and expenses when the project is completed.

## WHY JOB APPLICANTS MAY TRY TO DECEIVE YOU

Sometimes, job applicants who lie or exaggerate credentials don't feel they're in the wrong. Under the pressure to get a job, they may rationalize that *everyone* is, to some extent, engaging in deceptive practices and that it's not only understandable, but fair. Once on the job, they reason, they'll learn how to perform the various tasks and overcome the handicap of little or no experience or training.

Furthermore, the number of books, courses, and counselors teaching job search skills has increased enormously in recent years. Today's applicants are sophisticated and have learned that it's important to put the best possible face on their backgrounds, accomplishments, and abilities. Self-improvement books and resume-writing services don't counsel lying, but do suggest highlighting strengths and understating weaknesses. Some applicants take this advice too far.

> TIP: *Some applicants who are particularly adept at presenting the best image of themselves manage to remain technically truthful but IMPLY things that are untrue.*

## WHAT INFORMATION TO GATHER FROM APPLICANTS

The first line of defense when checking references and credentials is with the applicant. Even before you interview an applicant or begin your preliminary screening process, you should gather the following information:

1. Ask the job applicant to transcribe resume material onto your application form. That way, you're sure to get everything you need and the applications will be more uniform, and therefore, easier to compare.
2. Read the application critically and note questions to ask the candidate that will clear up uncertainties and ambiguities. (More on this below.)

> Sometimes, job applicants who lie or exaggerate credentials don't feel they're in the wrong.

> A signed
> application form
> gives you legal
> leverage if you
> learn later that a
> candidate
> has lied.

3. Have applicants note other names they used when they earned their degrees, attended school, or worked in other places. You'll need this information when you verify their credentials.

4. Ask each candidate to sign a statement that the information contained on the application form is true and that he/she accepts your right to terminate him/her if any of the information is later found to be false.

> **TIP:** *A signed application form gives you legal leverage if you learn later that a candidate has lied. Legally, there may be no limits (in terms of truthfulness) on what a candidate may claim on a resume because it is NOT a signed document. Thus, the candidate may disavow knowledge of its specific contents by claiming later that a resume service or other individual who helped prepare the resume fabricated or mistyped the information. However, a signed statement gives you strong legal footing.*

5. Also have each candidate sign a release giving you permission to contact references, former employers, schools, etc. This is an express waiver of the right-to-privacy laws. Tell the applicant on the application form that should you consider hiring him/her that you plan to check credentials and references.

## THREE RED FLAGS ON RESUMES/APPLICATIONS

Although it's very hard to uncover most falsified credentials without at least some digging, three red flags call for immediate clarification from the applicant:

1. **Education/Training Ambiguity:** A candidate may cloak educational credentials in uncertainty or describe them vaguely. For example, the two most common ploys are for the applicant to say that he/she:
   - "Attended" a school hoping that you'll conclude that he/she earned a degree when he/she didn't. In fact, an applicant can say without lying that he/she "attended" the school when he/she simply took a non-credit one-day course or when he/she was flunked out or was expelled for misconduct.
   - Graduated from a prestigious state university omitting the fact that he/she was a student at a less-competitive regional branch campus.

2. **Ambiguous Dates:** By providing an employment and education history in years rather than in months or dates, a candidate may try to imply longer past employment or hide periods of unemployment or imprisonment. He/she may also try to make it seem that he/she

obtained a degree in less time than he/she actually did. For example, suppose an applicant lists his/her past employment record in this way:

- 1999–Present: Receptionist, Children's Medical Associates
- 1996–1999: Receptionist, Office of Dr. David Kaufmann

From the dates above, it might *appear* that the applicant was employed continuously. But read it more critically. If you insisted that the applicant list *actual dates* of employment, his/her history could read like this:

- December 31, 1999–Present: Receptionist, Children's Medical Associates
- January 1, 1996–January 1, 1998: Receptionist, Office of Dr. David Kaufmann

Now you can see the truth quite clearly. The applicant was unemployed from January 1, 1998 until December 31, 1999. That's two full years! In the first example, when the applicant listed years rather than dates, he/she was able to disguise this fact without lying.

3. **Suspicious or Empty Awards:** Listings of awards and honors may contain substantial misrepresentations. The problem is most difficult to spot when the applicant lists "vanity" awards you've never heard of but that sound impressive. Membership in some organizations is a simple matter of completing an applicant form and paying dues.

## HOW TO COMBAT THESE RED FLAGS

Your best defense against false implications like those above is to ask the applicant directly for the information that will force the truth out of him/her. Specifically:

1. If you've never heard of an award or organization, ask about its purpose, requirements, and the organization's address and phone number.
2. If the applicant lists employment by year, ask for it by exact date or at the very least, by month.
3. If the applicant says he/she "attended" a school, ask whether a degree was earned, which degree, and the date it was awarded. If not, find out precisely which studies were successfully completed.
4. Ask the applicant to note the location of every school he/she attended by city and state. That will help you identify situations in which the applicant has attended a junior or community college before attending university. In addition, you will be able to see whether the applicant has transferred credits from lower institutions. If the applicant says he/she attended a state school with many

> Listings of awards and honors may contain substantial misrepresentations.

campuses, or a university with several colleges within it, ask which one he/she attended or graduated from.

## HOW TO VERIFY THE APPLICANT'S CREDENTIALS

Once you have screened applicants and are seriously interested in one or more, your next step is to verify their factual credentials including dates, certifications, employment, and degrees. Some tips:

1. Have the right person in your practice check the applicant's credentials. Don't delegate the task to an overburdened staff member who is hurt by the vacancy and anxious to fill the position quickly. He/she may not have the time to do the job thoroughly and may hear what he/she wants to hear to expedite things.

2. Begin with the academic credentials. Simple questions about degrees will be answered promptly by virtually every vocational, high school, college, and university. They'll tell whether a degree was awarded, what kind, and when.

   Schools don't usually give grades or course information by telephone. (Transcripts are confidential.) Thus, if the information is important to you (for example, if the applicant claims to have completed relevant courses or to have received a degree in a specific subject germane to the job) ask him/her to have the school send you a copy of his/her official transcript.

3. Next, verify past employment. A currently-employed applicant may ask you not to contact a current employer. However, don't let that keep you from checking with former employers.

4. Also check licensing or certification. Contact the appropriate agency to verify the credential and ask whether serious complaints have ever been lodged or disciplinary action ever taken against the applicant.

5. Check awards and honors. If a candidate graduated with honors or was elected to *Phi Beta Kappa*, his/her school should be able to verify this rather simply. Ask the applicant to provide the address and phone number of organizations you don't know.

> **TIP:** *If you require a candidate to prove certification, submit transcripts, or supply you with other specific documentation about his/her credentials, be sure to do so in a consistent manner for all candidates. If you fail to apply a uniform policy of documentation, you could leave yourself open to the possible charge of discrimination.*

> **TIP:** *Get official documents (transcripts, certificates, etc.) directly from original sources when possible. Photocopying and*

> The first line of defense when checking references and credentials is with the applicant.

*the use of digital computer equipment makes it possible for applicants to change names, date, and grades on seemingly official documents.*

## IN ALL THINGS—MODERATION

Although some job applicants may lie or imply untruths, keep in mind that the vast majority of applicants do present their credentials honestly. Preoccupation with resume fraud can lead to employee resentment. Therefore:

1. Do your absolute best to verify credentials and gather useful opinions about the applicant before you hire. It's nearly impossible to ask too many questions or to be too careful at this point in the employment process. In addition, recruitment is the time most applicants will be most cooperative. People generally don't mind being investigated or interrogated in order to secure employment. However, they usually do object to it once they have a job.

2. Once you hire, let it go. Don't continue to question an applicant's credentials after he/she is in your employment, unless, of course, he/she gives you good reason to suspect that he/she has indeed lied to you. Then,

3. Act quickly, decisively, and firmly. Remember, however, that you must assume that the employee is innocent of wrongdoing until he/she is proven guilty. Therefore, don't make accusations or take action until you have the proof you need. ▲

# Preoccupation with resume fraud can lead to employee resentment.

# Gathering Useful Opinions about the Job Applicant

*Getting people to talk to you about former employees' job performance can be like pulling teeth. It seems that everyone these days is afraid of saying the wrong thing and having even innocent remarks come back to haunt them. Most people say nothing. However, you can increase your chances of getting useful employment references by following a few basic guidelines.*

*This chapter describes the most effective methods for conducting reference checks. It suggests who is most likely to talk with you about a former employee and how to make your approach. It provides specific questions to ask and to avoid when seeking opinions about the job applicant. This chapter also offers simple and easy-to-implement techniques for using reference checking to build goodwill and referrals for your practice.*

Once you have verified a job applicant's factual credentials (see Chapter 1-6), your next step is to gather references from people who know the individual and his or her work. Here, you're looking for well-informed opinions from people with good judgment and inside knowledge of the person's abilities. As you might imagine, this is the hardest part of the reference checking process. And for good reason.

> Everyone these days is afraid of saying the wrong thing and having even innocent remarks come back to haunt them.

## WHY IT'S SO HARD TO GET THE TRUTH OUT OF PEOPLE

The next time you receive a glowing recommendation about an applicant, consider that very few employers answer completely candidly when they're asked to recommend former employees. Although most people want to tell the truth, they usually won't do so, at least not completely.

Perhaps it is simple human nature or good manners that make most of us reluctant to say bad things about other people behind their backs. Most of us will shy away from criticizing others when we know that doing so can seriously hurt the individual, such as by jeopardizing his or her chances for employment. Add to this that some people subscribe to the "every man for himself" philosophy. These individuals reason that they had to learn the truth about the applicant the hard way, therefore, so should you. They see no personal benefit to telling to truth so they don't.

Some reference givers may fear, perhaps justifiably, that even the smallest criticism will hurt the applicant's chances. Because other employers may give rave recommendations even for mediocre or marginal performance, they may fear that the applicant will look bad with anything less. This is akin to the problem teachers face in schools where grades are inflated. It is very hard (and perhaps unfair) to give a student a C for average performance when the other teachers are giving that grade for poor performance.

Finally, perhaps the most compelling reason that people hide the truth about job applicants is that speaking your mind these days can lead to a lawsuit from a former employee. Although the number of such suits is small, the stakes are alarmingly high. According to one litigation research firm, people who win defamation of character suits against former employers are usually awarded more than $100,000!

Thus the reference-giver perceives that his/her hands are tied. He/she may want very much to give you an accurate recommendation, especially when the former employee has been less than satisfactory. However, doing so may hurt the applicant, benefits the employer in no tangible way, and may even promote a lawsuit with fantastic damages. So to play it safe, reference givers usually stick to quantifiable facts and tell only the good. Or they may flat-out refuse to offer any opinion at all.

Also keep in mind that some people you contact don't have any choice at all about what they can say to you without risking their own jobs. Personnel policy in some firms prohibits employees from giving references. Others insist that everything be cleared through a personnel officer. Still others will verify dates of employment, title, salary, and other factual information and give no opinions.

> Most of us will shy away from criticizing others when we know that doing so can seriously hurt the individual.

---

**Sidebar 1.** Verify Factual Information About Job Performance

The easiest information to gather from references is of the factual kind, so that's usually the best place to start. To help organize your thoughts, you might prepare and run through the basics using this kind of form:

## JOB APPLICANT REFERENCE

Applicant: _____ Date: _____

Reference: _____ Conducted by: _____

Method of interview (circle one):        Phone        In Person

---

Question:                                    Response:

---

1. Ms. Brown states she worked for you from _____ until _____.

   Is that correct?

---

2. She lists her position with you as _____. Correct?

---

3. She said her salary when she left was $_____. Correct?

---

4. How many days was she absent this past year?

---

5. How many days was she tardy to work this past year?

---

6. Ms. Brown says she supervised four employees. Correct?

---

Fortunately, there are some things you can do to coax accurate and useful references from an applicant's former employers and co-workers, even those with tight lips. To increase your chances, you'll need to prepare carefully and know what to ask, of whom, and how to ask it.

## HOW TO CONDUCT THE MOST EFFECTIVE REFERENCE CHECKS

Reference givers are understandably reluctant to put judgments of former employees in writing, particularly ones that are negative or could be construed that way. Therefore, don't ask for or rely upon letters or references, at least without following up personally afterwards.

Former employers, supervisors, and co-workers tend to be more candid when approached in person, especially in a face-to-face interview. They usually take more time with you and answer your questions more seriously and thoughtfully. Moreover, the face-to-face meeting gives you a chance to observe body language and detect subtle nuances such as the raised eyebrow, deep sigh, or dubious expression behind a favorable comment. Nonverbal cues such as these may provide useful opportunities for probing follow-up questions and help you interpret the person's remarks more accurately.

If a face-to-face interview is simply not possible, the telephone is the next best thing. Avoid calling reference givers first thing on Monday morning or immediately following a holiday. They are likely to be swamped by other responsibilities at that time. Always ask the reference giver if it is a good time to talk, and if not, schedule your conversation for a more convenient time.

## WHO SHOULD CONTACT THE REFERENCE?

In almost every case, the worst person to do the reference checking is an overburdened employee who is most affected by the job vacancy and who is anxious to fill the spot. If an employee is to conduct the reference check on your behalf, that person should have strong people skills and the time and motivation to do the job right.

A doctor in the practice will be the best person to make contact personally when another doctor is being contacted for a reference. This sort of one-on-one meeting is often the most helpful. The reference giver is bound to take the matter seriously when a physician takes time out of a busy schedule to place a call or, better yet, pays a visit to her office to meet face to face. Although this isn't always going to be possible, it is a strategy you will probably want to use when trying to fill the highest-level positions in your practice.

If you are pressed for time, you might consider having a credential-checking firm verify that the applicant's claims are true and conduct the reference interviews on your behalf. In general, such firms charge several hundred dollars for services that include interviewing job candidates' former employers, confirming resumé details, running credit checks, and even examining court records to make sure the applicant has nothing unsavory hidden in the past. If you don't have the time to do the job yourself, hiring a good firm will be well worth the cost.

## WHO GIVES THE BEST REFERENCES?

Someone the candidate worked with closely such as an immediate supervisor or co-worker usually gives the most useful reference. The president or CEO of a large firm is not necessarily a great reference for

> Speaking your mind these days can lead to a lawsuit from a former employee.

## Sidebar 2. Sample Questions: What to Ask the Reference Giver

Once you get a chance to speak with a reference giver, it's best not to put him or her on the spot with lots of tough questions. Start with easy, factual information about employment dates, salary, etc. (see Sidebar 1). Then, once you've established rapport, slowly move over to the more delicate questions.

In so doing, you might begin by simply asking the reference giver to describe his or her work relationship with the applicant: how long he or she knew the applicant, what his or her job was, how much daily contact he or she had with the applicant, etc. Then, slip into the harder questions, always keeping your remarks as positive as you can. For example:

| Instead of Asking | You Might Ask |
|---|---|
| What would you describe as Ms. Brown's major weakness or flaw? | We have a good training program in our practice. In what areas do you think we might best concentrate our efforts with Ms. Brown?<br><br>Are there any areas in which Ms. Brown could have produced better results? |
| Did Ms. Brown have any problems interacting with others in your office? | How did Ms. Brown interact with her co-workers? Is she easy to get along with?<br><br>How do the other people in your office regard Ms. Brown? Were they sad to see her leave? |
| Was Ms. Brown's work better or worse than that of her co-workers? | How did Ms. Brown's work efforts compare with those of co-workers with similar responsibilities? |
| Did Ms. Brown ever get promoted? | Was Ms. Brown ever promoted or demoted while at your company/practice? Why? |
| Would you say that Ms. Brown ever exhibited an attitude problem? | What are Ms. Brown's philosophies on how a business/practice should be run? |
| Can Ms. Brown take orders? | Is Ms. Brown a good team player? |
| Did Ms. Brown ever have a positive impact on your business/practice? | In which areas in your company/practice did Ms. Brown have the most success?<br><br>Which part of her job did she seem to like most? |
| Who else can I talk to? | Are there any other references you might suggest, other people Ms. Brown worked with and knew well? Could they answer some of these questions? |
| Were you glad when Ms. Brown left your employment? | If you had the same position open, would you rehire Ms. Brown?<br><br>If you had it to do over, would you hire Ms. Brown? |

a candidate who worked in the rank-and-file because he will probably not be familiar with the applicant's daily work, shortcomings, contributions, etc.

At the end of your reference interview, it is helpful to ask the person you've spoken with for the names and titles of others in the organization you could speak with, such as the applicant's former co-workers or direct supervisors. Often, the applicant will give you the name of the person who will paint the best picture, not necessarily the person who know the employee's work best and can be the most accurate.

> **TIP:** *Ask the applicant to list at least five or six references. Then, start with the three who are listed last. Applicants usually list references in order of the most glowing to the least glowing. Names listed last are apt to offer a more balanced picture of the person.*

## HAVE APPLICANTS FUEL YOUR REFERENCE INTERVIEWS

When conducting your job interviews, or on your application form, ask job applicants to tell you what they think each of their references will say about them, both positive and negative. This gives you helpful insights into each reference's relationship with the applicant. It also gives you a good springboard for your conversation with him or her.

For example, based upon what the applicant tells you, you might explain to the reference: "Ms. Brown thought you might say that she had tremendous rapport with your patients. Would you?" or "Ms. Brown thought you might say that she had a problem coming to work on time." In this way, it is the applicant, not the reference, who is bringing up the topic, good or bad. Thus, the reference is apt to speak more freely on the subject.

## SHOULD YOU ASK FOR A PERSONAL REFERENCE?

Most recruitment experts warn that you must take whatever a personal reference tells you with a large grain of salt. Some go as far as to call personal references useless because they offer little information about job performance and are usually strongly biased.

However, the pattern of personal references may tip you off to something the applicant is trying to hide or play up. For example, did the applicant list only peers who worked with her on previous jobs? Does she omit important references from one or more previous employers for no apparent reason? If so, ask her to explain these omissions.

---

**Applicants usually list references in order of the most glowing to the least glowing.**

## USING REFERENCE CHECKING TO MARKET YOUR PRACTICE

By the time you conclude your interview with the reference giver, you will have spent a considerable amount of one-on-one time with him or her and, hopefully, made a positive impression about your care, thoroughness, and professionalism. Most practitioners simply say *thank you*, and let it go at that, squandering a fantastic marketing opportunity. Not only is the reference a good potential patient, but he or she may also be a great referral source, especially if he or she supervises many other people or is a personnel officer in a large company.

When you say goodbye, you might end the interview with a closing along these lines: "Mr. McCabe, I've really enjoyed our meeting (or conversation) today and I want to thank you again for your helpful comments about Ms. Brown's performance. As you know from personal experience, hiring is a difficult job but a very important one. Like you, I want to be sure to get the best people I can to work with me, my staff, and my patients. You've played a big part in the process and I'm grateful. I hope that you will not hesitate to call on me if I may ever be of help to you in any way. I will see to it that my office manager sends you some information about our practice as a follow-up to today's meeting."

Then, be sure to send a personally signed letter of thanks to the reference giver and enclose any printed material you have, such as your practice brochure, business card, and patient newsletter. Add the reference's name and address to your mailing list for newsletters, special marketing mailings, and invitations to open houses, speeches, and other practice building events.

When the reference giver is the personnel manager of a large company, you might send a stack of your business cards and other printed marketing materials to be given out to employees who may need your services. If appropriate, you might suggest or offer to conduct a program for company employees such as a workshop, lecture, or screening program. ▲

The reference giver may be a good potential patient and a great referral source.

# Making the Job Offer and Rejecting Job Candidates

*When you have a job opening, it is very important to choreograph how you make job offers and to whom, as well as how you reject unsuitable applicants. This chapter offers practical suggestions about whom not to hire and what to do when you can't choose between two or more candidates.*

*This chapter also offers tips about structuring the actual offer to your top job applicant. It suggests techniques and a sample letter for rejecting less-than-ideal applicants while maintaining their goodwill. Finally, this chapter explores the possibility of and criteria for hiring an applicant as an independent contractor.*

The final stage of recruitment efforts occur when you choose your top candidate, make your offer, have it accepted, and inform the other applicants that you have not chosen them. As simple as this part of the process may seem, a few precautionary steps should be implemented to make everything go smoothly.

## WHEN *NOT* TO OFFER THE JOB

Obviously, it makes sense to offer a job to your best candidate. However, you may find that for some positions, your best candidate is not of the caliber that you would have liked. Although compromise is sometimes unavoidable to fill a vacancy, you should not be willing to lower important standards.

When your best candidate is less than ideal, it is often prudent to offer him or her the job on a temporary basis and continue your job search. Alternatively, you might hire the individual for a probationary period and spell out exactly what training or skills must be acquired to keep the job permanently and by when. It is usually best *not* to offer the job to someone you can't fire (for example, your son's girlfriend, your mother-in-law, or your next-door neighbor). If such a person comes to you for a job, it is generally best *not* to hire him or her. However, you can offer to use your contacts to help him or her secure a job elsewhere.

> Although compromise is sometimes unavoidable to fill a vacancy, you should not be willing to lower important standards.

It is usually best **not** to offer the job to someone you can't fire.

## WHAT TO DO WHEN YOU CAN'T DECIDE

If you're having trouble choosing between two candidates, an on-the-job tryout, or "working interview," may help. Ask each of the top contenders to return for a brief on-the-job trial run, usually 1 or 2 days, for which you will pay them a fair hourly rate. This will give them the chance to see first-hand what they may expect on the job, and it will allow you to assess each candidate 'in the line of fire' before committing yourself to either one.

Some applicants may decline your invitation to the working interview. Of those who accept, some may not return after the first day. (One day may be all it takes to decide the job isn't for them.) That's good. The trial run will help you eliminate applicants who won't fit in or who won't be team players.

Remember, the paid working interview is a good investment, from a recruitment point of view. As well, the applicant you ultimately hire will already have one or two days of on-the-job experience in your practice. This will make the adjustment to the new job and his or her coworkers and your patients very easy.

> **TIP:** *Tell working interviewees in a letter that this is a trial run only and not a job offer. Ask them to sign and date the letter. That way, there will be no misunderstandings.*

## MAKING THE OFFER

When you have finally found your ideal candidate, be very exacting in making your offer. Spell out everything—pay, hours, benefits, start date, dress code, conduct, job duties, etc.

It is wise to put all new employees on a probationary period of at least 30 days. You cannot know for sure how an employee will work out from interviews and by checking references alone. Time and experience will tell you so much more. A probationary period gives you an easy out if you find that you were wrong.

## HOW TO HANDLE REJECTIONS

After you make your offer and have it accepted, it is smart to wait until the new employee has completed at least several days before you inform the other applicants. That way, the door is still open in case the new employee doesn't work out.

Rejecting applicants is difficult, but it can and should be handled gracefully and professionally, not only for the applicant's sake, but for yours, too. Although you may be reluctant to contact a rejected applicant, you owe this courtesy to the applicant. (This is especially true in a small community, where tongues may wag at a lack of courtesy.)

For one thing, if staff turnover occurs again, you may wish to reconsider one of your top choices for the opening. For another, rejected applicants can become patients, or even good referral sources, if they have been impressed with your practice and the manner in which you treated them. See Appendix 2-C for a sample rejection letter.

For example, a general practitioner in Innesfail, Alberta (Canada), has a florist send a long-stemmed red rose to each applicant he interviews and rejects. The cost is several dollars per rose, including delivery, but according to the doctor, the expense is well worth it. Rejected applicants are quite impressed with the V.I.P. treatment. This simple, affordable goodwill gesture keeps the line of communication open and has led to many new patients and referrals over the years.

In addition to or instead of this technique, you might give each rejected job applicant a one-year complimentary subscription to your patient newsletter. Finally, you might place all rejected applicants on your mailing list, so that you can include them in future practice-building mailings. For example, you might send them invitations to practice

## Ground Rules for Working Interviews

An on-the-job tryout, or "working interview," can help you choose between two job candidates. It can also help you decide about an applicant you're not 100% sure of. If you'd like to try using a working interview:

1. Be clear that the working interview is an interview only. Make sure the applicant does not mistake the working interview for a job offer. Put the details in writing if necessary.

2. Pay a fair hourly wage to the applicant for his or her time during the working interview. It is not reasonable to expect an applicant to work for you without pay.

3. Limit the length of the working interview to one or two days. Longer working interviews are not usually necessary and may lead to extreme disappointment for a rejected applicant.

4. Be reasonable in your expectations. An applicant will not know the specifics of your practice or your patients. Ask the applicant to perform tasks suitable to an outsider.

5. Do not spend large periods of time training the applicant during the working interview. If hired, the applicant can be trained later.

6. Choose tasks for the applicant that will help you assess his or her knowledge, personality, and working style. For instance, assign tasks that will help you assess whether the applicant is thorough, a fast learner, courteous, and professional and/or those that demonstrate clinical competency.

The trial run will help you eliminate applicants who won't fit in or who won't be team players.

events (such as open houses, office tours, and health fairs), holiday greeting cards, entry blanks to contests you sponsor, surveys, or new copies of articles published about you and your practice.

## INVESTIGATE "INDEPENDENT CONTRACTOR" STATUS

The vast majority of people you hire will be "employees." However, every now and then, you may have the opportunity to hire someone as an "independent contractor" (IC). If so, there may be several benefits to you.

An IC is someone who works for you on a freelance basis. Such relationships have been common for years in fields like publishing, real estate, and graphic arts. They can also make sense for some positions in professional practices. For example, it might be beneficial to hire freelancers to write or design your quarterly patient newsletter. You might hire a freelance consultant to do staff training or to conduct a survey of your patients.

The main advantage of using an IC is that you get work done but don't have to pay benefits such as Social Security and health insurance. In addition, you won't be paying the IC for down time such as vacations, holidays, and sick days. You also don't have to withhold money for federal and state income taxes or pay unemployment tax on the worker's behalf.

The IRS has strict guidelines, however, specifying who can be an employee and who can be an independent contractor. Generally speaking, the latter is just that—independent. An employer-employee relationship exists when the person for whom the services are performed has the right (even if it is not exercised) to control and direct where, when, and how the work will be done. If the only control you have is the right to accept or reject the finished project, the worker can generally be classified as an IC.

In determining whether a worker qualifies as an IC, the IRS must believe you have a reasonable basis for the classification. This is relatively easy to do if you act based on one or more of the following:

1. Custom. It's a long-standing practice to use ICs in certain circumstances, for example, on projects that require writing, photography, or graphic design.
2. Documentation. You may obtain a written opinion from the IRS that your worker is an IC by submitting the written agreement you have with the worker for evaluation. You might also have the freelancer sign a contract acknowledging IC status and responsibility for paying his own taxes.
3. Place of work. If the work is done at a location selected by the worker—his or her own office or home, for example—it supports

---

> Remember, the paid working interview is a good investment, from a recruitment point of view.

IC status. If the work is performed at your office, and the freelancer isn't charged rent, this suggests that the worker is your employee.

4. Hours. If you set the work hours, or you have the right to do so, even if you don't exercise it, this suggests that the worker is an employee. If the worker decides when to do the work, it suggests an IC.

5. Supplies. Does the worker use his or her own equipment? If you provide free supplies, it suggests the worker is your employee. The more costly the equipment the worker provides, the more weight it carries in proving IC status.

6. Pay. Workers paid on a regular basis (i.e., hourly or weekly) are usually employees. Payment on a per-job or commission basis supports IC status.

7. Benefits. Workers eligible for vacation pay, sick leave, bonuses, and a pension are usually employees, not ICs.

8. Supervision. Do you give instructions to the worker on a regular basis or require a progress report? If you're concerned only with the finished product, this reinforces IC status.

9. Accounting records. Workers who keep their own accounting records are probably ICs.

10. Other work. Does the worker offer his or her services to the public in general, or only to you? Someone who also works for others, or tries to, is usually an IC.

If you goof, and the IRS says your IC is really an employee, you'll owe a percentage of the employee's wages during the period of employment because you failed to withhold income taxes. You'll also owe the full amount of Social Security and unemployment taxes you should have withheld in the employee's name. Furthermore, the misclassified employee may be eligible for back benefits, such as vacation pay and insurance coverage. And, if the IRS finds that you intentionally disregarded withholding requirements, you may be assessed even harsher penalties.

## KEEPING APPLICANTS' RECORDS ON FILE

Once you have hired your new employee, you may be tempted to discard the other applications, resumes, and letters you received, especially those from unsuitable candidates. Don't. You may need these important papers someday to protect yourself in an employment discrimination suit.

Keep all applications, resumes, etc., on file for at least two years. Also, keep your notes from applicant screenings and interviews, both for rejected job applicants and those you hire. ▲

> Keep all applications, resumes, etc., on file for at least two years.

# Special Considerations for Hiring an Office Manager

*Medical practice office managers come in many varieties. They can be hired from the outside or promoted from within. They can have a great deal of experience working in medical practices or practically none. Which type of office manage is the best choice for your practice?*

*This chapter will help you decide. It describes three types of office managers and considers the pros and cons of each. It explores the characteristics, advantages, and disadvantages of lay administrators hired from the outside, office managers promoted from the ranks, and "super-aides" who are asked to manage while doing their old jobs.*

*This chapter also offers a list of 10 characteristics to look for in office manager candidates, as well as six areas of overall responsibility for your office manager. Finally, it includes a quick checklist of 20 required duties of typical medical practice office managers that can help you shape your office manager's job description.*

Medical practice office managers come in many varieties.

Recruiting an office manager for your medical practice is much the same as recruiting any member of your staff. The application process, preliminary telephone screening, interviewing, reference checking, and making the offer are essentially the same. The office manager position, however, has several extra concerns that need your attention.

## WHICH TYPE OF OFFICE MANAGER SHOULD YOU HIRE?

Medical practice office managers come in three basic varieties: lay administrators, promoted managers, and "super-aides." Each has particular characteristics and pros and cons worth considering:

### Lay Administrators

A lay administrator is almost always hired from the outside specifically to manage a medical practice, and may or may not have served in various office roles. The lay administrator generally has experience as a manager in another professional practice or even in a commercial setting. He or she may have a degree or other training in business administration or accounting and often has background, training, and experience with computers, marketing, and interpersonal communication.

**Pros and cons.** The lay administrator usually has significant management training and experience. He or she will have managed people and systems before and will be accustomed to making decisions and delegating to others. Lay administrators often pursue continuing education to keep abreast of new developments in the law, management systems, and computer technology, and to increase their communication and organizational skills. Many belong to a professional association for practice managers.

On the downside, any individual hired from outside your practice will not have an existing relationship with the doctor(s), patients, or staff, or knowledge of your practice-specific activities and goals. Thus, the adjustment period for any outside hire may be long. In many practices, existing staff may resent or even resist the intrusion of a manager from the outside, particularly at first. Often, at least one person on the staff feels that he or she knows more than the administrator hired from the outside. Occasionally, a staff member (or several) will undermine the authority of a lay administrator or leave the practice rather than take direction from someone hired from the outside.

### Promoted Office Managers

This type of manager is promoted from a staff position and is no longer performing previous duties. Selection of a promoted office manager

> Occasionally, a staff member (or several) will undermine the authority of a lay administrator.

# 20 REQUIRED DUTIES OF MEDICAL PRACTICE OFFICE MANAGERS

Medical practice office managers are often responsible for the following duties, which they can perform themselves or delegate to other members of the staff. (Delegated duties are still the office manager's responsibility, however.)

1. Determining present and future personnel needs.

2. Developing and updating comprehensive job descriptions with staff by listing all tasks each employee performs (and should perform).

3. Recruiting, hiring, training, evaluating, managing, and firing employees, using an organized system defined by the doctor(s).

4. Writing, updating, and interpreting the office policy and procedure manual. Seeing that staff members receive, read, and document that they have read the manual and are notified of changes.

5. Suggesting salary and bonus levels for each staff position based upon community standards, ability, experience, training, and standards established by similar professional practices.

6. Administering staff schedules, insurance, vacations, holidays, sick leave, and fringe-benefit plans.

7. Maintaining personnel files. Conducting performance reviews on a regular basis, with proper documentation. Documenting all pertinent staff matters including warnings for attendance infractions, substandard work, and insubordination.

8. Scheduling and controlling work flow among staff members.

9. Coordinating staff continuing education programs.

10. Planning and coordinating staff social events.

11. Arranging staff meetings: Distributing agendas, notifying staff of times and dates, attending meetings, ensuring that meetings are carefully prepared and facilitated, following up on matters that arise from meetings, seeing that follow-up minutes are prepared and distributed.

12. Conducting exit interviews and surveys when employees resign or are fired.

13. Evaluating office facility requirements such as leases, furnishings, supplies, instruments, files, security, and maintenance.

A good receptionist, clinical assistant, or bookkeeper doesn't always make a good office manager.

The most successful super-aides don't regard "office manager" as an empty title.

## 20 Required Duties of Medical Practice Office Managers (continued)

14. Identifying and recording inventory, warranties, and guarantees.

15. Investigating goods and services the practice intends to purchase by doing comparison shopping, obtaining competitive bids, and checking with consumer rating services, the Better Business Bureau, and references.

16. Assessing and overseeing all aspects of office maintenance such as utilities, housekeeping, security, grounds maintenance, and trash collection.

17. Assuming overall responsibility for public relations and marketing activities. This includes market research, the development of marketing tools (such as logos, brochures, and patient newsletters), publicity, media advertising, promotional events (such as open houses, speaking engagements, and office tours), and marketing education.

18. Working with the practice's accountant, attorney, and management/marketing consultant to solve problems and improve practice management systems.

19. Assisting the bookkeeper with practice billings, collections, accounts payable, payroll, financial statement, and budgets.

20. Regularly meeting with the doctor(s) to ensure ongoing executive communication, including written minutes. Informing the doctor(s) of all practice management emergencies and urgencies and other pressing problems when they occur or are anticipated. Following the doctor's instructions for keeping the practice operating in case of his or her absence.

should ideally be based upon the individual's supervisory and organization skills and perceived *potential to manage*. However, this isn't always the case. Many medical practices promote from within to reward staff loyalty and good performance or because the employee is a known quantity and seems like the safest choice. That is why many medical practices learn the hard way that a good receptionist, clinical assistant, or bookkeeper doesn't always make a good office manager. The person must also have managerial talent and potential.

**Pros and cons.** The promoted office manager has an existing relationship with the doctor(s), patients, and staff—presumably a good one—and is already acquainted with your office procedures and practice-specific activities and goals. In the best cases, the promoted office manager already has the respect of those he or she will manage and steps up to the position with the staff's support. Ideal candidates for promoted office managers are those who have already demonstrated leadership ability and a willingness and desire to face new challenges and learn. Some promoted office managers say that they find it difficult socially to be pulled up from the ranks. They can feel isolated from co-workers they formerly regarded as friends and miss being "one of the gang." Many find needed support and information when they join a professional organization for office managers.

In some cases, staff members may be jealous or resentful of the promoted office manager, particularly if staff perceives that there was more than one good candidate for the job. As in the case of the unwanted lay administrators, there are occasionally some resentful staff members who will object so strenuously to the promoted office manager's new authority that they take action, either by deliberately crossing or undermining the new office manager, giving him or her the cold shoulder, or quitting.

### Super-aides

The super-aide is usually the most senior or conscientious employee who is given the additional title of office manager. He or she is typically given no specific responsibilities except such vagaries as to "coordinate the staff," nor is he or she relieved of previous job duties.

**Pros and cons.** The super-aide, like the promoted office manager, is already acquainted with you and your practice. He or she may experience the same kinds of challenges as the promoted office manager and may feel the same kind of isolation and resistance from other staff members. The super-aide may, however, find it even more difficult to establish his or her own authority in the new position, particularly if he or she has vaguely defined authority and responsibilities.

Among staff and patients who know the super-aide, there is a natural tendency to continue to think of the person in the former role and assume that nothing has changed, because in reality, very little has. Of course, it may not be practical for you to relieve your super-aide office manager of all previous job duties. Super-aides, however, generally do best when they have their job descriptions adjusted to relieve them of at least some previous duties and when they are given new and higher levels of authority and responsibility. The most successful super-aides don't regard "office manager" as an empty title. Rather, they and everyone else in the practice see the step as a real promotion to a new level of responsibility. In many practices, much more can be accomplished if the doctor(s) and the individual can expand the role to promoted office manager and leave former responsibilities behind.

Some promoted office managers say that they find it difficult socially to be pulled up from the ranks.

> The first step toward shaping the role of the successful office manager for your medical practice is to write a complete job description.

## QUALITIES TO LOOK FOR IN AN OFFICE MANAGER

The best prospects to fill an office manager position in your medical practice will have usually had some verifiable experience in supervision and leadership, plus training in basic business management and accounting. Experience as a business assistant or clinical assistant in a medical practice does not necessarily indicate an individual's ability to manage. Nonetheless, such experience usually provides valuable insights and is desirable. In addition, here are 10 important general qualifications to look for in an applicant:

1. Education and/or experience in management or supervision; especially good experience supervising clerical or clinical personnel, including hiring, firing, and performance assessment.
2. Above-average intelligence.
3. A positive, can-do attitude and an even-tempered disposition.
4. Proven ability to make good decisions.
5. Organization and the proven ability to plan and carry out projects to successful completion.
6. Ability and desire to learn and grow.
7. Sensitivity toward diversity.
8. Superior communication skills in reading, writing, speaking, and listening.
9. Maturity.
10. Directedness—a proven ability to set and reach goals.

## WRITING THE JOB DESCRIPTION

The first step toward shaping the role of the successful office manager for your medical practice is to write a complete job description. This description should define not only the office manager's immediate role as it has existed so far (or as you imagine it will be), but also how the job will evolve over the next few years, no matter who holds the position.

Broadly speaking, the office manager of a medical practice has overall managerial responsibility for:

- Personnel
- Facilities
- Practice management systems (appointment scheduling, financial arrangements, collections, insurance processing, etc.)
- Patient relations
- Internal office communication
- Marketing

What do these responsibilities mean specifically? Should the office manager set policy or merely carry out your orders? Should he or she have hiring and firing authority? Should your office manager make decisions about spending, and if so, is there a dollar limit? These are some of the questions your job description should address.

Only you (and your partners) can decide how much authority you would like your office manager to have. To help, the sidebar that accompanies this article offers 20 duties required of typical medical practice office managers. Before you begin to consider an applicant for the job (or before you review the performance of an existing office manager), modify this list to suit your particular practice's circumstances, philosophy, and temperament. ▲

> Only you (and your partners) can decide how much authority you would like your office manager to have.

# Special Considerations for Hiring an Associate

*If you're thinking about hiring an associate for your medical practice, you will have many things to consider and many decisions to make. This chapter weighs the pros and cons of associateships and provides a 12-question quiz to help you determine whether an associate will be a good fit to your goals, philosophy, needs, and personality. It suggests helpful tips for recruiting and interviewing top-notch applicants to your associateship, including 15 effective interview questions. It also offers advice about evaluating associateship applicants and suggests typical associateship compensation arrangements.*

*As well, this chapter includes 10 questions to answer in your associateship contract and practical advice about restrictive covenants and externships. Finally, this chapter offers 12 suggestions for getting your new associate up to speed right away in your practice.*

Adding an associate to your medical practice is a big step that requires serious consideration, careful planning, and commitment. Before taking the plunge, especially for the first time, it's important to examine the pros and cons of associateships and to assess your practice's actual needs.

## FIRST EXAMINE THE POTENTIAL BENEFITS OF ASSOCIATESHIPS

To the plus side, the right associate can bring a lot to your practice and also bring personal benefits to the doctor(s) and staff. For example, the right associate can:

- Provide coverage for emergencies, extended evening and weekend hours, and the doctor's time off.

> Adding an associate to your medical practice is a big step that requires serious consideration, careful planning, and commitment.

Bringing an unwanted associate onboard is unfair to the associate and very unlikely to work in the long run.

- Relieve an excessive patient load.
- Increase practice income.
- Create a more stimulating professional environment.
- Maximize the use of office space and equipment.
- Spread fixed overhead costs over a greater number of practitioners.
- Shoulder administrative burdens.
- Become a ready buyer for the practice when the doctor/owner retires.
- Market the practice actively through community involvement, extended office hours, expanded scope of professional services, and participation in marketing projects.
- Market the practice passively by making it more demographically diverse. A medical practice that's varied by age, gender, personality, and ethnicity generally appeals to a larger market.

## NEXT CONSIDER THE POTENTIAL DRAWBACKS: A QUIZ

While there are many potential benefits to hiring an associate, you must also consider what you're willing to give up to make an associateship work. The quiz below can help you see what's at stake. Ask each doctor in your practice to answer the 12 questions below as honestly as they can with a yes or no. As well, you may wish to ask some or even all members of your staff to participate in this quiz:

____ 1.  Are you adaptable and ready to compromise?

____ 2.  Would you find it easy to share responsibilities for patients and make decisions jointly?

____ 3.  Will you be happy referring patients to the associate?

____ 4.  Could you accept the fact the associate might be better trained or better liked by your patients?

____ 5.  Are you willing to share your staff?

____ 6.  Can you relinquish more autonomy in consideration of your associate's needs and goals?

____ 7.  Do you have enough active patients and adequate office space and equipment to justify having the associate?

____ 8.  Does your office presently run smoothly?

____ 9.  Do you have the management skills needed to coordinate the operations of a larger practice?

____ 10. Will you need more staff to handle the extra appointment scheduling, bookkeeping, and case load?

____ 11. Can you deal with the friction that may occur as a result of personality clashes and changes in workload?

____ 12. Can you devote time and energy to guide your new associate through the initial honeymoon period?

YOUR SCORE: Ideally, every doctor in the practice should answer *yes* to each question before the practice takes on an associate. Every staff member should be able to answer *yes* to the questions that are relevant to them. Explore all *no* answers before proceeding to see if there are ways to fix problems or to compromise. Bringing an unwanted associate onboard is unfair to the associate and very unlikely to work in the long run.

## TAKING THE PLUNGE

Once you've determined that an associateship is compatible with your needs and situation, your recruitment process will be very similar to that used to hire most employees. As always, begin with the job description. Outline the required and preferred skills and the typical job duties. Then, try to attract suitable applicants for the position by using personal contacts and by advertising in appropriate media. Screen, interview, and check references for the applicants closely following the guidelines suggested in Chapters 1–6 and 1–7.

In addition to these usual recruitment techniques, you will also need to consider the unique nature of the associateship arrangement and incorporate a number of different strategies into your recruitment efforts. An associate is an unusual type of employee and recruiting one may be more time consuming. In many cases, you will need to look beyond applicants in your immediate geographic area, which leads to extra work, expense, and new concerns.

## ATTRACTING THE RIGHT APPLICANTS

Word of mouth is a great way to learn about prospective associates. Important contacts might include your professional association, management consultants, colleagues, bulletin boards, and placement services in professional schools.

When advertising for an associate, begin by studying the publication's current advertisements. They will help you with your own ad contents and phrasing. Unlike a daily newspaper, where you'd probably advertise for most other types of employees, the journals and tabloids where you'll advertise for an associate will usually publish monthly or bi-weekly. They will need more lead time to place your classified ad.

Generally, the more you tell in your ad for an associate, the more on-target your applicants will be. Start by indicating your city or area of the country and whether you prefer or require an applicant with a particular specialty or experience. Mention opportunities for part-time research, teaching appointments at local universities, and the benefits of your community (good schools, climate, culture and recreation, geography, etc.). Describe your practice, experience, strong areas of

> Word of mouth is a great way to learn about prospective associates.

interest, and compensation offerings. If the doctor/owner is planning to retire, estimate how long he or she intends to stay with the practice and a conservative estimate of income. Note partnership possibilities. End the ad by asking for the applicant's curriculum vitae.

## HANDLING THE LONG-DISTANCE INTERVIEW

When applicants travel considerable distances to attend your interview, you will need to make several arrangements beyond the ordinary:

- Be clear about the visit's duration, schedule, and purpose.
- State whether the applicant's spouse or significant other is invited.
- Decide upon overnight accommodations, method of travel, and transportation, as well as special social plans. For example, you might offer to set up an appointment for the applicant to meet with a local realtor for a few hours. If the applicant's spouse is invited, you might arrange a tour of the area for him or her. As well, you may wish to take the applicant to dinner or invite him or her to your home.
- State clearly who will pay for transportation, meals, hotels, and other costs, and how and when the applicant is to be reimbursed.

> **TIP:** *An out-of-town candidate will undoubtedly have questions about what it's like to live in your area. It is very helpful to gather relevant materials including maps, real estate listings, weather statistics, information about schools, crime, recreation, etc. Your Chamber of Commerce should be able to provide you with appropriate literature.*

## EVALUATING THE APPLICANTS

It may not be practical to conduct an in-person second interview with the top applicants if they are from out of town. However, it does make sense to do a follow-up telephone interview to answer any remaining questions and confirm your initial impression. Schedule the telephone call in advance at a mutually convenient time. Plan on spending approximately 20 minutes talking with the applicant once more.

As you assess each candidate, you'll need to prepare notes just as you would when trying to fill any position. In addition to the usual notes, you'll need to answer questions such as:

- Does this applicant see eye-to-eye with me on basic practice philosophy?
- Will his or her experience make it hard or easy for him or her to fit in here?
- Do the applicant's professional interests complement ours?
- Will the applicant be happy living in this area?
- Do I want this person to be treating our patients?

An out-of-town candidate will undoubtedly have questions about what it's like to live in your area.

### Good Interview Questions for a Prospective Associate

You'll want to ask a potential associate some excellent targeted interview questions. Here are 15 possible questions that can help you learn a lot.

1. Are there any kinds of patients you don't feel comfortable with or that you can't get along with?
2. Why did you go into medicine? Our area of specialization?
3. Where did you rank in your class in medical school? How do you account for this?
4. What do you want most from this associateship?
5. Why were you attracted to this community/practice?
6. What has been the most satisfying thing you've done so far in medicine?
7. Who in our field do you most admire?
8. How do you feel about our fee schedule and financial arrangements with our patients?
9. What would you do if a patient complained that you lack experience and that he would prefer me to treat him?
10. What would you do if a patient complained that your work wasn't satisfactory?
11. What would you tell a patient who realizes the need for recommended treatment but who says she can't afford it?
12. How would you handle a patient who appears to be fine but who complains repeatedly of a particular pain or condition?
13. What rewards to you foresee with this associateship?
14. How much money do you expect to earn this year? Next year? In five years?
15. How do you feel about our examining rooms (equipment, instruments, other facilities) that you'd be using?

> Adding an associate should be an asset to your financial health in the long run.

## HOW TO COMPENSATE AN ASSOCIATE

Adding an associate should be an asset to your financial health in the long run. While it may take a little time for the associate to become established and productive, he or she should eventually do so.

In general associates are compensated in one of three ways:

1. **Straight salary:** The associate is guaranteed a sum on a regular basis for performing set duties during set hours.
2. **A fixed percentage of production or collections:** This arrangement provides extra incentive for productivity. Usually, new associates on a straight percentage basis are given a "draw" against future commissions so they're guaranteed an income in the lean early days.

Restrictive covenants have several potential drawbacks that you will need to consider.

3. **A combination:** Usually, the associate receives a small salary (or base pay) plus a percentage of production/collections.

> **TIP:** *Many experts recommend switching from one payment option to the other as the associate matures. For example, you might begin by paying a flat salary until the associate becomes established and you've had time to determine his or her professional proficiency. This might take six months or so. Then, once the associate is on his or her way, you might change to a permanent percentage arrangement. A typical amount: 40% of production less expenses (lab bills, supplies, assistant's salary, etc.).*

## STRUCTURING AN ASSOCIATESHIP AGREEMENT

After you and the associate have decided to work together, the next step is to draft an associateship agreement. Here are 10 questions that are answered in such a contract:

1. **Length of contract.** Most associateship contracts are for one year and are renegotiable.
2. **Legal classification.** Is the associate an employee or an independent contractor?
3. **Financial responsibilities.** Will the associate cover his or her lab bills? Who pays the premiums for the associate's malpractice insurance? Who pays for supplies, billing, assistant's salaries, etc.?
4. **Management responsibilities.** Will the associate arrange his or he own appointment schedule? Manage staff? Supervise collections?
5. **Nature of work.** What duties will the associate perform?
6. **Compensation.** What formula will you use? To what (if any) fringe benefits is the associate entitled? Is a draw against future commissions available?
7. **Office coverage.** What hours, weekends, holidays, and nights will the associate work? Does he or she receive paid holidays? Sick leave?
8. **Potential ownership rights.** Have you made any promises to the associateship about future buy-in/partnership potential?
9. **Restrictive covenants.** See "How to Prevent Your Associate from Taking Your Patients" below.
10. **Provisions for dissolution.** How will practice-related expenses be settled? If applicable, how will patient records and office staff be divided? How much notice is needed for termination? (Usual: 30–60 days.)

TIP: *Seek the advice of consultants, accountants, and attorneys when drawing up the written associateship agreement.*

## HOW TO PREVENT YOUR ASSOCIATE FROM TAKING YOUR PATIENTS

Covenants not to compete restrict the associate from practicing within a set radius for a set period of time after leaving your practice. In states where such covenants are legal, courts will enforce them only if their terms are deemed reasonable, usually if they can answer no to these questions:

- Is the restraint on the associate greater than is necessary to protect the owner's legitimate interest?
- Is the restraint unduly harsh or oppressive?
- Is the restraint harmful to public interest?
- Is the set geographic area unreasonable?
- Is the duration unreasonable?

TIP: *Typical restrictive covenants set a radius of from 1-5 miles and a time frame of 2-3 years.*

Restrictive covenants have several potential drawbacks that you will need to consider. For one thing, they can be enforced only through costly litigation, which is potentially detrimental to your public image. For another, the courts are generally unreceptive to enforcing a restrictive covenant if it will give one practice a monopoly or severely restrict the public's access to efficient and cost-effective health care. And, patients may simply not understand why an established practitioner will sue a former associate to keep him or her from setting up practice nearby. The ill will generated by such a suit may harm your practice more than the associate ever could.

In lieu of a restrictive covenant, many employers provide in the employment contract that all records belong to the practice, including the patient list. They state that employees must surrender all records to the owner/doctor upon leaving the practice. Then, when a patient asks about the former associate, they respond honestly and without rancor and let them choose for themselves. Usually, patients who are satisfied with the care they are receiving stay where they are.

An alternative to an associateship is a position called an externship. (This will work only in certain types of practices.) In such an arrangement, the owner/doctor continues to do all examinations, diagnoses, treatment planning, case consultations, and post-treatment consultation for all patients. The extern (not called an associate) is brought in only to perform certain parts of the

Typical restrictive covenants set a radius of 1-5 miles and a time frame of 2-3 years.

treatment, as determined by the owner/doctor. Thus, the owner/doctor stays in control and is still perceived as every patient's doctor.

Obviously, working with an extern requires close teamwork. As well, the extern will not get the comprehensive experience he or she would have had an as associate. Because of this, it may be challenging to find good candidates willing to take such a position.

> **TIP:** *One benefit of externships is that you may be able to structure things so the extern does those parts of treatment you don't particularly like. Furthermore, you'll be able to supervise the extern's work and bedside manner easily because you'll be working closely with him or her and talking with every patient your extern sees. You might see whether an applicant would be willing to work for you as an extern for a set period of time before moving into a full-blown associateship.*

## A DOZEN WAYS TO KEEP A NEW ASSOCIATE BUSY

Once you've signed the associateship agreement, you'll want to pave the way for your new associate to succeed. Here are 12 suggestions for making sure that every minute counts with your new associate:

1. Announce the newly-formed associateship at a staff meeting. Make clear to staff members that the associate is your equal and not a junior partner whose orders can be ignored.

2. Add your associate's name to your office door. Print a business card, Rx pad, name tag, and other stationery for him or her.

3. Introduce your associate to your patients in your newsletter. Feature your associate in a reception area bulletin board display. Send a printed announcement to all patients to introduce the associate, enclosing a small gift (pen, bumper sticker, calendar, refrigerator magnet, etc.) in his or her honor. That will make your patients think positively about this new addition to your practice.

4. Seek media exposure for the new associate by sending press releases to media editors. Enclose action photos (not a mug shot) of your associate doing something—hanging his or her diploma on the wall, meeting a patient, etc. Or, consider placing paid announcements in local newspapers.

5. Write a colleague or other non-patient referral sources to introduce your new associate and describe his or her capabilities and training.

6. Review your patient charts to identify those who might benefit from the new associate's special training. Call or write them to explain how the new doctor can help them.

---

An alternative to an associate-ship is a position called an externship.

7. Begin to schedule appointments for your associate before he or she arrives.

8. Try to line up public speaking announcements for your associate. Or, if you're scheduled to speak in your community, bring your new associate along and let him or her give a portion of the presentation.

9. Schedule an open house, party, or other practice event in honor of your new associate. Invite your patients. Provide an incentive for attending, such as refreshments, freebies, or special attractions for children.

10. Sponsor a contest for patients having to do with your new associate. For example, contestants might guess the associate's birthday or middle name. Or, ask them to write the associate's full name on a standard postcard as many times as they can without overlapping. (The card with the smallest handwriting—the name on it the most times—wins.) Display the winning entries in your reception area. Or, send them to local newspapers and ask them to print them with a story.

11. Give patients good reasons when referring them to your new associate. Don't say that you're referring them because you're too busy or because your associate needs patients. Give a reason related to treatment or the doctor's special skills.

12. Have your receptionist give new patients good reasons, too. For example: "Because of the time your appointment requires, it will be several weeks before I can give you an appointment with Dr. Smith. However, I can appoint you much sooner with Dr. Jones. I'm sure you'll like her...." ▲

> Begin to schedule appointments for your new associate before he or she arrives.

# Getting the Most from Office Temporaries

*Practically every medical practice finds itself short-staffed at one time or another. In some cases, a temporary employee is all that is needed to keep the practice running smoothly. Because of this, many temporary employment agencies today gear themselves specifically to filling both administrative and clinical positions in medical practices.*

*This chapter explores when and how to hire a temporary employee. It suggests strategies for preparing for the temporary employee's arrival, orienting the employee to the practice and assigned tasks, and evaluating the temporary worker's performance. In addition, this chapter offers ideas about working well with temporary employment agencies, as well as likely policies one would encounter when trying to hire a temporary employee permanently.*

Your practice may have occasional need for or benefit from the services of a temporary employee. Fortunately, now there are many agencies that specialize in placing temporary employees—administrative and clinical—in medical practices. Be warned, however, that managing a temporary employee requires somewhat different techniques than those used to manage permanent staff members. In this chapter, we will explore some specific guidelines and procedures for finding and supervising a qualified temporary employee.

## DETERMINE YOUR NEED FOR THE TEMPORARY EMPLOYEE

When do you really need temporary help? There are many possible instances, such as:

- A permanent employee is on vacation or will be taking an extended leave of absence for illness or parental leave.

> Evaluate whether and how specifically an outsider can be of help to you and your practice.

> ## Good sources of temps are parents at home with young children, retirees, and college students.

- A permanent employee quits or is fired abruptly and you need someone to keep things going while you conduct a job search.
- Patient flow peaks temporarily and the workload becomes excessive or unmanageable for a short period of time.
- A special short-term project occurs, and your permanent staff isn't trained in that area or can't handle the extra work.

When considering the services of a temporary worker, evaluate whether and how specifically an outsider can be of help to you and your practice. You will get the most benefit from most administrative temporary workers if you assign them routine or repetitive tasks that require little training or inside knowledge of your practice. Typing form letters, alphabetizing files, collating, stamping, folding, stapling, and simple posting are all good temporary assignments. Likewise, a clinical temporary worker might also be limited to repetitive or relatively simple duties and procedures.

Avoid assigning a temporary worker to handle the tasks that require intricate knowledge of your profession, practice, or patients. For example, you probably won't want to hire a temporary worker to fill in for your lead receptionist. Greeting patients, scheduling appointments, and answering your telephone require extensive inside knowledge of your practice and its policies and procedures. If you must replace your receptionist temporarily, it may make the most sense to have another member of your staff pinch hit for him or her. Then, you can hire a temporary worker to assist him or her and do the routine filing, typing, etc. under his or her direction.

## MAINTAIN YOUR OWN "TEMP" LIST

If you regularly need temporary help, try to develop and maintain your own list of possible workers. Good sources of temps are parents at home with young children, retirees, and college students. Excellent: See if former employees (home with children or retired) would be willing to work on a temporary basis. Also look into senior citizen groups and similar organizations to see if their members would be willing to work on an as-needed basis.

## WHAT TO DO BEFORE THE TEMPORARY WORKER ARRIVES

You'll get so much more from a temporary employee if you give the matter a little forethought and planning:

1. Be specific about what you need when you call someone on your own temp list or enlist the services of a temporary employment agency. At the very least, it's smart to have the following:

   - Starting date and the length of the assignment. Estimate daily and weekly time expectations.

- The tasks the temporary worker will be expected to handle, and the specific skills you require, such as typing, filing, clinical skills, or familiarity with particular office equipment or computer programs. Give the employee and/or the employment agency an exact job description.
- The kind of clothing, appearance, and language skills you expect from the temporary worker.
- Relevant office policies that might make a difference. For example, tell the agency if you prohibit smoking in your office, or if the employee is expected to pay for parking.

2. Be clear that you, your office manager or a veteran employee will be the person in charge of the temporary employee. To avoid confusion, it's best to have the temporary worker report to just one person who can orient him or her, give assignments, and answer questions.

3. Tell your permanent employees when a temporary worker is coming, and why. Emphasize that the temporary worker will not affect their job security. This is crucial. Many permanent workers feel insecure when a temporary worker arrives on the scene. Be especially sure to discuss this with your staff when a temporary worker is replacing a worker who is ill or on vacation.

4. Make sure that the temporary's equipment (telephone, computer, etc.) is in good working order and that all necessary supplies for his or her work are easily accessible. It's a waste of time to hunt for basic supplies such as a stapler, paper, and scissors after the temporary worker is already in your office and raring to go. Remember, the temporary's "meter" is running the moment he or she crosses your threshold.

## SUPERVISING THE TEMPORARY WORKER

When the temporary employee arrives at your office, begin with a five-minute orientation. Greet the worker personally and invite him or her to meet with your privately. Describe your basic office philosophies and structure—your profession or area of specialization, how long you've been in practice, what you do, who your patients are, etc.

Explain the office policies that are most likely to affect the temporary employee:

- Where he or she is to park, hang his or her coat, keep personal belongings, etc.
- When and where coffee breaks and lunch will be.
- Restrictions about smoking and eating at his or her desk.
- How late he or she is to stay, and time-clock procedures, if any.
- Rules about personal phone calls.

Give the employee and/or the employment agency an exact job description.

> A temporary worker will be much more enthusiastic and diligent about a task if he or she has some broad understanding of what it is or how it fits in with the practice as a whole.

Take the employee on a tour of your office, and point out your bathrooms, break rooms, staff coat closet, his or her work station or desk, and other areas that will be important throughout the day.

As you go, introduce the temporary worker to your permanent employees. Acquaint him or her with your fire exits, and if appropriate, your phone system. Such an orientation takes little time and will allow the temporary worker to settle in quickly and get to work confidently. Don't skip this important first step, even if the employee is to be in your office only one day.

Once the employee is oriented to your practice, get down to the subject at hand: the work he or she will be doing. Start with a broad outline of the work. This step is extremely important. A temporary worker will be much more enthusiastic and diligent about a task if he or she has some broad understanding of what it is or how it fits in with the practice as a whole. Your explanation needn't be lengthy or complicated.

For example: "Joan, you're going to be helping us get out the spring issue of our patient newsletter. Here's a copy of it. We publish this newsletter every 3 months, and send it to every patient in our practice, as well as to other doctors and friends of the practice. It is an informational newsletter that helps us keep our patients up-to-date with the latest developments in our profession, and in our practice. Therefore, this newsletter is extremely important to our patients, and to us, since it is our way of staying in regular touch with them."

Now you can get down to particulars. Because temporary workers are usually not familiar with your organization, the instructions you give should be as thorough as possible, and you should be as helpful as you can.

> **TIP:** *Dole out the work piecemeal at first. Provide the worker with everything he or she will need—written instructions, samples of the finished work he or she is trying to duplicate, etc.*

Spell out exactly what should be done when the assignment is finished, so the temporary worker doesn't think the job is over when it isn't.

In the beginning, make yourself or a designated person in your office available to the temporary worker as much as possible, to stay in control of the work and to ask frequently if the temp has any questions or problems. Then, as you begin to get a feel for the temporary worker's abilities and speed, and as he or she becomes more and more familiar with the work, you can usually increase the workload and step back a little more.

## WHAT TO DO ABOUT AN UNSATISFACTORY TEMPORARY WORKER

It may be very tempting to put up with a marginal or unsatisfactory temporary worker for reasons like the following:

- It will only be for a day or two.
- At least he's better than nothing.
- That's about what I expected. No wonder she doesn't have a permanent job.

Don't allow yourself to fall into this kind of thinking. Many excellent workers take temporary positions, and you have a right to reliable, competent people. It may take some searching and effort to find the best temporaries, however.

If you aren't satisfied with the worker by the end of the afternoon of the first day, call the employment agency in time to get someone else by the next morning. Explain precisely what went wrong and review what skills and qualities you're looking for. The longer you wait, the harder it will be to make that call and the more damage the poor temporary may do to the smooth running of your office.

If the agency sends you another "dud," it's probably best to say goodbye and call another firm. Ask your colleagues to recommend a good temporary employment agency to you. Then ask the agency itself to tell you how it screens and tests its applicants.

*Important:* If the agency provides clinical temporary workers, determine precisely how it verifies certification, licensure, etc., and what proof you will receive of the individual's credentials.

## AFTER THE TEMPORARY WORKER HAS COMPLETED THE ASSIGNMENT

All too often, temporary employees leave an assignment with no feedback. Feedback is important, especially if you ever wish to work with that individual again.

At the end of the assignment, ask your temporary worker to meet with you in private. Review what was expected of him or her and what he or she accomplished while working in your practice. In essence, think of this meeting as a short performance evaluation. Let the employee know how you feel about what he or she has done, and specifically, what improvements you would like to see if he or she ever comes to work for your practice again.

Record the names of temporary workers who did particularly well. List the specific skills and attributes that made them valuable to you. Note the actual work they did and also how you feel they might be of benefit

> Many excellent workers take temporary positions, and you have a right to reliable, competent people.

Feedback is important, especially if you ever wish to work with that individual again.

to you in the future. That way you can request the best workers by name the next time you need temporary help.

## HOW TO MAKE THE TEMPORARY WORKER PERMANENT

If you find a good temporary worker through an agency, it will generally ask you to promise that you'll always hire that person through the agency. Read and honor your employment agreement.

If you'd like to retain a temporary worker permanently, your agency will probably offer you two options. Either:

1. You can "buy out" the employee at a negotiated fee based on the amount of time he or she has worked for you, and his or her contracted commitment to the agency, or

2. You can hire the employee through the agency for a minimum number of hours, usually approximately 500, at which time the employee is free to be hired as a full-time staff member, without further penalty or fee. ▲

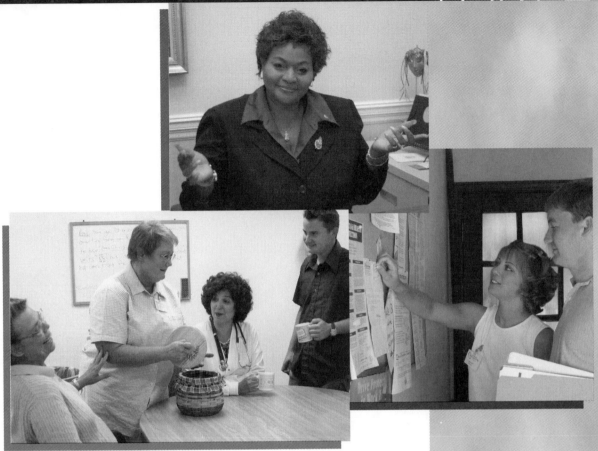

## PART 2

# Motivating a Winning Staff: Boosting Morale and Improving Communication

# What Do Employees Really Want?

*Each person who works in your medical practice is unique and has different goals, values, dreams, and perceptions. This uniqueness means that you can't make assumptions about what your employees want. By learning what makes the people working in your practice tick, you will be able to develop meaningful rewards and incentives and eliminate some nagging practice management problems once and for all.*

*This chapter suggests a simple exercise that enables staff members to rank 10 job features in order of importance. It shares the results of original research indicating common complaints medical office employees have about their doctor-bosses. It cautions readers not to solicit employee opinions unless they can live with the truth and keep from becoming bitter, defensive, or retaliatory. This chapter also offers two hands-on tools for helping practice managers find out what their employees really want: a ready-to-use staff morale survey and an employee suggestion program.*

> Each person who works in your medical practice is unique and has different goals, values, dreams, and perceptions.

People are motivated by so many different things. For some, there is no substitute for money. For others, recognition, achievement, independence, opportunities to advance, or a good old pat on the back are far more important. If you don't know for certain what is important to each member of your staff, it will be very hard for you to devise effective incentives and rewards for them. Furthermore, you may be contributing to your employee's job dissatisfaction without even knowing it.

## EMPLOYERS AND EMPLOYEES HAVE DIFFERENT VALUES: AN EXERCISE

You and your staff may have greatly different attitudes and values. As an exercise and starting point for discussion, you and each member of your staff might rank the following 10 job values from 1 to 10 (most important to least important):

- Interesting work
- Full appreciation of work done
- Feeling of being in on things
- Job security
- Good pay
- Promotion and growth
- Good working conditions
- The boss's loyalty to employees
- Help with personal problems
- Tactful discipline

Chances are that you will not anticipate your employees' answers accurately. For example, employers often believe their employees will rank good pay as the most important job feature. Employees, however, often place at least one other job feature (such as interesting work, job security, or full appreciation of work done) as more important to them than good pay. You may also find that your employees do not all rank job features the same way, depending upon their personal life experiences and of-the-minute needs. For example, job security is likely to be an extremely important job feature to employees who have others depending upon them or who have just taken on big mortgages, more so than to those who have no such obligations. Likewise, tactful discipline may be more important to an employee who has experienced humiliating discipline in the past than to those who have had no such painful experience.

It is very important to find out what each member of your staff wants most and least and to analyze whether your perceptions match reality. Only then can you develop rewards and incentives and eliminate problems that are going to have the most impact on your staff.

> You may also find that your employees do not all rank job features the same way.

## OUCH–WHAT EMPLOYEES HAVE TO SAY ABOUT THEIR DOCTOR-BOSSES

At the conclusion of several of my staff seminars, I conducted a survey of staff members to see what they had to say about their doctor-bosses. Presented here are 20 of their most eye-opening complaints, in no particular order. Naturally, we should not assume that these are the feelings of *all* or even *most* medical practice staffs. These are so startling, however, and appeared often enough in my research that I believe they deserve some consideration.

Each of these is a direct quotation that I gathered from written surveys and follow-up interviews with medical office staff. I promised to guard the anonymity of each staff member who took part in my survey, so participants knew that their bosses would never see what they had to say. Each complaint was corroborated by at least one other employee in the same practice. Thus, what you are about to read is not a listing of isolated comments by an angry few; in every instance, at least one other person in the practice agreed with what the dissatisfied employee had to say (Table 1).

Now, how did you feel reading these comments? Did they make you angry? Outraged? Defensive? Worried? Do you think anyone on your staff might feel any of these things about *you*? Whether these employees are right or wrong about their bosses, justified or not in their opinions, their attitudes don't bode well for employee satisfaction. When soliciting *your* employees' feedback for the purposes of boosting employee morale and finding out what's important to your staff, remember what you are trying to do. Your

---

### Checklist for Establishing an Employee Suggestion Program

An excellent way to increase your employees' satisfaction *and* improve your practice is to solicit and implement employee suggestions. Involving your staff in problem solving may lead to better ways of handling insurance claims, appointment scheduling, collections, inventory control, or dozens of other office procedures. At the very least, your staff's morale will soar when you demonstrate that their suggestions count.

Increasingly, employers are instituting formal employee suggestion programs. Elements of the best such programs can be adapted to your medical practice, even if you have only a few employees:

- ✔ Hold a meeting to define the areas in which you are seeking employees' ideas. Discuss specific problems (such as running late with patients) or simply encourage employees to suggest anything that will save money, bring new patients to the practice, make practice life better for patients or the staff, or simplify work. Explain your reasons for requesting their input.

- ✔ Describe how employees should submit their suggestions. For example, you might have them complete a survey questionnaire or form. Structure such devices to pinpoint problems and get your staff's step-by-step suggestions.

- ✔ Consider setting up a task force to work on a particular problem. Avoid gripe sessions that don't lead to solutions.

- ✔ Provide feedback on all suggestions promptly after receiving them. When possible, explain why an idea can't be used or other factors to consider. Thank employees for their suggestions and ask for more. Make them feel good about having tried.

- ✔ Grant cash or attractive merchandise awards to an employee whose suggestions are adopted.

- ✔ Publish congratulations to employees whose ideas are used in your patient newsletter, a routed memo, or on your staff bulletin board. Send them a personal letter of congratulations and keep a copy in the personnel file. If the idea warrants it, send a press release to local media.

> "He thinks he's better than everyone because he's the Doctor, with a capital D."

---

### TABLE 1
## What Employees Say About Their Bosses

1. "The doctor belittles me in front of patients, making me feel small and stupid."
2. "The doctor makes financial arrangements with patients and lets them set the payment schedule. Then, he's disappointed with me if I don't collect what he thinks I should."
3. "She meddles in the appointment book."
4. "He has no respect for the patient's time. He's always late in the mornings and after lunch. We're always behind schedule."
5. "The doctor is too good-hearted. He gives away so much for free that he's going to kill his practice with kindness."
6. "He doesn't allow enough time for his appointments so we're constantly squeezing in patients."
7. "She's very concerned with money, money, money all the time, but she doesn't pay me a living wage."
8. "He gives me a job to do, like collections, but he doesn't give me the authority I need to do it."
9. "He doesn't appreciate me. I rarely hear a kind word about my work, let alone a thank you."
10. "The doctor never returns phone calls. Then I look like the bad guy when a patient calls back for the third time and wonders if the doctor ever got the messages."
11. "I never know what I'm supposed to do first. The doctor throws a pile of work on me and doesn't give me any priorities. Then, he's mad when I don't have everything done right away."
12. "I can't read his handwriting. It drives me crazy."
13. "He makes me do personal work for him and his family. I wasn't hired to call his daughter's piano teacher or to buy a present for his wife's birthday, and I resent it. I'm not his personal slave, you know."
14. "She gives me too much work at the end of the day. It's all I can do to get things picked up and finished on time; then she comes along and throws a wrench into things."
15. "He's cheap with anything that has to do with us. If you think our salaries are bad, you should get a look at our office equipment. I see more of our photocopier repairman than I do of my husband."
16. "He doesn't trust me to make even the smallest decision myself. I hate having to go to him for every little thing."
17. "He takes my ideas and doesn't give me any credit for them. Sometimes he even makes fun of them or laughs when I make a suggestion, but he ends up doing it later."
18. "She overturns my decisions, usually in front of everyone. I end up looking like a fool."
19. "He thinks he's better than everyone because he's the Doctor, with a capital D. I'm just a lowly assistant here to meet His Highness's every need—at least he thinks so."
20. "He's such a phony. He's so charming and seems to care so much about his patients—that is, when he's with them. You should hear what he says about them behind their backs."

## Measure Staff Morale and Satisfaction with This Survey

How's the morale in your medical practice? Are your employees satisfied with the various features of their jobs? Here's an easy way to find out.

Photocopy the form below and have staff members anonymously circle the numbers that best describe their feelings. Average the answer to each question and add the averages together. Then compare your total with the Your Score analysis to take the pulse of the employee morale in your practice.

**Tip:** Averages are important but don't tell all. One huge area of employee dissatisfaction won't destroy your average, but it can lower staff morale fatally. Therefore, as you analyze your staff's responses, consider not only averages but also extreme responses. Remember that there may be job features not listed on this survey that are important to your staff. You might provide space at the bottom of the survey for employee comments and additional thoughts about their jobs.

Please rate the following features of your job by circling the answer that best describes your feelings:

A. Pay:
   1. Below par for position and geographic area.
   2. Adequate.
   3. Excellent.

B. Fringe benefits:
   1. Below par for position and area.
   2. Adequate.
   3. Excellent.

C. My relationship with the rest of the staff:
   1. Worse than I'd like.
   2. Adequate.
   3. Excellent.

D. Performance reviews:
   1. Performance never formally reviewed.
   2. Performance reviewed occasionally.
   3. Regular performance reviews.

E. Criticism from the doctor(s):
   1. Poor. Little to no communication or constructive criticism.
   2. Good. Doctor occasionally offers praise or at least helpful criticism.
   3. Excellent. Doctor offers praise and constructive criticism when deserved.

F. Workload:
   1. Way too much or way too little.
   2. Usually OK.
   3. Just right/fine.

G. Hours:
   1. Poor—too long, too irregular, and/or get out too late.
   2. Usually OK.
   3. Just right/fine.

H. Training:
   1. Nonexistent or almost nonexistent.
   2. Adequate.
   3. Great. In-office and/or out-of-office training and seminars.

I. Physical environment:
   1. Poor—depressing and/or unpleasant office, building, or location.
   2. Adequate.
   3. Pleasant—bright, clean, tastefully furnished, etc.

**Your Score:**

| | | |
|---|---|---|
| ☹ | Below 16 | Poor. Staff morale is dangerously low and needs reviving ASAP. |
| 😐 | 16–20 | Fair. It's not hopeless, but you've got room for improvement. |
| 🙂 | 21–25 | Good. Staff morale is strong and just needs a little tweaking. |
| 🙂! | 26–30 | Excellent. Staff morale is through the roof! |

goal should be to identify staff perceptions, whether you believe they are correct or incorrect.

Don't respond to negative criticisms with an urge to prove that you are right or to defend yourself. Rather, take critical comments, even harsh ones, as opportunities for straightening out misconceptions, improving communications with your staff, and finding ways to improve your own practice management skills.

## UNCOVER THE TRUTH

An anonymous survey of your staff can be an excellent way to discover problems like those just listed. A staff survey on sensitive subjects, especially those eliciting criticism of the boss, will work only if your staff members feel that they can be honest without hurting themselves professionally.

Don't administer a staff survey soliciting truthful opinions about your deficiencies unless you can live with the truth and can keep from becoming bitter, defensive, or retaliatory. If an employee is punished for speaking out when you've asked him or her to, you will do more damage to employee morale than good.

The two sidebars that accompany this chapter may prove very helpful as you try to find out what your employees truly want. The first sidebar provides a survey you can use to measure your staff's morale level; the second sidebar provides a useful checklist for initiating an employee suggestion program. These tools may be practical and nonthreatening ways for you to begin a dialogue with your staff about what they want most, particularly if you have staff members who are reluctant to speak up. ▲

> You and your staff may have greatly different attitudes and values.

# Starting Off on the Right Foot with New Employees

*How and when you begin with a new employee in your practice sets the stage for your future working relationship. With a little planning and effort, the new employee can have a positive start and quickly become a motivated and productive member of your team.*

*This chapter describes the specific strategies for choreographing the employee's first days on the job, including scheduling the first day, physical preparations of the new employee's workspace, holding a get-acquainted meeting, creating an individualized training program and checklist, humanizing the employee's orientation, and great first day assignments. As well, this chapter includes how-to guidance for introducing your new employee to your patients and for publicizing the new employee's arrival to your practice in a positive way.*

Imagine how you'd feel if you reported for the first day of work on a new job only to find there was nothing planned for you to do and no one ready to greet you. Unfortunately, this is how it goes in many medical practices. But it shouldn't be. The new employee's first day sets the tone for his or her entire career in your practice.

Don't blow the only chance you'll get to make a positive first impression with your new employee. Lay the groundwork for a great working relationship and maximum new employee productivity by planning a productive a meaningful first day and taking steps to introduce your new employee to your patients.

> The new employee's first day sets the tone for his or her entire career in your practice.

---

**Buy and wrap a small gift for the new employee.**

---

## GEAR UP PHYSICALLY FOR THE NEW EMPLOYEE

You can't possibly make a new employee feel welcome while you're scrambling to clean out a desk and find him or her basic office supplies. Start by making these physical arrangements well before the new staffer's first day:

- Prepare the employee's workspace—desk, cabinets, bulletin board, telephone, etc. Make sure the space is clean and stocked with fresh supplies and properly functioning equipment. Remove personal items left by former employees.
- Engrave a name tag for the new employee and a desk or office door sign with his or her name and title, if appropriate.
- Gather the materials the employee will need for orientation: insurance and tax forms, your policy and procedure manual, written job description, books, training tapes, office brochures, patient newsletters, etc.
- Buy and wrap a small gift for the new employee. A nice pen or coffee mug is appropriate for someone starting a new job and is certainly affordable.
- Arrange for the new employee's permit/space, security pass, etc.

## CHOOSE A GOOD DAY FOR THE START

Your new employee should report for work when you can give him or her attention and when the office is relatively calm. Ideally, choose a time when patients aren't scheduled. For example, have the new employee come an hour before your start to get acquainted and complete paperwork.

If this is not possible, choose a relatively light day. Most medical practices should avoid Monday mornings and days immediately after holidays, which are traditionally busy times.

## KICK THINGS OFF WITH A GET-ACQUAINTED MEETING

Meet with your new employee privately for a few minutes the first morning on the job. Welcome him or her to your practice and express your wishes for a good and lasting relationship. Give him or her the gift you've bought. Then:

- Restate the job for which you have hired the employee.
- Review the hours to be worked and your expectations about overtime.
- Review the salary and benefits you'll provide: vacation (and eligibility), holidays, insurance, uniforms, bonus programs, profit-sharing plans, sick leave, etc.

- Outline the basic elements of the job and your office policies: lunch and coffee breaks, absences (how reported), parking, smoking, dress code, time clock, etc.
- Give the employee a copy of your office policy and procedure manual and a written job description. Instruct him or her to read both thoroughly, and in a week, to sign a statement that says he or she has done so. Note the date of signing in your calendar.

> TIP: *Keep the signed statement in the employee's personnel file. It could become important evidence that you informed the employee of your policies should any legal action be brought against you.*

- Introduce the new employee to each member of your staff. Explain each person's responsibilities and job duties. If the employee will be supervised by your office or clinical manager, or another person, introduce him or her.
- Give the new employee a guided tour of your office. Point out the staff restroom, coat/storage closet, and break room.
- Have the employee complete all the necessary paperwork: Application form, social security number, work permit, tax and insurance papers, emergency information, etc.
- Outline what the new employee is to do that day and throughout the orientation period. Prepare a checklist of all the tasks to be learned and who in your office will do the training. (See Sidebar.) Choose trainers who have mastered the task and who are willing and capable teachers.
- Assign one staff member the task of being the new employee's "buddy" and give him or her a copy of the orientation checklist. He or she will serve as your new employee's mentor and troubleshooter.
- When the training is complete, have the employee fill in the dates and sign the checklist. Keep a copy in his or her personnel file and offer congratulations on a job well done.

## HUMANIZE THE NEW EMPLOYEE'S ORIENTATION

Socially, it can be stressful and lonely to start a new job. To make the first day go more smoothly:

- Eat lunch with the new employee on his or her first day. Or, have a staff member do this for you. This provides a warm welcome and gets the employee through what can be a stressful time.
- Give the new employee a button or tag to wear that says, "Be nice to me. I'm new on the job."
- Hold a 15-minute meeting at the end of the first day. Reiterate your welcome and give some praise and words of encouragement. End on a smile and handshake. Give the employee good reason to want to come back tomorrow.

> Outline what the new employee is to do...throughout the orientation period.

## Sample Orientation Checklist for a New Employee

| Assignment: | Trainer: | Date Completed: |
|---|---|---|
| 1. Introduction to practice history, philosophy, etc. | Dr. Lee | _____ |
| 2. Introduction to staff | Dr. Lee | _____ |
| 3. Office tour | Janine | _____ |
| 4. Completion of insurance, tax, and social security paperwork for new staff | Janine | _____ |
| 5. Use of time cards | Shirley | _____ |
| 6. Telephone techniques | Shirley | _____ |
| 7. Introduction to the computer system | Shirley | _____ |
| 8. Other office equipment: postage meter, copier, phone, fax, etc. | Shirley | _____ |
| 9. Appointment scheduling | Maya | _____ |
| 10. Bookkeeping methods | Donna | _____ |
| 11. Collection methods | Donna | _____ |
| 12. Insurance processing | Donna | _____ |
| 13. Fee schedule and financial arrangements | Luis | _____ |
| 14. Filing methods/creating new patient records | Luis | _____ |

## GREAT FIRST-DAY ASSIGNMENT #1

Observation usually teaches us a great deal. As a first assignment, have your new employee observe in your reception area and elsewhere in your office for at least 30 minutes per area. Instruct him or her to look, listen, take notes, and pay particular to both verbal and non-verbal communication between staff and patients. Provide structure with these questions:

- List 3-5 positive non-verbal cues you observed between a patient and a staff member.
- List 3-5 positive comments you heard a staff member make to a patient.
- Did you observe any patient-staff interaction you thought could have been improved? If so, how?

- List five goals you've formed for your own communications with patients.
- What else have you learned?

> **TIP:** *Inform the rest of your staff about the observation before it begins. Meet with the new employee afterwards to discuss his findings and to answer questions.*

## GREAT FIRST DAY ASSIGNMENT #2

Do your patients encounter new staff members by chance and draw their own conclusions? If so, you might try to orchestrate a more careful introduction so the new staff member looks good (and you do, too).

On the first day, have your new employee write and send a letter of introduction to all of your patients of record. In it, he or she should stress the enthusiasm and qualifications he or she brings to the practice and explain how being there will benefit patients overall. If the employee being replaced has left for a neutral or positive reason (such as to retire, have a baby, or move far away), mention that in the letter, too (with the former employee's permission).

This assignment serves two important purposes. First, it gets the staff member into personal contact with your patients in a positive way, which will make meeting them easier. But more importantly, a carefully-crafted letter will make your patients more receptive to the change and to your new staff member.

> **TIP:** *You might want to word this so the letter is from you. If so, take a look at the example of such a letter in Appendix 2-B).*

## GREAT FIRST DAY ASSIGNMENT #3

Another great first-day assignment is to have your new employee prepare for meeting the patients in your practice. Specifically, the new employee can study material about you and your practice so he or she will be able to answer patients' most basic questions. "I don't know, I just started working here" is usually avoidable with a little bit of preparation.

Before the new employee meets even a single patient, have him or her memorize a list of facts about you and your practice. Then give him or her a verbal test to see how well he or she has mastered the material. At the very least, your new employee should know:

- Each physician's name, pronounced and spelled correctly.
- How long each physician has been in practice and where he or she took professional training.
- Awards, honors, memberships, licenses, board certifications, etc. held by each physician.

A carefully-crafted letter will make your patients more receptive to your new staff member.

Write an article about your new staff member in your next patient newsletter.

- Your practice address and phone number.
- Locations and phone numbers of satellite offices.
- The correct pronunciation and spelling for your speciality, particularly if it is difficult to say or spell.
- A lay explanation of what you do.
- A short practice philosophy statement.
- Directions to your office, including parking and public transportation information.
- Your hours.
- Names and titles of all employees.
- The correct way to answer your telephone.
- Answers to your most frequently asked questions (about the services you offer, fees, appointment availability, etc.). Ask your other staff members to list these questions and their ideal answers.

> **TIP:** *Have one of your staff members prepare flashcards for this material to make learning easier for the new employee.*

## CAPTURE YOUR NEW EMPLOYEE'S DEBUT ON FILM

The day will come when you introduce a new employee to his or her first patient. This is a big moment for many employees and particularly for new associates fresh out of school. Don't let this moment come and go unnoticed.

Take an action photo of your new employee's first time "up at bat." Depending upon his or her position, it may be his or her first time answering your phone solo, his or her first collection call, the first patient he or she treats, or his or her first lab order completed.

Enlarge and frame the photo and present it to the new employee with some degree of ceremony at your next staff meeting. Just like the first dollar bill a new business frames and hangs on the wall, the photo will remind your employee of his or her humble beginnings and how much he or she has grown professionally since joining your practice. Your employee will come to cherish the photo as they years go by.

## FOUR MORE WAYS TO START OFF ON THE RIGHT FOOT WITH A NEW STAFF MEMBER

Here are four more ways to make your new employee feel special while helping your patients get to know him or her:

1. Write an article about your new staff member in your next patient newsletter. Focus on the wonderful asset this person will be to your practice and the new and interesting things he or she will be doing.
2. Feature the new staff member on your reception area bulletin board. To make it lively, create a display that looks like one you'd see

in a theater lobby to introduce the cast of a play. Put a headline above the employee's 8" × 10" black-and-white photo that reads, "Now Playing in Our Office . . ."

3. Run a contest that in some way features the new staff member. For example:

   - Have patients come up with as many words as they can using the letters in the new employee's name.
   - Have patients guess something personal about the staff member —where he or she was born, went to college, etc.
   - Give a prize to the patient who first sees your new staff member outside your office and repeats a designated phrase to him or her, like, "Rosa Valdez is the best new medical receptionist in town."
   - Run a poster contest for the children in your practice. Ask them to draw a picture of your new employee. Make the prizes enticing and publicize both the contest and the winners.

4. Take out a newspaper ad to announce the addition of the new staff member, particularly if you are expanding the scope of your services.

## WHY GO TO ALL THIS TROUBLE?

What you do from the moment your new employee steps into your office can determine whether he or she becomes an asset or a liability to you. Just a little bit of extra attention at this critical time can reduce your turnover and speed the new employee's acclimation to your practice.

Think of the new employee as a guest in your office. Welcome him or her as you would welcome a guest to your home. A well-planned, well-executed orientation program takes some effort, but is worth it. The time and energy you invest in orientation at the start will be paid back many times over by a loyal, well-trained, and highly motivated employee. And, employees who have had the benefit of an excellent orientation will in turn be able to provide the same for future new employees. ▲

What you do from the moment your new employee steps into your office can determine whether he or she becomes an asset or liability to you.

# How to Make Staff Training More Effective

*An employee-training program offers many benefits both to employees and to the professional practice. However, it takes time, effort, and know-how to structure an effective training program.*

*This chapter offers guidelines for staff training and explores specific training techniques that work. Among these are narrated demonstration, role-playing, flashcard training, study motivation exams, and tuition reimbursement programs. In addition, this chapter offers a script of a sample role-playing session.*

Good training for your staff assures a strong foundation for your employment relationship. When trained properly, your staff will know correct work methods, and they'll learn faster and easier. They'll understand the tasks they're responsible for and see how their duties fit into the total operation of your practice. In addition, they'll work with greater self-confidence and make fewer mistakes. Overall, their performance will be better.

Good training takes time, effort, sensitivity, and teaching ability. It is not always easy to help your staff master complicated material. Because we all learn differently, one teaching technique will not work for every employee, or for all the material they must master.

## GENERAL RULES FOR GOOD TRAINING

Which training technique you should use will depend on several factors: the material, the student, resources available, and the time you have, to name a few. In general, however, there are several rules common to all good training:

1. Have the right person do the training. For some tasks, another employee may be the ideal teacher. For others, you may be. For others, outside consultants, teachers, seminars, books, audio and videotapes, and other learning aids will be the best trainers.

> It is not always easy to help your staff master complicated material.

Occasionally, you may want to send a staff member to a colleague's office to observe and learn something new. And sometimes, the employee will need a combination of people, experiences, and training tools to help him or her learn best.

2. Learn to see things through the eyes of the beginner. When we have mastered tasks or material ourselves, it is easy to assume that the student shares our knowledge. Try to imagine how the material would seem to you if you had never encountered it before. Learn to anticipate impediments to learning, typical questions, and gaps in the employee's background that need to be filled.

3. Break down complicated material into steps or smaller units. It is very difficult to absorb a great deal of material at once. Likewise, training sessions should not be too long or try to cover too much material.

4. Explain the purpose in everything the employee learns. Don't get involved in the details before giving the material proper perspective. Doing so thwarts learning in the long run.

**Example:** *Suppose you're trying to teach a new assistant the correct procedure for sterilizing instruments. Before explaining the various steps, try motivating learning first by briefly describing why sterilization is so important. That way, not only will the assistant learn better now, but he or she will also be more likely to follow the procedure correctly later on, and not cut corners.*

5. Demonstrate visually whenever you can. Most people learn best when they can see and hear about the material at the same time.

**Example:** *When teaching an employee to prepare the exam room for a new patient, motivate him or her first by explaining why a fresh exam room is so important. Then, narrate as you run through the procedure. That way, he or she can associate your words with your actions.*

> **TIP:** *To maximize retention of the material, have the employee run through the procedure after your demonstration. Ask the employee to narrate as he or she goes.*

6. Be encouraging. Employees learn easier and faster when the trainer is patient and doesn't scold them for mistakes.

7. Prepare. Successful trainers prepare for their lessons and have all the supplies and equipment they'll need on hand. If you don't, your trainees may have to sit on their hands while you rush around trying to find missing items. That makes you look disorganized, and they may become confused; in addition, delays cost time and money.

New employees will greatly benefit from role-playing.

8. Set aside adequate time for staff training. Don't rush it or allow it to become catch-as-catch can.

9. Establish an individual training program for each employee. This should be among the first things you do for the new employee. Established employees should update their training plan at their regular performance reviews. To create on-target training programs, list all of the procedures and materials the employee is to learn. Then, establish priorities and a training schedule, including the study materials the employee will need, when the training will occur, and who will do the training in each subject.

   **TIP:** *When possible, train during regular working hours, not at night or on weekends. Set specific learning goals and the dates for beginning and completing the training.*

10. When training new employees, set aside 15 minutes at the end of each workweek to evaluate training programs. In your review, determine what's being done well, shortcomings, and areas for further training.

11. When training established employees, remember that doing the same things over and over can lead to boredom, dissatisfaction, and personnel changeover. Cross training is a great way to relieve the monotony. For example, you might cross-train a clinical assistant to do clerical duties, such as checking on insurance claims. Or, you might cross-train a business assistant to do clinical procedures.

   **TIP:** *Cross-training benefits your staff because they get to do a wider variety of tasks, which makes their jobs more interesting. It also benefits your practice by providing trained backup when the office is shorthanded.*

## HOW TO USE ROLE-PLAYING AS A TRAINING TOOL

Role-playing is an effective way to improve your staff's patient relations skills. It can teach your business assistant how to greet patients properly, handle patient concerns, persuade patients to pay on time, make and keep appointments, and refer others to the practice. It can also teach a clinical assistant how she might help a nervous child relax for a certain procedure, reinforce a patient who has been following your recommendations, or persuade a non-compliant patient to change his ways.

Unlike most other training tools, such as manuals, tapes, or lectures, role-playing is active and participative. Because of this, training is often more fun and the learning rate is traditionally very high.

New employees will greatly benefit from role-playing. However, even veteran employees will find the sessions helpful. After all, there's almost

> Your telephone receptionist is your front-line employee.

> The best tuition reimbursement plans are those that are coordinated with practice training goals.

always a better way to handle a tough situation. In addition, role-playing reveals annoying habits and mannerisms the employee may have.

Before beginning a role-playing session, make a list of the scenarios you want your staff to run through. Schedule the session so you'll have plenty of time and privacy. Meet in your office, not in a restaurant or other public place.

> **TIP:** *Use a video camera to tape the sessions (with everyone's permission) so staff members can see their actions more objectively.*

In addition to these suggestions, here are some other important tips for holding purposeful role-playing sessions with your staff:

1. Focus the activity by giving every session a subject, such as greeting patients, making financial arrangements, making collection calls, or handling a specific type of patient (child, elderly, etc.).
2. Create challenging situations. Encourage those who portray patients to be demanding, aloof, or resistant according to the exercise. As your staff develops greater competence, have the "patients" increase the challenge level.
3. After the exercise, have the featured staff member tell the group how he or she could have been more effective. This makes the staff member concentrate and reinforce the learning process. Moreover, he or she may preempt potentially threatening criticism from others.
4. Seek comments from the observers on what the staff member has done especially well. Stressing the good points draws attention to excellence and heads off defensiveness.
5. Ask observers to identify areas that need improvement. Keep the tone positive and insist on specific constructive criticism. Don't allow any staff member to be humiliated. Remember that it's difficult for many people to stand before their peers and hear critiques of their performance.
6. End the session by summarizing the points made.
7. Remember that there's no single best way to respond to a circumstance with a patient. Role-playing encourages participants to use their imaginations and instincts to respond to the many situations that confront them. Your staff should feel free to be themselves, not parrots of someone else. See the Sidebar for a sample script of a role-playing session.

## SPECIAL TIPS FOR TRAINING YOUR RECEPTIONIST

Your telephone receptionist is your front-line employee. He or she represents your practice to both people you know and people you've

## Sample Role-Playing Session

LEADER: Today, we'll do some role-playing and concentrate on greeting a patient. Our objective is to be friendly, pleasant, and helpful. We want to tell the patient that we're happy to see him and that we regard him as a whole person, not just a body we treat and a checkbook. We want to develop good rapport with our patients so they come back and refer others.

When greeting patients, avoid hackneyed phrases such as "May I help you?" Keep in mind a picture of yourself meeting a stranger at a party and starting a conversation. This situation isn't strictly comparable to meeting a patient, but it might help you.

(Now select a "staff member" and "patient" from the group.)

Let's begin with Ms. Thompson, a new patient who has just arrived for her first appointment.

STAFF MEMBER 1: Good morning. You must be Ms. Thompson.

PATIENT: Why yes, that's me.

STAFF MEMBER 1: Hello. I'm Susan. Welcome to The Family Practice of Springfield. We've been looking forward to meeting you.

LEADER: (Interrupts.) Good! Let's pause here. (To the staff member.) Anything you could have done even better?

STAFF MEMBER 1: I caught myself avoiding eye contact with the patient. And I didn't smile.

LEADER: (To others.) What did she do well?

STAFF MEMBER 2: She seemed in control. She introduced herself and the practice by name.

STAFF MEMBER 3: She knew the patient's name, which means she was expecting her. That shows the patient is important.

LEADER: OK. Good. Now is there anything she could have done even better?

STAFF MEMBER 4: She was right about the lack of eye contact. Also, she could have stood up when she greeted the patient.

STAFF MEMBER 5: It might have been nice if she had walked closer to greet the patient, away from the computer terminal. I always feel like distance puts me too far away to be really friendly.

LEADER: Thanks for the comments. Overall, I thought she did an excellent job. I'd feel welcomed to the practice. A warm smile, standing, and perhaps coming closer might have improved the greeting, but this is a still a great start.

(Ask the same "staff member" and "patient" to take another crack at the exercise, this time incorporating the group's suggestions. Afterwards, reinforce the positive changes.)

Now, let's have other people take the parts of the staff member and the patient. This time, let's greet Ms. Marino, an elderly lady who has been our patient for 15 years, but whom we haven't seen for a while. . . .

> Role-playing encourages participants to use their imaginations and instincts to respond to the many situations that confront them.

never met. Undoubtedly, he or she will be asked many questions. For these reasons, any employee you hire to be your receptionist should be trained to answer typical questions before picking up the phone the first time.

Your departing receptionist can probably make the transition go more smoothly. Several weeks before he or she leaves, instruct him or her to list all the typical questions callers ask. For example:

- How much is an exam?
- Where are you located?
- How do I get to your office?
- What are your hours?
- Does my insurance cover this?

After your receptionist makes the list, add questions you feel a competent receptionist should be able to answer. For example, you might add:

- How do you pronounce and spell each doctor's name?
- Where did each doctor go to school?
- What exactly is a gastroenterologist (urologist, ophthalmologist, etc.)? Who are the paraprofessionals in your practice and what do they do?
- Where did each doctor get his or her professional training?

Have your departing receptionist write each of these questions on a separate flash card, with the correct answer on back. Give the stack of cards to your new receptionist right away and explain that the first assignment is to memorize the information. Then give your new receptionist an oral test before he or she starts answering your phone, perhaps using a role playing session as described above.

> **TIP:** *This flashcard training method could be used for virtually any position in your practice.*

## USING TRAINING TOOLS WITH YOUR STAFF

There are many good materials, some specifically designed for professional office staffs, that can help your staff become more motivated, knowledgeable, and adept at personal and professional skills. Many offices establish a budget for these newsletters, magazines, books, and tapes for the office and set up a training library.

One doctor tells about an unusual method he uses to motivate his employees to learn. He found that when he provided his staff with books and tapes in the past, they didn't always use them. Now, he runs a contest for his staff. He assigns one book or tape per month. At the month's end, he gives his staff a voluntary written exam on the material. Staff members who pass the test receive a small bonus.

**Flashcard training can be used for virtually any position in your practice.**

The bottom line: He reports that his staff is now exceptionally motivated to use the books and tapes. Most importantly, they learn the material much more thoroughly than they had previously.

## TUITION REIMBURSEMENT INCREASES STAFF LEARNING

Reimbursing an employee for tuition payments is a long-established fringe benefit in the industry. However, a well-constructed program can also be productive in a professional practice and may be a drawing card for attracting top job applicants.

The best tuition reimbursement plans are those that are coordinated with practice training goals. Thus, you'll want to create a plan to increase your staff's competence, eliminate specific deficiencies, and reduce turnover. Some suggestions:

1. Require that the course, degree, or certification program be related to the staff member's development in your practice. For instance, for a business assistant, you might approve a course that addresses keyboarding speed and accuracy or your office's new computer software. You might even reimburse the employee for a course in Spanish if you practice in a Spanish-speaking area, or sign language if you treat (or would like to treat) deaf patients in your practice. Or, you might pay for assistants to take the Dale Carnegie course, to increase self confidence, communicate ideas more effectively, solve problems, think on their feet, overcome worry and tension, make better decisions, and get along better with people. All of these courses would be related to their tasks in your practice.

2. Consider reimbursing staff members for courses that would help them earn a promotion in your practice. For example, you might reimburse a business assistant for courses that would prepare him or her to be your office manager. You might pay for nursing or other clinical courses that would enable an assistant to perform new procedures or earn new certification. These kinds of opportunities are good for everyone. They reduce turnover because staff members can work on their own career goals and still remain in your practice.

   TIP: *If you structure this kind of program, make it available to staff members who have been in your office for a prescribed minimum amount of time, such as 2 years. Also include some sort of repayment provisions so the employee does not get you to pay for his or her new credential and then get another job somewhere else. For example, you might require the employee to pay back 75% of your tuition payments if he or she quits within a year of earning a new certification or degree, and 40% if he or she quits within two years.*

A well-constructed tuition reimbursement program may be a drawing card for attracting top job applicants.

3. Limit the number of courses you will reimburse the employee for at one time. Typical limit: Two courses. As well, limit the total dollar amount you will reimburse per year per employee. Finally, limit the amount of time an employee can take off from work to satisfy course requirements.

4. Consider tying reimbursement to grades. For example:
   - 100% reimbursement for an A
   - 85% reimbursement for a B
   - 70% reimbursement for a C
   - 50% reimbursement for a D
   - No reimbursement for failure or a dropped course. ▲

Limit the number of courses you will reimburse the employee for at one time.

# When and How to Use Monetary Incentives

*Will money motivate your staff to perform better? While some practice managers prefer not to use bonus incentive programs, others use them frequently and report excellent results. This chapter explores the benefits and pitfalls of using monetary incentives with your staff. It explores the effectiveness of bonuses compared with raises. As well, it considers the four qualities of effective incentive bonus programs and gives examples of both percentage bonus programs and flat dollar bonus programs. In particular, this chapter includes how-to advice for structuring a new patient incentive bonus program along with the potential problems of such programs as reported by two doctors who tried them. Finally, this chapter explores the benefits of using merchandise rewards rather than cash and includes innovative ideas for maximizing bonuses by implementing a "cookie jar" system and dividing annual bonuses into two installments.*

Design incentives for your staff that motivate and reward the performance you truly want and that don't lead to problems.

> Employees must know specifically what they must do to earn the bonus.

A monetary staff incentive is a reward system designed to motivate staff members to improve their job performance. Some practice managers prefer not to use bonus incentive programs because they believe that bonuses will reward only specific performance and not overall achievement. Other practice managers believe that bonus systems are very effective and recommend them highly. One thing is clear; if you're going to use incentive systems of any kind in your practice, you must design incentives for your staff that motivate and reward the performance you truly want and that don't lead to problems.

## RAISES OR BONUSES?

Which do you think will give you better results with your employees—raises or bonuses? The answer will depend upon your employees and the results you're trying to achieve.

In general, salary raises increase employee performance over a long period of time. They are usually linked to accomplishment of specific, personal objectives for each employee, such as mastering new skills or improving current ones. For example, a business assistant might qualify for a raise if she masters the procedure for making financial arrangements with patients by the time of her next salary review. Or, a clinical assistant might earn a raise if he learns how to perform a designated new procedure by the end of the next three months.

Bonuses, unlike raises, improve performance only for a short period of time. Like sales commissions, they can sometimes thwart long-term improvement by making employees concentrate on immediate objectives at the expense of long-term goals. That's why it's usually best *not* to target a bonus to a new, unlearned skill. Instead, the most effective bonuses create an incentive for employees to improve some skill or activity they have already learned.

For your bonus or raise to function as a true incentive for your staff, it should be justified by and clearly linked to the employee's performance. As well, make sure that the raises or bonuses you create are worth your expense. Remember that compensation of all employees in your medical practice, including raises and bonuses, should not exceed a reasonable percentage of your total practice income.

## FOUR QUALITIES OF EFFECTIVE INCENTIVE BONUS PROGRAM

All effective incentive bonus programs share four common qualities or characteristics. Specifically, the most effective incentive bonus programs:

1. **Ensure that employees know about and understand the program.** Employees must know specifically what they must do to

earn the bonus. Bonuses given on whim or automatically (such as a holiday, birthday, or vacation bonus or an unexpected bonus for a job well done) do not directly motivate better performance and may be quickly taken for granted. Such bonuses are not *incentive* bonuses, though they can function as thoughtful gifts and can help generate goodwill.

2. **Encourage employees to stretch.** A too-ambitious bonus program will cause employees to give up. On the other hand, bonuses that are too easy to earn won't improve performance significantly.

3. **Provide immediate reinforcement when an employee earns a bonus.** Make sure that prizes are awarded quickly and that the employee is aware of and appreciates the extra he or she has earned.

   TIP: *If you want your cash bonuses to have the most impact, don't include them in your employees' regular paychecks. Doing so dilutes their effectiveness, especially when the bonus is for a small amount such as $10. Instead, write separate checks for all bonuses and note on them that they are bonuses and what they are for. For example: "Bonus for three new patients in April." Writing separate bonus checks may seem like unnecessary extra work, but it's a sure way to make employees appreciate that their bonuses are indeed extra. Moreover, your staff will get two morale boosts from the extra check. The first boost will come when they receive it; the second will come when they endorse the check at the bank.*

4. **Need not be a permanent program.** When introducing a new bonus incentive program, you might establish it for a short time only, such as one month. That way you can assess the effectiveness of the bonus program, change it, or take it away without disappointing your staff.

   TIP: *Many practices establish short-term bonus programs in slow months when production, recall, and collections are traditionally at their lowest.*

## EXAMPLES OF PERCENTAGE BONUS PROGRAMS

In a percentage bonus program, the staff shares bonuses each month or quarter for increased production or collections. By giving staff a "piece of the action," so to speak, they feel that the practice they work in is *their* practice as well as yours. A percentage bonus program stimulates staff to keep the practice running at capacity. As well, the total share of gross practice income spent on staff compensation always remains acceptable.

> A too-ambitious bonus program will cause employees to give up.

Make sure
that prizes
are awarded
quickly.

## Cookie Jar Bonus Plan Keeps Costs Down

Providing $5 and $10 bonuses may fail to motivate some
employees. But for only $300, or an average of $13.64 per bonus,
you can devise an incentive reward program that is effective and
exciting for almost anyone. Here's how:

1. Buy a cookie jar and 22 small, identical opaque containers.
   Coin envelopes, film canisters, and jewelry boxes work well.
2. Fill the containers with money as follows:
   - 10 with a crisp new $5 bill
   - 5 with a crisp new $10 bill
   - 5 with a crisp new $20 bill
   - And two with a crisp new $50 bill
3. Write a list of what's in the small containers on a card and
   attach it to the cookie jar. Then seal the small containers and
   put them in the jar.
4. Explain to your staff what you've done and tell them specifically
   what they must do to take a container from the cookie jar. For
   example, they might have to refer a new patient or improve
   collections by a certain percentage.
5. When an employee qualifies for a bonus, call everyone
   together and allow him or her to take a container from the jar.
   With a few well-chosen words, you can turn this event into a
   small ceremony.

Percentage bonus systems vary from one practice to the next. Here are
a few of the most common ones reported by medical practices around
the country:

- One doctor pays his financial secretary a bonus equal to 1% of
  collections over a set dollar amount each month. His appointment
  secretary earns a bonus of 1% of production over a set amount
  monthly.
- Another doctor pays his clinical assistant a bonus based upon a dollar
  amount for production she helped produce. His receptionist gets a
  percentage bonus based upon kept appointments and another
  percentage based upon recall appointments. The posting/insurance
  clerk gets a percentage bonus based upon collections. The office
  manager's bonus depends upon the total office production and on
  new patients.
- A number of doctors use a shared bonus program. In one practice,
  the entire staff splits 10% of the increase in production over the
  previous month. In another, the staff divides 22% of collections over
  their goal. In another, the staff divides 18% of collections over goal,
  but they divide it according to the proportionate hours worked.

- In another practice, the doctor established that if the collection ratio compared to staff salary is below a set percentage, the staff gets the difference split equally among them.

## EXAMPLES OF FLAT DOLLAR-BONUS PROGRAMS

The most common flat dollar bonus is the bonus given for new patient referrals. (See "Special Tips for the New Patient Incentive Bonus" below.) Most practices providing such a bonus pay a flat $10-$75 bonus for each new patient a staff member refers to the practice.

Flat dollar bonuses are as varied as percentage bonuses. Here are a few of the most common ones medical practices use:

- A "jackpot" bonus for new patient referrals, paying $10 for every new patient referred by the staff. This is paid NOT to the staff member, but into a common pot. When the pot is large enough, the money is used for a staff outing or party of their choice.
- A $25 bonus for the best suggestion of the month.
- One doctor pays a flat $10 bonus to every clinical assistant working on a day the practice exceeds its production goal.
- Similarly, another practice averages gross production for the last six months and rewards each staff member with a flat dollar bonus based upon the increase over the previous six months. Bonuses range from $25 to $5,000, depending upon the size of the production increase.
- In another practice, a staff member can earn a flat dollar bonus if he or she convinces a patient to accept the doctor's elective treatment recommendations (if the patient has not already done so).

## SPECIAL TIPS FOR THE NEW PATIENT INCENTIVE BONUS

To encourage staff members to promote their practices, many practice managers award flat dollar bonuses for patient referrals. Although money is certainly an effective motivator for generating staff referrals, be aware of the potential problems of such bonus programs.

One doctor tells it this way: "I had a staff member refer a friend, so I gave her the usual bonus. This friend ended up bringing in five new patients—her husband, mother, and three children. Now my assistant wants to be paid the bonus for each of them. What if that friend refers someone else in two years? Do I owe the staff member for that referral, too?"

Another doctor reports yet another problem: "I give a $15 bonus for each referral. One of our new patients recently told us she came to the practice because of our receptionist's referral. Naturally, I gave the bonus to the receptionist. Now, however, another assistant claims that she was responsible for the patient's visit. I assumed they both had a

> If in doubt,
> pay the
> bonus.

> Take a lesson
> from large
> companies that
> offer sales
> incentives such
> as trips,
> televisions, and
> appliances.

hand in it, so I offered to split the bonus. However, my receptionist refuses. She doesn't want to give half of the money back. I don't mind paying them both the full bonus this time. But I have six employees. What if they all want to be paid the full bonus for every new patient? I've got to set some limits, but how?"

Not having a clearly-defined policy for such situations can turn what should have been a morale booster into bitter resentment. Here are several policies for nipping such problems in the bud:

- If in doubt, pay the bonus. In the case of the doctor who had two assistants claiming to be the referral source, he should pay the full bonus to both employees—this time. However, once this case is settled, he should set a policy to prevent it from happening again.
- When instituting a bonus program, state the date it takes effect. Tell employees that all referrals made before this date are appreciated but that they won't be compensated. You are opening yourself up to a sticky mess if you try to reconstruct the past.
- Make a rule about referrals from referred patients. Although one option is not to pay a bonus for them at all, a more motivating policy is to set a time limit, perhaps 30 or 60 days.

   **TIP:** *To eliminate arguments and resentment, specify that patients must call to schedule appointments on or before your deadline day. Also require that the staff member be in your employ the day the patient calls.*

- Consider placing bonuses in an office pool. Use the money for a staff outing, something new for your staff break room, or divide it equally among employees each quarter. This may stimulate friendly competition among staff members because everyone will know what everyone else is doing. However, avoid this strategy if you have one very strong referral source on your staff. He or she may not appreciate the fact that other employees are not pulling their weight and are benefiting from his or her efforts.

   **TIP:** *If you do choose to put new patient bonuses in a kitty, divide the amount equally among full- and part-time staff. A part-timer is just as likely to make a new patient referral as a full-timer and should be rewarded equally.*

---

### "Christmas" in July Gives Oomph to Annual Bonus

If you give your staff only one bonus annually, why not split it into two payments? One can be given at the year's end, the other in July.

The split means your staff enjoys the pat on the back your bonus gives them twice. Even though it's the same amount of money, and in smaller increments, your staff may appreciate the bonus more. As well, splitting the bonus can improve your cash flow by giving you use of half the money for an extra six months.

   **TIP:** *If you decide to make "Christmas" in July this year, be sure your staff knows they will receive only half their regular bonus this December. Try timing the summer bonus to vacations or a slow or difficult time.*

## THE RIGHT STUFF MAY BE BETTER THAN CASH

Most people are motivated by the lure of earning a substantial cash bonus. But will a smaller, $10 or $20 bonus serve as much incentive for your staff to work harder? Not always.

To some people, a small sum will be absorbed quickly into the household budget and go virtually unnoticed. In some cases, a small bonus can actually backfire. Employees may feel that token sum is inadequate compensation for the effort they put forth. Even worse, they may find the small sum insulting.

For these reasons, many employers opt for giving merchandise rather than cash, especially when small sums are involved. The employee who receives wanted merchandise will remember that it came from his or her employer each time he or she uses it or someone comments on it. Take a lesson from large companies that offer sales incentives such as trips, televisions, and appliances. They give gifts rather than cash precisely so employees will remember where they got the merchandise.

What merchandise will appeal to everyone? Rather than choosing and risking doing the wrong thing, a practical solution is to order a gift certificate to a catalog of items from which the staffer may choose bonus merchandise. Or, give staff members gift certificates to local stores, restaurants, or theaters.

> TIP: *One doctor asks employees to name the luxury merchandise they'd most like to have. Then he sets up personal incentive programs to help them earn them. For example, his senior employee (who has been with the practice for more than 20 years) has earned substantial bonuses over the years, including a fur coat and a trip to Hawaii. The employee says she would never have been able to afford these things if not for the bonus incentive programs. The doctor says employees earn their bonuses fair and square and that every penny he spends on bonuses is well spent, not only in increased performance, but even more so in staff loyalty.* ▲

One senior employee has earned substantial bonuses over the years, including a fur coat and a trip to Hawaii.

# Nonmonetary Incentives and Rewards Can Motivate Your Staff

*Staff bonuses of cash and merchandise are widely used as a performance incentive tool, and they have steadily increased in popularity in medical practices during the past decade. Bonuses paid to staff, however, often do not work as intended, and they unintentionally can create new practice management problems.*

*This chapter explores why popular employee bonus programs may fail. It provides alternative ideas to help motivate and reward outstanding staff performance, ideas that have proved to be very effective and less trouble ridden than bonus systems. Suggestions include the use of regular performance and salary reviews, promotions, redistribution of job duties, special events, letters of commendation, and an employee-of-the-month program.*

Cash bonuses and bonus merchandise have long been used in medical practice management to encourage better job performance from employees. In my work with professional practices, however, I have found that money alone rarely motivates employees to reach their fullest potential. Simply put, monetary bonuses do not help people find satisfaction and fulfillment in their work. Many practice management consultants agree with me that monetary bonuses are so badly misused, and so often backfire, that most practices should use them sparingly or not at all (see Sidebar, next page).

Obviously, each person who works in your practice is different and has different motivations. It is not likely that a single management technique

> Money alone rarely motivates employees to reach their fullest potential.

Dangling financial bonus "carrots" in front of your staff will not always produce the employee performance improvements that you expect.

## Why Bonus Systems Fail

Monetary bonus systems designed to increase staff performance often do not work. Although many medical practices were drawn to using bonus programs, particularly during the past decade, and although some do find them useful, dangling financial bonus "carrots" in front of your staff will not always produce the employee performance improvements that you expect. Worse, bonuses very often backfire and create enormous and unanticipated management problems. Bonus systems do not work for the following reasons:

- **Production and collection-based bonuses are often unfair.** For example, luck might increase your practice, e.g., a large employer moves into your backyard and you gain a huge number of new patients. Or, the physician might take continuing education courses so as to offer more services to patients or to increase practice marketing efforts. If the practice increases in these ways, production and collections will go up, yet employees will have done nothing to attract this new business. Likewise, if the physician gets a divorce or his or her attitude takes a nosedive, production might drop off, and bonuses will, too. Again, staff behavior will have had nothing to do with the change.

- **It can be tricky deciding which employee deserves a bonus.** For example, if you pay a cash bonus for bringing a new patient into the practice, several staff members might feel they had a hand in bringing a particular individual to the fold. Who would get the bonus in such a case? (See Chapter 2-4.)

- **Money is not the root cause of desirable performance improvement.** Many bonus programs encourage employees to focus on the short term, rather than on what is best for the practice. For example, in one practice, the long-term patient retention rate dropped from 95 to 90%, but the short-term production was increasing. Employees thought that a downturn in the long term was fine as long as they were making more in bonus dollars today.

- **Profit-based bonus plans make financial adversaries of practice owners and employees.** Bonuses paid on the profitability of the practice prevent the physician from taking full advantage of the tax laws to minimize annual tax payments. The business owner wants to minimize profits to avoid paying higher taxes, and the employees want the practice to report as much profit as possible, because it increases their bonuses. Some practices try to get around this by paying bonuses on production, but this is risky. A practice can produce $500,000 a year, yet it can cost $500,00 or more to produce it.

- **Shared bonuses make adversaries among employees.** Some practices divide a bonus "pot" among all staff members, rather than rewarding individuals. Although such a system seems fair, some staff members might feel that they did all the work and that it is not fair for others to enjoy a free ride.

- **Bonus programs are one-sided.** If you have a bonus system, then you are in some ways making every employee a working owner of the practice, but only a "fair weather" owner. If the ownership concept is truly to work, you would have to have employees share in your losses as well as your profits. Few would agree to taking this chance.

will work with everyone. And, there is no substitute for paying a fair wage. For most of us, however, the number of dollars in our paychecks is no more important (and might even be less important) than nonmonetary factors such as agreeable working conditions, recognition of our accomplishments, flexibility of hours, challenge, variety, and friendships among co-workers.

Fortunately, there are many things an astute practice manager can do to motivate employees other than dangling "cash carrots" in front of them. These non-monetary incentives and rewards require sensitivity to the individual needs and desires of employees, and, in some cases, time, planning, and imagination. The results, however, will be infinitely superior to any that money alone could buy.

## PROMOTIONS CAN MOTIVATE AND REWARD

The potential to move up within the practice structure can be a great motivator and an incentive to work harder. Advancement in job duties, responsibilities, title, and pay means that staff members are progressing and being recognized for their achievements. For some, earned promotions can be the ultimate motivator and reward throughout their working lives.

The decision, however, of when and how to promote employees is not always an easy one to make. Also, when the practice is small, there will not always be lots of openings in higher level positions. Therefore, keep these tips in mind when making promotion decisions that are intended to provide performance incentives:

- Discuss with staff members their dreams for promotion, and clarify exactly what employees must do to be promoted. These discussions will be most effective when they are incorporated into the semiannual performance reviews.
- Ask staff members where they would like to be in 5 or 10 years. Then, discuss the ways in which this growth could happen within your practice, and the specific actions that employees would need to take to accomplish these goals. For example, describe the additional education, mastery of new skills and technology, or better performance in specified areas employees would have to demonstrate to earn promotions.
- Promote employees only on the basis of their accomplishments, not their seniority. It can be very discouraging for employees to know that they have no shot at an upcoming promotion because there are so many employees with longer service records. Certainly, such an environment will not stimulate better performance, and it might encourage a motivated junior employee to leave.
- Promote truly, not in name only. Some "promotions" are empty titles for people who are still doing their old jobs, perhaps with few new

The potential to move up within the practice structure can be a great motivator and an incentive to work harder.

responsibilities. A real promotion, however, should bring a new level of responsibility. It might be impractical for you to relieve your promoted employees of all of their previous duties. Nonetheless, do try to relieve them of some, to adjust their job descriptions, and to give them new authority and responsibilities.

- Do not assume that every staff member wants to be promoted. Some might prefer more input or increased responsibility in their current jobs. Some might prefer to stay exactly where they are, with no new responsibilities or challenges. Identify employees for whom promotion holds no appeal but who might be motivated by other means.

## REMOVE DISTASTEFUL TASKS TO IMPROVE PERFORMANCE

Some employees do not seek promotions. They would be much happier staying in their current jobs, with a few alterations. For this reason, it pays to ask your staff members to share their dislikes and pet peeves concerning their jobs at your next performance review. On the basis of what you learn, you might promise to take away a staff member's most dreaded task, if he or she meets specified new goals.

For example, suppose you learn that your business assistant hates making collection calls. If so, you might offer the chance to get rid of the task and to do something else productive instead, if the assistant improves your no-show and cancellations rate by a specified amount and time. Then, if the assistant accomplished this task, reassign job duties accordingly. Do not assign dreaded tasks to another employee unfairly. It is usually easiest to make changes in job assignments when you have a new job opening or are creating a new position.

In a recent consulting assignment, I met Stephanie, a very capable front desk employee who reluctantly told me that she disliked practically all of her job duties. The front desk was dull, she said, not where the "action" of the practice was. She told me that the duties of the clinical staff looked much more exciting. I recommended that when an opening in the clinical staff occurred, Stephanie should move into a clinical aide trainee position, and a new business assistant should be hired to take over her front desk duties. This happened in short time, and the results have been fabulous. Although Stephanie took a pay cut, she is now much happier and more productive in her work, and the practice has a new business assistant who loves doing that job. Knowing an employee's likes and dislikes and offering opportunities to make the job more enjoyable and fun can be extremely motivating to job performance. To pull this off, however, your employees must feel that they can be honest in expressing their negative feelings about their job duties. This strategy will not work if the employees fear that speaking up

Do not assume that every staff member wants to be promoted.

might mean losing their jobs. You must make your staff feel secure if you wish to use this technique to motivate and reward good performance.

## EVENTS AS INCENTIVES OR REWARDS

A special event for your staff can be used to reward good performance and to instill a team attitude. For example, a practice party, picnic, banquet, theater outing, or retreat are all effective events that can boost team spirit and morale.

To be a true incentive, the event should not be automatic; it should be given only for achievement of specified goals. For example, you might promise your staff a fancy dinner or an outing to a show if they exceed your quarterly production goals. Or, you might promise them an old-fashioned picnic or the chance to go to a meeting out of town if they improve their collections ratio by a specified amount and date.

The key is in suggesting a truly motivating event (or better yet, a choice of events) and then explaining precisely how your staff can earn it. Do not confuse an incentive event with a general staff appreciation event that is not tied to specific new job achievements. For example, if you hold an annual holiday party or summer picnic for your staff, regardless of particular performance, the event will not motivate specific new achievements or performance.

Consider, as an alternative, a new addition to your staff breakroom that could take the place of an event. For example, you might promise your staff a refrigerator, microwave, or other wanted item for the breakroom if the employees achieve specified goals by a specified time.

## OTHER NONMONETARY REWARDS

Just saying "thank you" or "well done" to deserving employees can go a long way toward improving productive performances, as can catching them in the act of doing things right. In addition, try some of these nonmonetary rewards for your staff:

- Write a letter of commendation to an employee who has done an exceptional job on a particular project. Be specific about what the employee has achieved, and how much you appreciate it. Mail the letter to the employee's home, and keep a copy in the employee's personnel file.
- Announce an outstanding staff achievement at a staff meeting and solicit a round of applause.
- Start an "Employee of the Month" program and create a bulletin board display in your reception area that features your chosen employee. If you have a large practice and a busy parking lot, have a sign erected to designate a choice space as the "Employee of the Month" space.

> Just saying "thank you" or "well done" to deserving employees can go a long way.

> Medical practices can easily get trapped by "union mentality" employees.

- Brag about your staff's outstanding accomplishments in your patient newsletter.
- Make your staff's accomplishments the focus of press releases or even paid advertisements.
- Create awards for your employees and bestow certificates or small trophies when the awards are earned. You might even plan an annual awards ceremony to draw more attention to staff accomplishments.

## THE BEST INCENTIVE PROGRAM OF ALL

Medical practices can easily get trapped by "union mentality" employees and begin production-only bonus systems, automatic cost-of-living increases, automatic raises every year, and similar financial programs. I think that this is the exact opposite of what these practices should be doing to survive and prosper.

The very best way to motivate employee performance is to develop accurate job descriptions, to assign accurate and fair wage scales, and to monitor performance. The employee's income should be based upon the job performance, as measured against job goals and expectations, and it should not exceed the maximum wage designated for that particular position.

Many practice managers fear that it is too difficult or too stressful to manage the staff in this manner. Doing it right, however, actually produces less stress and greater improvements. By conducting semiannual performance and salary reviews and by tying raises to goal achievements, you can reward employees for good, desired performance that has been documented and measured against the expectations of the practice.

In the end, goal setting, performance evaluations, and raises will improve staff performance much more effectively and more meaningfully than any bonus program has or ever will. ▲

# Developing a Competitive Benefits Program

*Offering your employees the right fringe benefits can help staff morale soar, foster loyalty, and increase the chances that a top-notch job applicant will say yes when you offer him or her the job. This chapter suggests practical ways to offer a competitive benefits program without breaking the bank. It includes specific guidance about offering a uniform allowance and shares one practice's unusual method of providing uniforms for its employees. It describes the best way to offer day care as a fringe benefit and reviews six fitness incentive programs from industry that can work in a medical practice.*

*As well, this chapter suggests a dozen more extra benefits employees value and a sample cafeteria-style fringe benefit plan. Finally, this chapter includes guidelines about creating and using your own benefits statement with your staff, along with a model statement form you can use or adapt to your needs.*

The usual fringe benefits such as health insurance, paid holidays, and vacations are certainly important to employees. Most medical practices offer their staffs the basics. However, you can make a big difference in the quality of the applicants you attract to your medical practice, and in staff morale and motivation, by topping off your benefits package with a few unexpected extras.

Extra benefits you offer your staff need not be expensive or difficult to implement or administer. The key is that the benefits be desirable and appreciated, particularly if they are not benefits typically offered in other jobs.

> A uniform allowance is almost always a desired benefit in medical practices.

Day care
as a fringe
benefit is best
offered under
a cafeteria-
style plan.

## PROVIDING A UNIFORM ALLOWANCE AS A FRINGE BENEFIT

Your attorney can advise you about any legal obligations you may have to provide a uniform allowance for minimum wage employees. But even if it turns out that you don't have to pay for a uniform, you may still want to. It is almost always a desired fringe benefit in medical practices.

A uniform allowance is used for the purchase, laundering, and mending of uniforms. Uniforms can be a considerable expense to an employee and one that he or she may resent, especially if he or she doesn't like having to wear a uniform or doesn't like the one you require. Typically, the allowance in most practices is a few dollars a week, roughly the equivalent of one hour of minimum wage pay.

## PROVIDING DAY CARE AS A FRINGE BENEFIT

If you're considering offering day care as a fringe benefit, you'll have to decide what form and amount of the benefit to provide. The three most common methods of providing day care as a fringe benefit are:

1. Choose a single day care center near your office. Make an arrangement with it to provide care for employees' children and bill you directly. If you wish to pay only a portion of this cost, have the remainder of the fee withheld automatically from the employee's paycheck (with his or her knowledge).
2. Participate in a day care center in your building. This is most likely to occur if you are in a large office complex. Again, you may wish to pass some of your costs on to your employees.
3. Provide an allowance for day care. Let the employee choose any accredited day care center.

The third option is the easiest to implement. For one thing, it is usually better for you *not* to choose a particular day care facility. You don't want to be blamed for a poor program or other problems. If the employee makes the choice, he or she is responsible. For another, employees will generally prefer choosing their own programs. They may want a special type of program or prefer a certain location, such as near their home or spouse's place of employment.

In fairness to all employees, day care as a fringe benefit is best offered under a cafeteria-style plan, described below. Since only some employees will have use for such a benefit, it is best to provide alternatives of comparable value for the remaining employees.

## ESTABLISHING FITNESS INCENTIVE PROGRAMS

An employee fitness program can be a great attraction for superior job applicants and one of the best investments you can make in your practice. Healthy employees are happier, absent less often, higher spirited, and save money for their employers. Below are six alternative fitness programs that have worked well in industry. Each of them, perhaps with some modifications, can work equally well in a medical practice.

1. Company A paid employees a bonus to lose weight or stop smoking. Employees who enrolled in the weight loss program received $5 a pound for up to 50 pounds they lost in six months. (However, the employees had to pay $10 a pound to the company's charitable fund for each pound they gained back in the next six months.) Employees who quit smoking for six months earned up to $200. (Again, the employees had to pay double the bonus to the charitable fund if they later resumed smoking.)

2. Company B bought racquetball court time for employees.

3. Company C provided aerobic dance classes for employees. You might encourage your employees to take fitness classes at a nearby facility. If so, tell them that while you expect them to pay for the classes, you will reimburse them later, based upon their attendance.

4. Company D offered employees memberships to local health clubs. Many clubs offer discounts for group memberships.

   **TIP:** *To keep costs low, you might pay half the club fee the first year and pay the entire renewal fee based upon attendance records. As well, look into YMCA's, community recreation departments, and other less-expensive fitness programs.*

5. Company E sponsored an annual race series in which they challenged employees of other companies to run against their employees. Most companies pay for T-shirts and entry fees. Consider challenging other medical practices in your community to a race. This can also be a great way to get media coverage to promote your practice. Donate entry fees to a worthwhile cause.

   **TIP:** *One practice rant this sort of program and challenged colleagues to see who had the fastest practice in town. The event was a huge success, not only in dollars raised for charity, but also in goodwill, staff morale, and positive media exposure.*

6. Company F sponsored a company bowling program. Bowling is a very popular and easy benefit to offer. Simply, enroll your practice in a bowling league in your community. Have shirts made with your practice name on it. Then consider giving your staff nice bowling

> Healthy employees are happier, absent less often, higher spirited, and save money for their employers.

### How One Practice Provides Uniforms as a Fringe Benefit

One doctor reports that he designed his own uniforms when he couldn't find the exact right look for his staff. The cost was $700 per employee which covered everything—shoes, purse, jacket, ties, pants, blouses, skirts.

Although the practice buys the uniforms, it provides them to the staff for their use at no cost. The practice also pays for the uniforms to be altered to fit. (There is a maternity version of the uniform available for pregnant employees.) The uniforms are the property of the practice, not the employee, and must be returned if the employee leaves.

Although not a true uniform "allowance," issuing uniforms in this manner will cut the employee's expenses and resentment considerably. At the same time, it allows the practice to have absolute control over the color and style of the uniform and accessories worn and to decide when a uniform needs to be replaced because of wear.

balls, bags, shoes, and other bowling equipment for a holiday present. This can be a great way to build morale and develop a team attitude.

**TIP:** *If you have only a few employees, invite their spouses and grown children to be on your team.*

## ONE DOZEN EXTRA BENEFITS EMPLOYEES VALUE

Here is a list of 12 additional fringe benefits being offered by professional practices around the country:

1. Preferred parking. If you practice in a busy downtown location, you might pay for a reserved parking space in a nearby garage. If you have a parking lot, you might reserve a section for staff parking.

   **TIP:** *Employees may especially appreciate seeing their names on their parking spaces. Ask them.*

2. A safe, covered area to park and lock bicycles, if employees are inclined to ride them to your office.

3. Transportation allowance to defray the costs of commuting to and from your office.

4. Grooming allowance to be used for hair cutting and styling, manicures, etc.

5. A pleasant break room. Your employees will appreciate a nicely decorated staff lounge, especially if it has a few extras like a refrigerator, microwave oven, coffee pot, hot water dispenser, or lockers. As well, they may make good use of a simple outdoor picnic area in your building's backyard.

6. Paid memberships. These include memberships to AAA (the Automobile Association of America), video rental clubs, and warehouse discount stores. As well, some employers provide books of discount coupons. These are offered in many communities for reduced prices at restaurants, stores, salons, movie theaters, pharmacies, and other establishments.

7. Free or discounted professional services for your employees.

8. Free or discounted professional services for the employee's family.

> Your employees will appreciate a nicely decorated staff lounge.

9. A shower in the office. Employees who like to jog or bike to work will appreciate this, but so might those who take exercise classes before work or who need to go to meetings or classes directly from work.

10. Organized van or car pools.

11. Matched saving. This is a program in which employees save a certain amount and the employer matches it.

12. Profit sharing. These plans benefit long-term employees. Because of this, some management consultants caution that younger employees usually prefer salary or other benefits to a profit sharing plan.

## CAFETERIA FRINGE BENEFIT PLAN LETS EMPLOYEES CHOOSE

Cafeteria-style fringe benefit plans emerged many years ago to meet the growing need for flexible employee benefits. Under such plans, employees are given an allowance and are offered a list of benefits from which they "buy" the ones that are most practical or appealing. Each employee thereby adjusts the benefit package to meet his or her own needs.

One doctor instituted a cafeteria plan for his employee. He says, "Personally, I like it. We're a large group practice with about 40 employees, but I don't see why a similar plan wouldn't work in a smaller office." His office manager adds, "The employees in our practice really value having some say over their benefits. Many of them especially like the uniform and grooming allowance, but not all opt for it."

Here are the components of this practice's cafeteria plan:

1. All full-time employees receive a contribution to their fringe benefit account at each pay period.

2. The amount of the contribution relates to the employee's length of employment. It starts at 8% of base salary and increases by 1% each six months from the date of employment to a maximum of 24%.

3. Employees may use the funds in their accounts for fringe benefits or they can choose to have the account paid out as income, after appropriate taxes have been withheld. The fringe benefits offered are:

   A. Health insurance
   B. Uniform allowance
   C. Grooming allowance
   D. Monthly parking
   E. Sick days (following set guidelines)

Employee benefits can cost more than 30 cents for ever dollar paid in wages.

> ## A benefits statement should be accurate, informative, and attractive.

F.  Personal days. These must be schedule in advance. Employees may take no more than two per year, except with the office manager's permission.

G.  Vacation days (as soon as the employee has 50% of the cost of that vacation accumulated in the account). Vacation days must be scheduled in advance and approved by the doctor and office manager. Vacation must be taken in increments of at least four successive days. To calculate the cost of a vacation day, divide the current annual salary by 52 weeks (week rate) and divide the week rate by five.

H.  Professional meeting days. These must be scheduled in advance and are charged to the fringe benefit account at a half-day rate.

I.  Expenses for attending professional meetings.

J.  Professional dues/subscriptions.

K.  Life insurance.

L.  Retirement program.

**TIP:** *You will probably want to make some fringe benefits mandatory, such as vacation and health insurance. Then, you may make the remaining benefits options on a cafeteria plan, such as child care, grooming allowance, and a parking allowance. That way, you will ensure that every employee takes a vacation each year and has a certain level of insurance protection.*

## YEARLY BENEFITS STATEMENT REVEALS HIDDEN COSTS

Employee benefits can cost more than 30 cents for every dollar paid in wages. Because benefits are so costly, it is extremely important to offer the benefits your employees want most, making every dollar work hard.

**TIP:** *When calculating the total percentage of gross income you spend on staff compensation, remember to include your costs for employee benefits.*

One way to inform your employees of the value of their benefits is through an annual employee benefits statement. Such a statement creates an awareness of the additional financial protection employees have through the practice's employee benefits program.

Benefits statements can range from the simple to the complex. They can cover only one area, such as the practice's pension plan. Or, they can be more comprehensive and cover all aspects of employee benefits.

Essentially, a benefits statement should be accurate, informative, and attractive. Some tips:

## Sample Comprehensive W-2 Form

Year: _____

Employee: _____

Gross Wages.........................................$ _____
Matching Social Security ..........................$ _____
Workers' Compensation Insurance..................$ _____
State Unemployment and Disability Insurance ......$ _____
Federal Unemployment and Disability Insurance....$ _____
Profit-Sharing Contribution ........................$ _____
Medical Insurance..................................$ _____
Mid-Year Bonus ...................................$ _____
Uniform Allowance.................................$ _____
Continuing Education .............................$ _____
Miscellaneous.....................................$ _____
**Total** ...........................................$ _____

- **Restrict the information.** A benefits statement should be limited to the employee's annual salary, bonuses, what was received in terms of vacation, holidays, sick leaves, insurance payments, leaves of absence, uniform allowance, tuition reimbursement, and any other fringe benefits offered in the practice.
- **Seek help.** Good sources are your accountant, bookkeeper, and pension plan administrator.
- **Time it right.** The end of the year is a logical time to issue benefits statements to your staff. However, January can be a good time too, as can performance and salary review time.
- **Keep it simple.** The statement's format need not be elaborate and extensive. A single page with a simple straight-forward list is most effective. Briefly explain each benefit as well as the conditions associated with collecting it. Be sure to assign an accurate value to each benefit and to list the employee's total earnings for both salary and benefits.

When completed, step back and read the benefits statement as the employee would. Before you distribute it, be sure to add a cover letter expressing your thoughts about each employee's contributions to the practice. A benefits statement is a great way to make employees aware of the value of the benefits you provide, as well as an opportunity to acknowledge and thank them for the valuable roles they play.

Employees may especially appreciate seeing their names on their parking spaces. Ask them.

Add a cover letter to your benefits statement expressing your thoughts about each employee's contributions to the practice.

## DOCTOR ISSUES BENEFITS STATEMENT ALONG WITH W-2S

The first week of January was traditionally a stressful time in the office of one doctor. "That's when my staff receives their W-2 forms," the doctor explains. "They'd compare the forms to their weekly paychecks and wonder where all the money had gone. On the other hand, I felt frustrated because the W-2s didn't really reflect my outlay for each employee," he says.

After dreading this scene for several years, this doctor decided to do something about it by designing an employee benefits statement (see sidebar, preceding page) which he called his own "Comprehensive W-2 Form." The federal W-2 is attached to the top. "This form makes me and my employees feel better about the total costs of employment, which had otherwise been hidden," the doctor says. "But it also serves another valuable purpose. It reminds my staff of their mid-year bonuses and continuing education expenses. These are usually long forgotten by January," he explains.  ▲

# Nonverbal Aids for Improving Staff Communication

*Speaking face-to-face is the most common form of communication between doctor(s)/office managers and members of the medical practice staff. However, several nonverbal aids can enhance understanding tremendously and may be used in addition to or instead of speaking.*

*In this chapter, we will explore when and how to use the best nonverbal communication aids. These include memos, a staff bulletin board, an office mail center, correspondence routing, paycheck inserts, a staff newsletter, and staff surveys. This chapter also includes a sample staff survey and suggests situations that are not appropriate for using nonverbal aids.*

A bulletin board is an ideal place to post memos.

G ood, active communication with your staff depends upon the ability to have frequent opportunities to talk freely and openly. No other communication method can take the place of the face-to-face exchange of ideas between you and your employees.

However, talking is only one form of communication. There are many other communication methods that will help you improve your communication with your staff. The trick is to know which form of communication to use in which situations.

## THE POWER OF MEMOS VS. THE SPOKEN WORD

In most practices, internal memos to staff are rarely used. However, memos can be a powerful communication tool that should be used more often for many reasons:

- Face-to-face contact has limitations. Many listeners filter out a good part of spoken communications and misunderstand much of what is being said. Rather than listening carefully for content, the person receiving the spoken message may be busy wondering, "Why am I being told this now?" "What's behind all of this that affects my job?" and "What can I say to show I'm not to blame?" In addition, listeners sometimes have their minds on other things when receiving the message. The result can be message distortion.
- The receiver of a written memo may still ponder some of these questions, but the message has the advantage of impersonality. There's no need for an immediate response, so there's time to reflect and absorb the contents. The receiver can reread the message for better understanding when he has nothing to distract him.
- Many people have an easier time following written directions rather than oral ones.
- The written word is ideal to spell out the details of a complex new proposal or procedure, to summarize the pros and cons of a subject, or to get difficult ideas communicated thoroughly and in an organized manner.
- Being required to explain ideas in writing for another person forces you to think your ideas through completely and more logically. In the process, flaws and missing elements often become clear.
- When you need to give directions, memos can save time and unnecessary repetition. Instructions presented step-by-step can be followed sequentially. Everyone receives the same instructions in exactly the same way, so nothing is left out.

   **TIP:** *Do NOT use memos for sensitive issues, when the subject may be better explored through conversation. In addition, do NOT use memos when staff members have firm positions that*

## Writing forces you to think your ideas through completely.

*you are trying to change. Do NOT use memos when a give-and-take atmosphere is essential to the subject. Finally, do NOT use memos to deliver bad or confidential news, or when it is important that everyone hears the news at the same time.*

## OFFICE MAIL CENTER SIMPLIFIES STAFF COMMUNICATION

If you have more than a few employees, delivering memos, phone messages, and mail can be a time-consuming task. To streamline the job and eliminate mistakes, establish a staff mail center in your business office. Provide trays or boxes that are sturdy and large enough to accommodate letters, journals, and other mail your staff normally receives. Clearly label the bins in alphabetical order.

Staff members should check their mailboxes regularly, at least every morning and afternoon. That way, messages won't get lost on cluttered desks, and you won't waste time going to each work station delivering mail.

## HOW AND WHEN TO ROUTE CORRESPONDENCE

You may wish to route certain items to all or a few of your staff members, such as clinical or practice management books, journal articles, greeting cards that must be hand-signed, or brochures about upcoming conferences and seminars. Clip a note to each item pointing out why you think staff members would be interested in seeing it. Add anything specific you want staff members to read or do. Then date and sign it.

Design a simple routing form listing each employee's name. At the top, ask each staff member to read the attached information, cross off his or her name, and route it to the next person on the list. Stress timeliness if that is a factor. You also may want to provide a line or two for individual comments. Photocopy the form and keep a stack near your mail center. Then, when you do have something to route, attach a copy of the form to the item.

> **TIP:** *As an alternative to routing, you may want to post messages by your office mail center for everyone's attention. This saves unnecessary photocopying and routing. However, when it's important that all staff members read a message, list each staff member's name on the notice and post it with a pencil nearby. Instruct your employees to cross their names off the list after they've read the message.*

**Do NOT use memos to deliver bad or confidential news.**

## Sample Staff Survey

Read each statement and give the best response: Strongly Agree, Agree, Don't Know, Disagree, and Strongly Disagree.

| | Strongly Agree | Agree | Don't Know | Disagree | Strongly Disagree |
|---|---|---|---|---|---|
| Our office is well-organized. | | | | | |
| My duties are clearly outlined. | | | | | |
| My workload is just about right. | | | | | |
| The doctor(s)/office manager lets me know what he/she expects from me. | | | | | |
| My co-workers are friendly. | | | | | |
| My co-workers do their jobs well. | | | | | |
| I feel free to discuss problems or complaints with the doctor(s)/office manager. | | | | | |
| I am well-informed of changes in the practice that will affect me. | | | | | |
| I am paid fairly compared with the other employees in this practice. | | | | | |
| I am paid fairly compared with employees in other practices. | | | | | |
| The doctor(s) asks for and uses my ideas. | | | | | |
| Office policies are stated clearly. | | | | | |
| Our fringe benefits compare well with other practices. | | | | | |
| Staff members are willing to help each other out. | | | | | |
| I have the authority I need to perform my job well. | | | | | |
| My working hours are satisfactory. | | | | | |
| I am satisfied with the number of paid holidays and vacation days I receive. | | | | | |
| I am satisfied with my potential for advancement within the practice. | | | | | |
| I like my job the way it is. | | | | | |
| I know where I stand with the doctor(s)/office manager. | | | | | |

## INSTALL A STAFF BULLETIN BOARD

A small bulletin board above or near your office mail center is an ideal place to post memos, as suggested above. In addition, you can use a staff bulletin board to post minutes from staff meetings, employee vacation and holiday schedules, announcements of upcoming staff meetings and outings, notices of employee recognition, and announcements of upcoming meetings or continuing education opportunities.

In addition, you may allow staff to use the bulletin board to post non-confidential personal messages from patients and one another. For example, you might use the bulletin board to post thank-you notes from patients, postcards from vacationing staff members, newspaper clippings about births and marriages, inspirational quotes, amusing cartoons, party invitations, and photos.

> TIP: *A good morale booster: Allow staff to post their own notices, e.g., when trying to sell a car or sublet an apartment.*

## PAYCHECK INSERT CAN BOOST MORALE

Generally, staff will be in a good mood when they open their paycheck envelopes. An inserted message or small gift is your opportunity to praise a job well done and keep morale at a high level.

> TIP: *Insert only short, positive messages into paycheck envelopes. This is not the place to criticize or give bad news.*

## PUBLISH A STAFF NEWSLETTER

If you have more than four employees, consider publishing a quarterly newsletter/letter for your staff. In addition to being a morale booster, a staff newsletter can review practice news and procedures and publicize upcoming events.

A staff newsletter needn't and shouldn't be elaborate. All you need is some enthusiasm. Delegate responsibility for it to your office manager or another employee.

## STAFF SURVEYS OPEN LINES OF COMMUNICATION

Ideally, staff communication should be a two-way street. Especially in larger practices, it can be hard to gather everyone's opinion on an important issue. That's when a survey can come into play.

A staff survey might be used when contemplating a major change where staff opinion will count. It is a method for conducting a vote or for

A staff newsletter can review practice news and procedures and publicize upcoming events.

eliciting creative suggestions. In addition, a survey can help you assess how well you or your office manager is doing as a personnel manager. A good way to structure staff surveys is to ask each staff member to give the best response to a series of statements (Sidebar).

> **TIP:** *A staff survey will work only if staff members feel that they can be honest without hurting themselves. Do not give a survey on a sensitive subject unless you can take criticism well. In addition, do not conduct a survey unless you intend to use the results to make changes. It can be frustrating for your staff to be asked for their opinions and then have nothing happen.*

## MULTIPLE COMMUNICATION AIDS WORK BEST

One-shot communication of important or complex material rarely does the job. People tend to absorb information the way they eat from a buffet; they choose what they like and ignore the rest. In addition, most of us need to see a message over and over again before it registers. Testimony to that is the number of times we see the same television commercials. Advertisers know we will not remember the message until we get a large and repeated dose of it.

When significant or complicated information must be transmitted to your staff, your best bet will be to present your message in a variety of ways, using more than one medium. For example, you might call a meeting in the beginning to announce the news. Then, you might follow up afterwards with a memo, poster, routed correspondence, and/or one-on-one meetings. That way, your staff members will have multiple exposures to the message, increasing the likelihood that they will understand and remember it. ▲

One-shot
communication
of important or
complex material
rarely does
the job.

# Becoming a Better Delegator

*Most medical practice managers know that delegation is a useful practice management tool to streamline both personal and practice efficiency. However, delegation is often underused, misused, and misunderstood. What, precisely, should be delegated in a medical practice and to whom? What are some of the obstacles to successful delegation, and how can the astute medical practice manager identify and overcome them? Which tasks should not be delegated? Finally, why do members of the professional practice staff sometimes resist delegation?*

*This chapter provides answers to these intriguing questions, as well as a useful self-quiz to rate delegation skills. In addition, this chapter provides strategies and sample language you can use with your staff to make your own delegated tasks and responsibilities more enthusiastically accepted.*

Being able to delegate tasks and authority is central to good staff management. However, knowing how much to delegate, to whom, how, and when is not always easy. In addition, it may be hard to recognize which thing should not be delegated.

> Knowing how much to delegate, to whom, how, and when is not always easy.

## WHAT YOU CAN'T OR SHOULDN'T DELEGATE

Recent cases of malpractice and staff embezzlement suggest that medical practice managers/doctors should *not* delegate certain tasks to members of their staffs. Of course, what you can delegate will depend in large part on the kind of practice and the qualifications of your staff. However, in most cases, your staff should not:

1. **Evaluate medical histories.** You may choose to delegate to an assistant the tasks of:
   - Asking the patient every question on medical history,
   - Recording his/her responses, and
   - Obtaining his/her signature on the form.

Delegation must be in both word and deed to be truly effective.

## ARE YOU A DELEGATOR?

1. Do you work later than anyone else in the office most nights of the week and Saturdays?

2. Is it hard to find time for planning and setting long-range goals for your practice?

3. Are you constantly fighting to stay on schedule?

4. Is your desk always piled with paperwork and journals no matter how much you work?

5. Do you make regular trips to the post office to pick up and deliver mail?

6. Do you open and sort the office mail?

7. Do you go to the bank regularly to drop off deposits and withdrawals?

8. Are you your own bookkeeper?

9. Do you order supplies and/or unpack them when they arrive?

10. Have you failed to take an annual vacation at least a week long during the last three years?

11. Do your office operations slow down greatly when you're not there to supervise?

12. Do you find that it is usually easier to do tasks yourself than to delegate them? Do you doubt your staff's ability to do tasks as you would like them to be done?

13. Do your assistants defer all decisions to you?

14. Has none of your staff ever come to you with new ideas?

15. Do you delegate according to status, seniority, or salary, instead of personal abilities?

YOUR SCORE: Did you answer *no* to each question? Great! Give yourself a grade of 100%. If you answered *yes* once or twice, that's still pretty good. However, many *yes* answers may indicate a serious delegation problem. Rethink what you're doing at once. Make the changes you need to make in order to delegate better and more often.

However, it is *the doctor's* responsibility to continue the discussion with the patient based upon positive findings in the written history. Therefore, the doctor should go over the material with every patient and review questionable or unusual responses. The doctor should then write notes directly on the history form to show that all existing or potential medical problems have been investigated.

2. **Have the final word on collections.** Of course, you will need to establish a good collection procedure and delegate responsibility for it to your business assistant. However, you will probably not want any employee to make decisions about altering your policy or loosening it for a particular patient. Instead, hold regular billing review meetings to discuss delinquent accounts and to make decisions about special cases.

3. **Have exclusive control of financial records.** Your office manager should have responsibility for overseeing the day-to-day transactions and financial record keeping of your practice. However, you should periodically do your own spot checks of employee time sheets or cards, receipts, etc. Spot checks are a simple way to retain authority and control and at the same time deter sloppiness and theft.

4. **Handle all patient relations duties.** Do not make the mistake of delegating patient relations entirely to your staff. Some doctors surround themselves with capable, outgoing staff and assume that they don't have to worry anymore about building relationships with their own patients. This is short-term thinking. Loyalty and confidence can be developed in patients best if the doctor communicates concern, expertise, and quality of care. For example, the doctor might make some post-operative calls, write a few important notes to patients, or spend a little extra time chatting with patients during their office visits.

## MISTAKES THAT SHORT-CIRCUIT DELEGATION

Delegation must be in both word and deed to be truly effective. If the delegator neglects steps or takes short cuts, the entire process can fail. The most common mistakes are:

1. **Delegating in form but not in substance.** A medical practice manager who assigns work to an assistant but dictates all of the procedures and makes every last decision does not truly delegate. Staff must be given freedom to exercise judgment, and practice managers must accept their methods (as long as they are reasonable and achieve the desired results).

2. **Delegating only undesirable tasks.** Medical practice managers who use delegation simply to dump unwanted work do not generally develop their staffs to their fullest.

3. **Lack of objectives.** Medical practice managers and staff must come to an understanding about what is delegated, what the precise results should be, and the timeframe for progress and completion.

> Spot checks are a simple way to retain authority and control and at the same time deter sloppiness and theft.

| Why Staff Resists Delegation | What To Do | Example |
|---|---|---|
| It's easier to let you make all the decisions. | Show how it is better for the staff member to make that particular decision. | "Since you, Sally, will be the one to work with a printer to produce our patient newsletter, it will be better if you decide which of these printing bids we should accept." |
| They are not prepared to accept responsibility. | Begin by delegating small tasks. Then reinforce good performance and work up to larger ones. | Start with the tasks that require the person to investigate something or produce a rough draft. Next time, ask him/her to make recommendations. Next, have him/her put the project into action. Finally, turn over a whole project. |
| They don't see what's in it for them. | If possible, choose tasks to delegate that will benefit staff. Emphasize the benefits. | "Joan, we're going to give patients an incentive to pay their accounts in cash at their appointments. You'll be the one to explain the new policy to patients. I think you'll find that it will cut down on the number of collection calls you'll have to make." |
| They've made mistakes in the past that have embarrassed them or made you angry. | Choose tasks that will not exceed your staff's capabilities, and be encouraging. | "Nancy, everyone makes mistakes, and I appreciate your concern. However, I believe you are very bright and capable, and I know that you can take over the appointment schedule for Shirley while she has her baby. She will work with you in the next month to teach you how to do it and answer all your questions." |
| They don't know that you've actually delegated something to them. | Be specific and very clear. | "Now that we've talked about remodeling our reception area, I'd like to give each of you an assignment that you'll need to complete before our next meeting. Consuela, you will find out who did Dr. X's remodeling job. Betsy, you will . . ." |
| They feel that they already have too much to do. | Be realistic about current and future workloads. Monitor change in workload and establish clear priorities. | "Janice, I'd like you to make collection calls three hours every week. I've postponed our open house until November so you will have time to assemble our information packets." |
| They think the task is inappropriate for their job category or temperament | Show how the task is related to other existing duties. | "Reza, as my clinical assistant, you work very closely with our patients and know how to put them at ease. From now on, I'd like you to be the one to meet them in the reception area and escort them to the exam room." |

4. **Poor preparation.** Staff must be trained and given the experience they need to accomplish delegated tasks.

5. **Lack of confidence.** Medical practice managers must have faith in themselves and in the abilities of their staffs. Unfortunately, many practice managers don't delegate for fear that the staff will make serious mistakes that will lose patients and cost money.

6. **Failure to let staff represent you.** Not allowing assistants to interact with people outside your practice interferes with their ability to get things done. Medical practice managers who fear that a staff member may "show them up" should remember that a competent staff reflects well on them. Those who feel that a staff member is a poor representative of the practice should consider very seriously why this individual is on the staff at all.

7. **Withholding information.** Staff can't effectively carry out their work unless they have all the necessary data.

8. **Not allocating funds.** Staff can't succeed on some projects without necessary funds. Delegating authority includes the authority to spend money and to decide how it should be spent, within reasonable limits and with accountability.

## WHY MEDICAL PRACTICE MANAGERS FAIL TO DELEGATE

In addition to the reasons already cited, medical practice managers sometimes fail to delegate because:

1. **They are perfectionists.** Do you insist that everything be done perfectly and get upset when it isn't? If you constantly criticize your employees, they'll lose confidence in their own abilities and will bring their problems to you instead of trying to solve them on their own.

2. **They don't like change.** Training an assistant to handle part of your practice takes time and energy and can cause headaches, especially in the beginning. It is important to remember that training is a worthwhile investment of time and energy that will pay off later.

3. **They are afraid of being outdone.** Perhaps an employee will show more skill at handling certain duties than you do. However, insecurity is poor justification for not delegating. If your employee can do a job better than you, all the more reason to turn it over to him/her.

## HOW DO YOU RATE AS A DELEGATOR?

Do you spend time needlessly on chores that could be delegated? Test your delegation skills and see if you're making the most of yourself and your employees (see *Are You a Delegator?* earlier in this chapter).

> Insecurity is poor justification for not delegating.

## WHY STAFF MAY RESIST DELEGATION

Sometimes, you may find that you delegate a task and it ends up back in your lap. Some people naturally resist delegation. The chart on page 142 shows the most common reasons and what you can do to turn them around. ▲

Some people naturally resist delegation.

# How to Make Staff Meetings More Enjoyable and Productive

*Staff meetings are a wonderful practice management tool if they are well-planned and well-run. This chapter offers practical advice for planning and running productive staff meetings. It suggests calculating the actual cost of staff meetings and provides a formula for doing so. It describes three basic types of meetings—daily, regular, and special event—and all the how-to's you'll need for running each kind.*

*This chapter also offers relevant advice for preparing and circulating a meeting agenda and minutes. It describes how to chair a meeting and suggests when to call meetings and when not to. Finally, this chapter establishes reasonable meeting expectations and provides a self-quiz to help you measure the effectiveness of your own staff meetings.*

The well-run staff meeting can be an unparalleled morale builder and an excellent way to assure that everyone gets "the word" about new policies and procedures. It can also result in positive change and serve as an open forum for your staff.

With proper control, meetings can also reduce conflict and the stress such conflict causes. Yet, poorly run meetings waste valuable time, achieve little, and cause frustration.

## HOW MUCH DO STAFF MEETINGS ACTUALLY COST?

An easy way to make staff meetings more effective is to estimate the cost of a meeting per minute. Here's how:

1. Add up the salary per minute of all staff who regularly attend meetings. Estimate 24 cents per minute per $10,000 annual salary.

> Meetings can also reduce conflict and the stress such conflict causes.

> Most importantly, daily meetings create a team feeling among staff members.

2. Add the cost of the other work these people might do if they weren't in a meeting. A good estimate is twice the person's salary, or 48 cents per minute per $10,000 salary.

3. Include your own salary and lost production per minute in your estimate.

4. Add in the cost per minute of refreshments, photocopying, and other meeting expenses. Divide this total by the average number of minutes of your last meeting.

5. Share your cost-per-minute total with your staff at the start of each meeting or post it at the front of the meeting room. Doing so may make you and your staff more mindful of digressions, long-winded speeches, and idle conversations that eat up precious time.

## HOW OFTEN SHOULD YOU MEET?

The frequency of your staff meetings will depend upon what you are trying to accomplish. Generally, three types of meetings will work well in a medical practice:

1. Daily meetings (usually first thing in the morning)
2. Regular meetings (weekly, bi-weekly, or monthly)
3. Special event meetings (as needed)

Each of these is discussed separately below.

## WHAT TO ACCOMPLISH AT YOUR DAILY STAFF MEETING

Daily meetings occur at the start of each day before the first appointment. Their purpose is to review the day's schedule so everyone knows what to expect and can anticipate problems. Most importantly, daily meetings create a team feeling among staff members. Without a few minutes together before the challenges of the day begin, the staff and physician may lose track of their relationship with each other, and feel they're functioning alone in their jobs.

Daily meetings should last no longer than 10 to 15 minutes, following the same format each day. Have one person chair all your daily meetings.

Before meeting, each staff member should review the charts for patients who will be seen that day. Look for patient's special needs, possible problems, questions, concerns, etc. Then at the meeting, your staff should:

- Address these issues, patient by patient.
- Review what each staff member will try to accomplish during their time with patients.

- Reinforce one another whenever and however needed.
- Help fine tune the day's schedule to account for emergencies and other changes.

> **TIP:** *Be strict about your daily meetings, in their length and scope, and in attendance. Keep discussion exclusively on your daily schedule. Other topics belong on the agenda of one of the longer meetings discussed below.*

## WHAT TO ACCOMPLISH AT YOUR REGULAR STAFF MEETINGS

Regular meetings will be scheduled weekly, bi-weekly, or monthly, depending upon your needs. They are your staff's forum for participating in the larger concerns of the practice—goal setting, tackling problems, reviewing progress, etc. Regular meetings generally last approximately 45 to 60 minutes but should probably go no longer than 90 minutes. They are best run with a rotating chairmanship.

Attendance and attitudes about regular meetings will be best if you incorporate them into at least part of your regular working hours. However, don't schedule them at the end of the day or week when everyone is tired and anxious to go home.

Many practices schedule regular breakfast meetings on their slowest mornings. With office appointments looming, breakfast discussions move quickly to their conclusion. In addition, while the breakfast meeting is a treat, it is a relatively economical one. (Breakfast is usually the least expensive meal you can buy.) Some tips about breakfast meetings:

- Begin your meeting 30 to 45 minutes before your regular starting time and leave the first 30 minutes in your appointment book free.
- Make reservations at a quiet restaurant that won't rush you. Investigate local hotels that can arrange breakfast meetings in a private room.
- Instruct the wait person to clear dishes promptly so you can use the table for papers.
- Don't discuss confidential matters in a restaurant, even if you have a private room. For sensitive discussions, serve breakfast in your office. (Many restaurants package complete hot breakfasts in keep-warm containers.)

## WHAT TO ACCOMPLISH AT YOUR SPECIAL EVENT MEETINGS

Special event meetings are called as needed. They generally have one of the following purposes:

> Daily meetings should last no longer than 10 to 15 minutes.

- To find a solution to a pressing problem. Examples: patient visits have declined; the doctor is frequently running behind schedule.
- To prepare for an upcoming event or big change. Examples: an open house; a new associate is coming on board.
- To hear an important announcement that's best delivered to everyone simultaneously. Examples: the doctor is going out of town unexpectedly; the practice is moving.

## ESTABLISHING AN AGENDA FOR THE MEETING

Successful meetings start with an agenda—an outline of the topics to be discussed and what the group is to accomplish. The agenda will always be the same for daily meetings. However, you must prepare a new agenda for each regular or special event meeting. Good: Estimate a starting and finishing time for each agenda item.

Most agendas are too vague or brief. For example, the phrase "Children's Tour" tells very little. The longer explanation:

> "To set up a schedule and divide responsibilities for the upcoming office tour by the fifth graders from Frost Elementary School"

gives meeting participants enough information to form some view, do some research, and brainstorm in advance of the meeting.

For best results, circulate the agenda 1 or 2 days before a regular or special event meeting. Invite staff members to submit their ideas to the chairperson no later than 3 days before the meeting.

## HOW TO CHAIR A MEETING

To be a successful chairperson, regard yourself as the group's facilitator, not boss. Steer the group toward the best decisions or conclusions as efficiently as possible. Ask questions to interpret, clarify, or move the discussion forward. But don't get carried away by your role. Do:

1. Start on time. Delaying for stragglers rewards them and encourages punctual members to come late next time.
2. Seat all participants face-to-face so they can see and talk to one another. Many practices hold meetings in the reception area.
3. Discuss the most important items first. That way, if you must end the meeting before the agenda is completed, you will have covered the most important items.
4. Before delving into a subject, explain where you should be by the end of your discussion. Make sure everyone understands the issue and why they're discussing it. Example: "The fifth graders from Frost Elementary School are scheduled to tour our office in two weeks. It's important that we set up a workable agenda to reduce

---

Many practices schedule regular breakfast meetings on their slowest mornings.

confusion and make the trip more enjoyable, both for the children and for us. Today, let's see if we can set up a schedule for the children's tour and divide the responsibilities for the preparations."

5. Control the meeting so no one dominates. If one member is starting to do so, break in quickly and tactfully. Examples:
   - "Janet, that's a very interesting point. I think it ties in with . . . "
   - "Janet, what you're suggesting is very interesting. I'd like to move on now."
   - "Mary, what do you think of Janet's idea about sponsoring an essay contest for the children?"
   - "Mary, what are your feelings on that? Janet, thank you."

6. Encourage a clash of ideas, but not of personalities. If two members get into a heated argument, call a time-out. Or, ask a neutral member to answer a question that requires a factual, not judgmental response. Examples:
   - "Sally, you ran the essay contest last year. How long did it take you to read and judge all the entries?"
   - "Stephanie, your daughter goes to Frost Elementary School. Have the students there participated in any other contests lately?"

7. Keep the discussion on track. Example: "Karen, you may be right about our answering service, but we have to move on and finish this schedule for the children's tour."

8. After an item has been discussed, give a brief summary of what has been agreed upon. Then, push on to the next item on your agenda.

9. Give all suggestions serious consideration and a fair chance. If you immediately squash a new idea, the person who offered it may be reluctant to share ideas next time.

10. If a member of the group comes up with a new project or idea, don't automatically assign him or her responsibility for it. Doing so discourages suggestions.

11. End the meeting on a positive note. Even if the final item is left unresolved, refer to an earlier item that was handled successfully prior to closing the meeting.

## HOW TO FOLLOW UP WITH MINUTES AFTER A MEETING

The chairperson may delegate the job of taking the minutes. However, he or she is still responsible for them.

Most practices find it fairest to rotate the chair of regular meetings, having the chairperson write and distribute the minutes. This should be

> To be a successful chairperson, regard yourself as the group's facilitator, not boss.

> **How Productive Was Your Last Staff Meeting?**
>
> Answer YES or NO to each of these questions to determine whether your last regular staff meeting was productive:
>
> - Did we begin and end the meeting on time?
> - Did everyone know the meeting's goals in advance?
> - Was an agenda prepared and distributed before the meeting?
> - Were all required staff members present?
> - Were only required staff members present (versus ones who could have been omitted)?
> - Did we devote enough time to important issues?
> - Did we stick to the agenda?
> - Did the chairperson give everyone ample time to speak and offer suggestions?
> - Did we achieve our goals for the meeting?
> - Were all projects assigned to someone for completion?
> - Were completion dates established?
> - Was the next meeting date set and a chairperson chosen?
> - Were all problems resolved?
> - Was time used effectively rather than wasted through small talk and interruptions?
>
> YOUR SCORE: The more YES answers, the better: If you answered all 14 in the affirmative, you get an "A+" in meeting productivity. If you missed 1 to 3, you're doing well. Just focus on your few problem areas. If you missed 4 to 6, that's average. However, you're only using about 35% to 50% of your staff meeting productivity. Try harder next time. If you missed 7 or more, better get cracking! Reorganization is called for, or your meetings may be unproductive, or even destructive (to staff morale and smooth office operations).

*If a member of the group comes up with a new project or idea, don't automatically assign him or her responsibility for it.*

done no later than 2 days after the meeting. For consistency, establish a format for minutes that all chairpersons can follow:

- The date of the meeting, starting and finishing times, and the chairperson's name.
- Names of all present and absent.
- All agenda items (and other items) discussed and all decisions reached. Record any action that was agreed upon and the person(s) responsible for the assignment.
- The date, time, and chairperson of the next meeting.

## WHEN TO CALL A MEETING, AND WHEN NOT TO

Sometimes, you won't know whether to distribute a memo about something, call a meeting, talk to each person separately, or let your office manager handle the whole thing. These guidelines should help.

It makes sense to call a meeting to:

1. Get participation. Meetings are a good option when you need a fluid exchange of ideas.
2. Be uniform. Call a meeting when you need everybody to hear the same thing, at the same time, and in the same way.
3. Pack more weight behind decisions. A group decision is apt to carry more weight than the same decision argued by one person (you), no matter how persuasive you are.

It makes sense to AVOID a staff meeting to:

1. Make a fast decision. Meetings can stall action.
2. Generate big ideas. No committee ever wrote a great novel or painted a masterpiece. Brainstorming aside, highly creative tasks rarely benefit from "group think."
3. Resolve a crisis. When Lee Iacocca set out to pull Chrysler out of bankruptcy, he didn't form a committee to study the situation. He knew it called for someone who could provide clear orders and strong leadership. Group decision-making in that crisis probably would have meant Chrysler's demise.

## WHAT YOU CAN AND CAN'T EXPECT FROM STAFF MEETINGS

Well-run staff meetings can realistically accomplish one or several of these objectives:

- Learning
- Setting goals
- Reviewing progress
- Sharing information
- Identifying and/or solving problems
- Training
- Planning

However, do NOT expect to accomplish any of these:

- Group therapy
- Discipline session
- Party
- Gripe session
- Lecture

Realistic expectations are critically important. ▲

> For consistency, establish a format for minutes that all chairpersons can follow.

# Why and How to Organize a Practice Retreat

*Medical practices are often so busy that physicians and their staff have difficulty seeing the big picture. A well-organized practice retreat can provide needed time and space for tackling large practice management problems and establishing new goals. In addition, a practice retreat can enable staff members to get to know each other better and learn new ways to function as a cohesive team.*

*This chapter describes the similarities and differences between single-task and team-building retreats. In addition, it shares practical do's and don'ts for organizing worthwhile medical practice retreats and makes suggestions about possible locations for retreats, recommended follow-up, and team-building exercises.*

A practice retreat can enable staff members to get to know each other better.

Many busy physicians complain that they don't have enough quiet time to make important decisions about their practices' futures. They are so caught up in the day-to-day problems of their practices that they can't step back and look at the big picture. They also complain that when they are really busy, they don't have the time they need to iron out ongoing problems in their practices or to work on getting their staff to function as a "team."

A practice retreat can be the perfect answer to these problems. A change of scenery and a block of uninterrupted meeting time can help busy physicians and their staff confront management issues once and for all and clear the air of nagging problems. A retreat can also enable staff members to get to know each other better and learn more effective ways to communicate with and work with each other. However, a worthwhile practice retreat must be carefully planned.

## DEFINE THE PURPOSE OF YOUR RETREAT

To make a practice retreat worthwhile, begin by defining the real purpose of your retreat. A successful practice retreat definitely is NOT:

- A series of half-hour presentations by departments or individuals about what they are doing;
- A gripe session;
- A forecast of the next couple of years; or
- A summary of new projects under development.

This sort of information sharing is strictly operational. It can and should be done within the timeframe of your regular daily, weekly, and/or monthly staff meetings, or with memos.

Retreats are relatively costly meetings, both in terms of time and dollars. They should therefore be used only to accomplish very important goals that can't be reached through the usual staff meetings, memos, and other staff communication methods. For example, you might:

- Organize a "single-task" retreat to work on a specific task or solve a specific problem (and only one such task or problem). For example, you might call a retreat to decide how to solve your problem of staying on schedule if you find that you are chronically late for appointments.
- Hold a "getting-to-know-you" retreat. Typically, you'd organize such a retreat in a larger practice to get together individuals who must mesh efforts but who don't really know each other well.
- Organize a "team-building" retreat. Such an event is useful when you feel that staff members are not working together as well as they might or that tension is particularly high in your office. Or, you might plan such a retreat after a particularly rough spell in your office as a reward for your staff's extra hard work.

Break your staff into smaller groups.

## ORGANIZING THE SINGLE-TASK RETREAT

The single-task retreat is an excellent way to review alternatives and get staff input when you must make a major or sensitive decision. For example, you might organize a single-task retreat to figure out what you can do to build the practice in the next year. You might call a retreat to decide practical ways to increase your practice production without sacrificing quality or service. In addition, you might call a retreat to solve an important ongoing problem, for instance, with patient retention or staff turnover.

## Team-Building Exercises for Your Practice Retreat

### Exercise 1: Didactic Sharing Using Drawing

Ask each of your staff members to draw or write three things that help describe who they are. Then, put your staff in pairs and have them share what they've produced with each other. You can then ask your staff members to explain to the group what they've drawn or written. You could also have the staff members introduce their partners and explain their partners' productions.

### Exercise 2: Scavenger Hunt

Ask staff members to circulate around the room looking for co-workers who fit certain categories. For example:

- Someone who is an only child.
- Someone who has lived abroad.
- Someone who speaks more than one language.
- Someone who has more than three siblings.
  **TIP:** Include additional statements that revolve around your profession or practice. For example:
  - Someone who has worked in more than three medical practices.
  - Someone who has worked in a medical practice in another state.
  - Someone who has worked in a medical practice for more than 10 years.

Tell your staff that when they meet someone who matches a category, they should write down the person's name. Encourage your staff to meet different people, even if the same person might fit more than one category.

When you reconvene the whole staff, process the exercise by asking your staff to introduce the people they've met and share what they've learned about them.

### Exercise 3: Staff Disclosure Exercise

Give a 3×5 index card to each member of your staff. Have your staff write their names on one side of the card and, on the other side, something distinctive or special about themselves they would not mind others on your staff knowing. Then, ask your staff to circulate, sharing what they've written about themselves. You can participate in the circulation as well.

Collect the cards and read the backs of them aloud. You can then either ask your staff to introduce themselves as their cards are read, or ask your staff to identify the individual.

The single-task retreat is most effective if:

- It has only one focus.
- The discussion can be specific.
- Decisions can be made.

To keep the discussion on track, prepare a tight agenda for the single-task retreat, preferably with your staff's help. Circulate the agenda well in advance of the retreat. When appropriate, don't preside over the entire session yourself. Rather, assign a discussion leader (or several) who has thoroughly prepared to lead the discussion. Perhaps the practice's office manager, administrator, or another staff member can be in charge of planning and running a single-task retreat.

## ORGANIZE PEOPLE-BUILDING RETREATS

The getting-to-know-you retreat and the team-building retreat balance work sessions with generous time off for socializing and fun. Some but not all of such retreats' social activities are planned for groups or sub-groups of practice employees. In addition, staff is usually given at least some time off in the retreat's schedule for impromptu socializing.

Unlike the single-task retreat, the team-building and getting-to-know-you programs can address several subjects, such as a series of small problems or new ideas for the practice. To keep things lively, you might assign discussion leaders for each short topic. You might engage the services of outside consultants, teachers, or even your colleagues, who can conduct workshops and other programs on interesting, relevant, and useful topics.

If you are in a large medical practice with many employees, you will find it helpful to break your staff into smaller groups for various discussions and activities. Later, rotate the groups. That way, you will encourage your staff to mix and get to know people in the practice they otherwise might not.

At these retreats, it is extremely important to organize fun group social activities that get people to mingle. Focus social activities on those that require dialogue, group discussion, and team spirit. For example, attending films, plays, and other spectator programs should not be the whole emphasis of the social program because they don't require interaction. Instead, try running group volley ball games, boat rides, hay rides, a round-robin ping-pong tournament, or old-fashioned picnic games such as three-legged and potato sack races. These activities will literally force your staff to interact.

---

> Focus social activities on those that require dialogue, group discussion, and team spirit.

## GROUND RULES FOR ORGANIZING SUCCESSFUL RETREATS

Retreats, like any good staff event, require careful planning and thought. Below are some helpful do's and don'ts of successful retreat planning:

- All retreats should be work-oriented, even the most social ones. To eliminate distractions, don't invite spouses and children to attend your working or team-building sessions. Depending upon your purposes, however, you may wish to invite them to some or all of your social events.
- Do not invite your staff's spouses or families to attend an intensive single-task problem-solving retreat. They will only distract the employees, and their presence may confuse things and cause resentment.
- Hold a retreat only if you can develop an agenda around specific topics on which action can be taken.
- Hold overnight or weekend retreats no more often than once each year. It is generally a burden to ask staff to leave their families and other personal obligations more frequently.
- Never mix a single-task retreat with the social ones. All working sessions of the single-task retreat must relate to the single subject. Don't digress by discussing other subjects or by emphasizing socializing.
- If possible, have the retreat away from your office. You needn't choose a luxurious spot, especially for a single-task retreat. Rent a suite or conference room in a local hotel. See if you can use a meeting room at your local public library or community center.
- Plan enough time. The minimum should be a long half-day program. A one- or two-day program is usually better. Critically important decisions or team-building require that sort of focused time and attention.
- Be mindful not to plan your retreat around the December holidays, in June during busy graduation and wedding season, or during other busy times of the year.
- Publicize the dates of the retreat well in advance. Make it clear that everyone is expected to attend. Pay for all expenses and compensate your staff for their time (for the work sessions). Be sure to pay any overtime your staff works while at the retreat.

## FOLLOWING UP AFTER YOUR RETREAT

Unfortunately, some retreats seem successful while they are in session but nothing ever gets done because of them. The best retreats lead to positive change. Therefore:

- Assign a retreat secretary to record and afterwards distribute copies of the proceedings and decisions.

> All retreats should be work-oriented, even the most social ones.

- Within a week of the retreat, set priorities and give specific work assignments to key members of your staff to fine-tune decisions made at the retreat.
- No later than three weeks afterwards, deliver specific assignments with deadlines to all staff members.
- If the retreat's main purpose was for your staff to become better acquainted or team-building, plan additional follow-up activities that will keep the team feeling going. For example, you might start a practice bowling team or plan a regular bi-monthly dinner outing with your staff, to keep the spark alive. Try some short team-building exercises at your regular monthly staff meetings.  ▲

Try some short team-building exercises at your regular monthly staff meetings.

# Innovative Ways to Boost Morale In Your Practice

*Employees with high morale are likely to work harder, contribute more to your practice, and stay with you. With a little ingenuity, almost anyone can come up with affordable, effective morale boosters that can add fun and excitement to your practice.*

*This chapter suggests tried-and-true morale boosting techniques to be used with your staff, such as meeting enhancements, contests, and outings. It explores how morale can soar when you allow an employee to personalize his or her workspace. It suggests an innovative technique for honoring your staff during their professional association's special week. In addition, it offers many good ideas for building staff loyalty with thoughtful, affordable, and easy-to-implement surprises.*

> Unexpected fun boosts morale and is an often-overlooked, yet highly effective personnel management tool.

## Fun on the job may encourage creative thinking.

Is your office a fun place to work? Do you hear laughter in your practice very often? Do you ever surprise members of your staff by doing something unexpected or nice?

Unexpected fun boosts morale and is an often-overlooked, yet highly effective personnel management tool. If your staff has fun at work, and there is appropriate laughter in your office, it is likely that you are providing a creative and productive atmosphere for your staff, yourself, and your patients.

## HAVING FUN IMPROVES PRODUCTIVITY

Having fun at work can greatly affect employee productivity. Generally speaking, people who have fun at work usually perform better and get along better with co-workers than those who are satisfied with their jobs but don't consider them to be fun.

Furthermore, people who have fun at work look forward to going to work each day and are loyal to their employers. They also tend to have a positive attitude while they are working and form better relationships with and attitudes about their supervisors. In addition, fun on the job may encourage creative thinking. Fun increases a person's ability to think in broader terms, seeing relationships that might otherwise be elusive. This mental skill is critical for determining creative solutions to problems.

## HOW TO MAKE ALMOST ANY OFFICE MORE FUN

Unfortunately, many of the day-to-day operations of a medical practice are not inherently fun—or funny. In many offices, laughter is rare. At times, the routine practice management and clinical tasks can become monotonous and boring. Patients can be difficult. In addition, depending on the type of practice and the patients and conditions treated, a medical practice can sometimes be stressful, and at other times, a very sad and depressing place.

The good news is that with a little ingenuity, almost anyone can come up with little things to do that will liven things up—and in so doing, boost morale. An occasional dose of well-timed, well-targeted fun can change an employee's negative attitudes, reinforce positive behavior, and develop a team attitude in your staff.

> **TIP:** *In this chapter, you will learn about some unusual morale builders other employers have used successfully. Every idea will not appeal to you, nor would it be appropriate to try too many of them at once. As you read, remember that there is a definite line between making your office a fun place to work and being inappropriate. Do not cross this line. Rather, be true to your basic*

*instincts and personality and avoid morale-building tactics that may hurt someone or interfere with your ability to run your practice. Never do anything that risks your own respect, or that of your staff, patients, colleagues, or community.*

## 12 UNUSUAL WAYS TO BOOST MORALE WITH FUN

Here are 12 affordable, simple techniques just about anyone can use to make a practice more fun:

1. **Lighten up your memos.** Do you sometimes post notices for staff on a bulletin board or send around memos? Why not write your next notice as a limerick, riddle, or as a series of puns. For example:

   ### MEMO
   Riddle: What do you call it when one germ meets
      another germ?
   Answer: A staph meeting.
   When and Where: Tues., May 7, 5 p.m., Staph lounge.

2. **Bury stupid mistakes.** If you have said or done things you shouldn't have, and your staff still talks about them, you might try burying your mistakes, literally. Write every dumb thing you did on individual slips of paper. Then call a meeting and say, "I'd like you to help me bury my mistakes." Then, read each one aloud, and drop it in a homemade miniature coffin (a cigar or shoebox). Then, lead everyone out to your back lot for a funeral. Dig a hole, bury the "coffin," and erect a grave marker.

3. **Apologize for losing your temper.** If your anger gets the better of you and you blast an employee unjustly, give the person a large package of bubble gum. Then explain, "I have found a better way to chew someone out."

4. **Stop talking.** Do you talk too much at staff meetings? At the next meeting, explain that you know you have a hard time keeping your mouth shut. Then announce that you are going to put tape over your mouth. First, take bets on how long everyone thinks you can keep it there.

5. **Celebrate in style.** Did your practice recently achieve a new high in production or collections? Is it a big practice anniversary? If so, do what you would do at any other celebration. Get banners, a cake, noisemakers, and trophies and lead the hip-hip-hoorays.

6. **Have the staff take a bow.** Has one of your staff members done something exceptionally well or creatively? Call a staff meeting and have everyone give him or her a standing ovation.

7. **Catch them off guard.** Do you use videotapes for staff training and continuing education? If so, tell staff you are going to show an

With a little ingenuity, almost anyone can come up with little things to do that will liven things up—and in so doing, boost morale.

## Acknowledge when you bomb.

educational videotape. Instead (or first), show a funny tape such as the Abbott and Costello routine "Who's On First?"

8. **Acknowledge when you bomb.** Have you tried something in your practice that just didn't work out? Rather than announcing the change quietly, or not at all, dramatize it by calling staff together and doing something ceremoniously. For instance, if the first issue of your patient newsletter turned out poorly, call everyone together to burn a copy before starting on a revision. If your new schedule hasn't worked and needs to be changed, gather everyone around the paper shredder to bid it a fond farewell.

9. **Run a morale-building contest for your staff.** For example, you might have them write a fictitious press release telling why your practice was recently awarded the title of "World's Best Medical Practice." Then, post the finished entries and award a certificate and prize to the winner.

10. **Display humorous materials.** You might set aside an area of your office where you will display funny posters and comic strips. Or, hold a "Joke of the Week" contest, and post the winning entries.

11. **Plan a fun outing.** Take your staff on an outing to a local comedy club or amusement park as an incentive or reward for good work on a specific project.

12. **Have staff plan humor for patients.** There are many opportunities for appropriate humor in patient communications, and your staff may be able to come up with some good ideas and enjoy themselves in the process. For example, you might enlist their help in developing humorous postage meter imprints. They may come up with a good activity for April Fool's Day. Get them to help you develop funny patient giveaways or birthday cards.

## ALLOW STAFF TO PERSONALIZE THEIR WORKSPACES

In addition to humorous tactics like those described above, there are other things you might do to make your office more fun. One of the easiest is to allow your employees to personalize their work space or break area.

Some practices discourage staff from "nesting." However, a policy of bare walls and clean desktops can be dreary and devoid of personality. The freedom to personalize one's own work area (within limits) produces several benefits for the practice. For example, staff can express creativity through the objects they display, not only to one another, but to patients. As well, staff will feel important. By allowing your receptionist or bookkeeper to lay claim to a piece of your practice territory (namely, a desk or bulletin board), you are recognizing his or her individuality, and in effect, asking others to respect it. In addition, staff who can personalize their workspaces usually feel that they will be there permanently.

> **TIP:** *When allowing staff to personalize their work areas, advise them to limit themselves to a few items only, and to select these carefully. Most articles, like photos of children, will tell visitors something positive about the individual's private life, beliefs, or taste. Therefore, you might insist that they avoid pictures that are potentially unflattering, such as those that show them drinking with pals. In addition, you might steer staff away from objects and symbols that others might interpret negatively.*

## HONORING STAFF ON THEIR DAY BUILDS MORALE

Almost all professional practice staff have a day or week set aside each year by their association in which they are to be honored. If not, Administrative Professionals Day can be celebrated by many members of your staff. Of course, you should celebrate such an event with your staff, perhaps by taking them to lunch, giving them flowers, taking an ad in the newspaper, etc, but here is an unusual idea.

One family practice physician asks his patients to help him honor his staff each year during Medical Assistants' Week. Starting about a month before the special week, he hands every patient he sees a note at the end of the appointment that says:

> *October 19–24 is National Medical Assistants' Week. My office staff (names them) are all members of the American Medical Assistants Association. They are fine people who do an excellent job. Many times, the doctor gets the credit for what is truly a team effort. I'd appreciate it if you'd do me a favor. If you'd take the time during the week of October 19 to send them a little note or card of appreciation, it would mean a great deal to them and me. Thanks.*

The doctor reports a tremendous response. The first year he tried this, his patients sent his three assistants the following:

- 90 laudatory messages
- 15 floral arrangements
- Assorted food packages and goodies
- Bracelets for each member of the staff
- Restaurant gift certificates

In addition, the assistants got further recognition in a newspaper column, which resulted from the doctor's publicity efforts.

This unusual approach serves triple duty: it rewards your staff for their excellence and builds morale. It involves your patients in your practice in a positive way. In addition, it gets people in your community talking positively about your office.

Staff who can personalize their workspaces usually feel that they will be there permanently.

> What you do or give your staff is not nearly as important as the fact that you cared and did anything at all.

## TEN MORE PLEASANT SURPRISES FOR YOUR STAFF

The unexpected keeps things interesting and fun for your staff. Everyone likes a surprise gift from time to time, and there are a lot of things you can do easily, without spending an arm and a leg. For example, you might:

1. Buy a bud vase for each employee's desk and surprise each member of your staff with a fresh flower every now and then. Of course, you can bring them flowers on holidays, like Valentine's Day and St. Patrick's Day. But also catch them off guard occasionally. For example, most of us wouldn't expect a flower on the first day of Spring, Halloween, or Ground Hog's Day.

2. Put a small surprise in each employee's pay envelope. It might be a little note, a joke, a tiny bottle of cologne, candy, a fun comic strip, or balloons for their children.

3. Spring for refreshments for your next staff meeting. If you normally supply food, look for something fun and out of the ordinary. For example, have a cake decorated humorously, or serve funny fortune cookies.

4. Buy something new for your staff break area. Examples: A microwave oven, small refrigerator, snacks, drinks, a hot water dispenser, artwork, nice paper plates, cups, and napkins.

5. Invite a surprise guest to a staff meeting. For example, hire an image consultant, time management expert, or motivational speaker to do a program.

6. If a big employment anniversary is coming up for an employee, make a fuss about it and plan something very special for him or her.

7. When you go on vacation, bring back a small souvenir for each member of your staff.

8. One morning, give everyone a nice new coffee mug, for no reason at all.

9. Buy some extras for the bathroom in your staff area— fancy soap, a lighted make-up mirror, potpourri, or hand lotion.

10. Buy some extra-nice coat hangers for the staff coat closet.

> **TIP:** *What you do or give your staff is not nearly as important as the fact that you cared and did anything at all. Surprises like those above make work fun and will build staff appreciation and morale. However, a well-timed surprise note, card, or phone call home to say "well done" or "thanks" can be as or more effective than a tangible gift.* ▲

# 32 Ways to Spark Your Staff's Creativity and Productivity

*Staff creativity can help your practice run more smoothly and give it a competitive edge. In most cases, however, your staff's creativity needs to be fostered. You may do this in three very specific ways. First, you must communicate to your staff that their creativity is wanted and valued. Second, you must establish a climate that is conducive to creative thinking. And, third, you must reinforce staff creativity so it will continue to grow and flourish.*

*This chapter offers 31 specific methods for achieving these goals, thereby improving your staff's creativity and achievement, as well as your practice's productivity and excellence.*

Every medical practice has a pressing need for people with good ideas. Individuals who say it is the doctor's or the office manager's job to think creatively, and the staff's job simply to work, are missing a great opportunity. Still, some doctors and managers may want their staff's good ideas but not know how to tap into the staff's creative energy or to direct and reward it.

One of the most persistent myths about creativity is that it is the exclusive province of only a few, talented, naturally "creative" people. The truth is, everyone has at least some imagination and creative talent. True, in some people, these qualities are highly developed, as in the case of artists, writers, and inventors. However, in most people, creative talents lie dormant and untapped.

This chapter provides insight into the creative process and how your practice can harness and focus people's energies to achieve innovative results. It describes 31 specific methods for improving your staff's innovation, achievement, and productivity.

> In most people, creative talents lie dormant and untapped.

> When the physician or office manager treats every employee in exactly the same way, creativity may be stifled.

## 1. Hire people with a high capacity for creativity

People with high creative potential often possess one or more of these traits: curiosity, openness, flexibility, and the ability to think in images as well as words. Look for self-confident job applicants who are able to toy with ideas and tolerate ambiguity. Actively seek out individuals with special creative talents and aptitudes that might be useful in your practice, such as interior design, photography, graphic arts, writing, computer programming, and analytical thinking.

## 2. Provide an environment that fosters creativity

A creative environment is one in which the need for creativity is expressed openly. Try to provide a warm environment that offers the creative person recognition, prestige, and a chance to participate.

## 3. Involve staff in work planning

When possible, give your staff opportunities to be involved in planning their work and in making decisions about how it should be done. They will begin to feel that they have your confidence and respect and will form a more positive attitude about their work and themselves. From this, they will be more committed to your practice and push harder for creative solutions to problems.

## 4. Empathize

Managing for creativity means taking time to identify, understand, and act on a staff member's needs and expectations. Some creative people may need a bit more individual attention. Learn to put yourself into the employee's place to understand his or her situation, even when you don't see eye to eye with him or her.

## 5. Respect individual differences

When the physician or office manager treats every employee in exactly the same way, creativity may be stifled. It sends a message to every employee that the boss doesn't care enough to find out what makes him or her unique.

> **TIP:** *An easy way to recognize individual differences is to allow each employee to personalize his or her workspace.*

## 6. Be patient

Impatience tells your staff that you have "quick-fix" expectations of them and encourages shallow thinking. An astute physician or office manager knows when to let a staff member have the time to work through a problem and when to intervene.

## 7. Be open to staff creativity

To some physicians and office managers, staff creativity can be threatening. It modifies or even reverses established, traditional roles, in which the boss comes up with all the new ideas. That change makes some practice leaders feel that they've lost authority and control. In fact, this is not the case. You can remain in control and still encourage creative thinking.

## 8. Be positive about any idea offered

It is important to be enthusiastic about creative ideas, even when they seem silly or impractical. For example, you might say something like, "I see where that might take care of the one part of the problem." In so doing, the idea will be given some worth, in the eyes of the person making the suggestion and of any others on the team. Everyone will be encouraged to build upon the idea, identify ways to improve on it, and so forth, rather than brush it aside or ridicule it.

This strategy is important. Employees may be reluctant to present creative ideas and recommendations if they fear your reactions. In such a negative setting, creativity requires considerable psychological risk—one many employees will be unwilling to take.

## 9. Institute an employee suggestion program

A simple suggestion program encourages staff to generate and submit ideas. If possible, design your program to preserve anonymity until the suggestion award is made.

For example, you might have staff members submit their ideas in writing in a sealed suggestion box. Another option is to have staff meet with you one-on-one in private to offer their suggestions. That way, the staff member is free of the threat of public embarrassment if the idea is not practical.

Small cash awards can be an important stimulus for suggestions. However, the strongest motivation usually lies in seeing a suggestion implemented and receiving recognition for it. Therefore, be sure to play up the creative idea and the person who suggested it so that everyone in the practice can congratulate him or her for being so creative.

For example, you might announce the suggestion program winners at your next staff meeting or circulate a special office memo about them. (This is especially effective in a larger practice.) Not only will the winner be pleased, but the hoopla may entice other staff members to try harder.

> Impatience tells your staff that you have "quick-fix" expectations of them and encourages shallow thinking.

**TIP:** *Provide feedback on all suggestions promptly after receiving them. Explain why an idea can't be used. Thank the employee for the suggestion and ask for more. Make him or her feel good about having tried.*

## 10. Talk less at staff meetings

In most meetings, a leader (usually the physician or office manager) dominates the discussion. He or she talks a lot, not only in total "air time" but also between everybody else's comments. Even if you don't talk continuously, constant intervention may stifle creativity. Staff meetings to solve problems or to plan upcoming events should be opportunities for your entire staff to brainstorm and share risky ideas.

## 11. Show interest in new ideas

When a staff member comes up with a creative idea, he or she may be very excited about it. It is important that you show immediate interest to keep the enthusiasm going. Immediate interest reinforces creativity and encourages staff to risk presenting something new and unusual.

## 12. Express negatives as concerns

When an idea has problems, say, "I'm concerned that a part of your solution doesn't fit just right." Don't say that the idea won't work. Let your staff try to come up with creative ways to salvage the idea. Another way to react might be, "I wonder just how to overcome the problem," or "I'm curious. Do you think there's a way we can get around this problem?"

## 13. Don't assume the first idea is the best idea

Encourage maximum creativity by saying, "Let's not choose a solution until we think about at least three alternatives." Brainstorming may take less than 5 minutes, but if it's done consistently, the quality of your practice's decision making will improve.

**TIP:** *Have a chalkboard or paper and easel at your staff meetings. Tell your staff they will have 3 minutes to call out any idea they have to solve a particular problem and have one person write these in order on the board/paper. As a rule, don't evaluate any of the ideas until after the time limit.*

## 14. Don't set too many ground rules or restrictions

When it comes to finding creative solutions for problems, overly strict criteria can box your staff in, preventing them from expanding their thinking. Therefore, when describing a problem to be solved, try to leave your staff's hands untied as much as possible during the brainstorming process.

## 15. Clearly define the problem to be solved

Provide your staff with a list of the problems for which you are actively seeking creative solutions. Such a list might be posted by your suggestion box. As well, encourage staff to submit new problem areas that need creative attention.

## 16. Match projects with abilities

As much as possible, try to match project tasks and objectives with the abilities and true interests of each of the individuals involved. Provide stimulating work that gives a feeling of personal and professional growth. Doing so helps your staff get excited about their responsibilities.

For example, if you are thinking about building an addition to your office, you might assign one staff member the job of investigating architectural options, another the job of learning about building codes and restrictions, and another the job of gathering ideas and costs for interior decoration. Ideally, these assignments would be based upon each staff member's creative interests and abilities.

## 17. Help staff see problems as challenges

Instilling an attitude that there are opportunities in most problems will help staffers regard problems in a more positive light. It also makes them more willing to overcome the obstacles standing in the way of their goals. Example: When a valued employee quits suddenly, it is easy to focus on the staff vacancy purely as a problem. However, it is also an opportunity to change the job description for the position and to seek an individual with different training, experience, and qualifications. It also may be an opportunity to shift responsibilities among remaining staff.

## 18. Set high but reasonable standards

Even the most lofty ideas eventually must be subjected to realistic technical and financial constraints. However, by setting high goals initially, you will increase the chances of some people coming up with breakthrough ideas. For example, when planning a staff holiday party, you will have to work within a limited budget. However, by setting your sights very high for the party, thinking will be broader, and your staff may find creative ways to overcome financial constraints.

> **Let your staff try to come up with creative ways to salvage the idea.**

### 19. Don't overburden your staff

Is your staff over involved in putting out fires and coping with urgent, immediate problems? If so, they probably don't have much time or energy to be creative. Be sure you have adequate staff to handle your everyday workload properly, with time left over for new, stimulating practice growth projects and creative thinking.

### 20. Provide a safe atmosphere for failure

In many practices, the penalties for failure far exceed the rewards for success, which is often taken for granted. In some, the penalties for failure are even greater than the penalties for doing nothing. Even one failure can brand an individual as a loser.

To encourage creativity, it is extremely important to reward success and tolerate failure as much as possible. Try to use mistakes and setbacks positively, as learning experiences. For example, if your staff runs an open house or participates in a health fair that bombs, don't berate them for the failure. Rather call them together for a post-mortem brainstorming session to figure out what they might have done differently.

### 21. Don't penalize the idea person

Avoid giving all the work to the person who comes up with the creative idea. For example, if a staff member suggests that you publish a patient newsletter or run a contest as a way to draw new interest from members of the community, don't insist that that staff member also do the bulk of the work on the project. Doing so is a sure way to discourage creative suggestions in the future. Your staff will learn that it's easier to keep their mouths shut and that the only reward for coming up with new ideas is more work.

### 22. Share your long-term vision

Make sure that staff members know at all times where your practice is going and how individual contributions are helping to meet long-term goals. Without that, they will focus their creativity and energy on the day-to-day problems and see only the trees, not the forest.

### 23. Modify the seniority tradition

Your employees should know that they can be promoted from any level, strictly on merit. That way, all staff members will try harder to come up with creative ideas. On the other hand, if raises and promotions come only with seniority, staff members will feel less motivated to push themselves.

> To encourage creativity, it is extremely important to reward success and tolerate failure as much as possible.

## 24. Provide personal recognition for accomplishment

When one person has come up with or executed a truly creative idea, emphasize the importance of the individual. For example, you might write a letter of commendation to the employee who comes up with a creative idea and place a copy in his or her personnel file. This "celebrates" individual contributors.

## 25. Don't "over-departmentalize" your practice

If you have departments in your practice, such as front office, nursing staff, laboratory technicians, bookkeeping, etc., try to make them less rigid. A looser structure encourages greater interdepartmental communication, which in turn, encourages greater creativity and exchange. This allows staff members to offer ideas concerning not only their own jobs but also concerning problems outside their direct responsibility.

## 26. Teach creative thinking

There are many ways to teach staff how to be more creative. For example:

- Provide in-house creativity training and workshops. Numerous consultants and teachers can run such a program for your staff.
- Enroll staff in creativity classes offered by university extension or adult education programs.
- Enhance your own creative ability through seminars and books. This sets an excellent example staff members can follow.
- Practice creative exercises and games with your staff. Your local bookstore or library will have numerous books on this subject in self-help or self-improvement sections.

## 27. Discover creative "bents"

Try to learn in what ways individuals think they are most creative or would like to be most creative. Discuss with staff which sort of creative contributions they would most like to make. Almost every practice has some people who would be creative enthusiastically, frequently, and naturally, if given the chance.

## 28. Get rid of impediments to creativity

Do merciless "housecleaning" of yesterday's projects that absorb valuable creative resources and energy but do not contribute to practice growth. For example, suppose you publish a quarterly patient newsletter that is getting no results. After you've exhausted all the creative solutions that might fix it, it would probably make sense to abandon the project and go on to another with greater potential.

> Your employees should know that they can be promoted from any level, strictly on merit.

Do merciless "housecleaning" of yesterday's projects that absorb valuable creative resources and energy but do not contribute to practice growth.

## 29. Evaluate creativity at performance reviews

Make it known that part of a staff member's career success—including raises and promotions—will hinge upon his or her creative contributions to your practice. Discuss each staff member's creativity at your next regular performance review.

## 30. Establish a mentor program

Identify the individual(s) inside and outside your practice who have the greatest capacity for helping others realize their creative potential. Let these individuals become mentors to those who show the most promise.

## 31. Be careful with criticism

Criticism kills creativity faster than anything known. Creative people may be sensitive to criticism even if it is well-intentioned. For this reason, it is extremely important that criticism be given thoughtfully, positively, and constructively.

## 32. Commit to staff creativity

Staff creativity will give your practice a fresh point of view and a competitive edge. It can make you more efficient, less harried, and more productive. However, it rarely happens spontaneously. You must communicate explicitly that creativity is expected and establish a climate that is conducive to creative thinking. From there, it is important to reinforce staff creativity with sincere praise and tangible rewards.

Some employers approach staff creativity as a short-term management technique. To develop the creativity in your staff truly and fully, however, creativity must be an integral part of your overall management philosophy. You must value creativity in yourself and the people who work for you, not only when special problems come up, but every day, in everything you do.  ▲

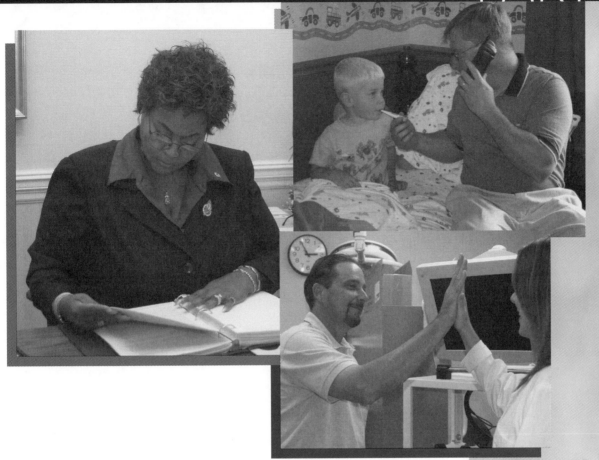

# Managing a Winning Staff: Establishing Personnel Policies, Evaluating Performance, and Anticipating Problems

# Using an Employee Handbook to Head Off Problems

*Most medical practices agree that an employee handbook is a great idea. However, many don't know how to write a good handbook. This chapter provides a helpful overview of the kinds of materials that should and should not be included your practice's employee handbook. It explores the many benefits of employee handbooks and identifies four policy topics that you should avoid. It suggests the benefits and potential uses of a glossary in your employee handbook and provides an example of the terms that might be included in a medical practice glossary. This chapter also suggests the appropriate language and tone for employee handbooks and offers advice about distributing handbooks so your staff will read and understand your personnel policies.*

*Finally, this chapter offers a blueprint for creating your own employee handbook with references to the many chapters in this book that will help you develop strong personnel policies.*

You may be frequently called upon to make rules and enforce them.

B eing an employer is sometimes a lot like being a parent. You may be frequently called upon to make rules and enforce them—and watch out if you're not consistent! If employees believe you showed favoritism to another employee, they can harbor resentment that may someday boil over and lead to a legal dispute. Without written policies to back you up, your chances of winning such a dispute are poor.

Legal protection is one of the strongest reasons that every medical practice needs to use an employee handbook. A well-written policy and procedure manual tailored to your practice would spell out your office policies and employee benefits in the impartiality of print and back you up in a court of law. However, a good handbook has value beyond legal protection. It can save time by answering routine questions once and for all. It can prevent misunderstandings, miscommunications, and mistakes. And, an employee handbook can make future personnel decisions more objective, providing the back-up support you need when you have to make a tough call.

A good employee handbook can also speed a new employee's orientation to your practice. Ultimately, a handbook may help you reduce your staff turnover rate and improve morale. Once your staff knows where they stand with the practice and what benefits they will earn over time, they will be much happier and more secure. Employees like to know your expectations and they are usually comforted to know that the rules in your handbook apply evenly to everyone.

> **TIP:** *Have your attorney review a draft of your employee handbook before you distribute and use it. Work with your attorney to eliminate ambiguity, potential discriminatory remarks, and other material that may lead to practice management and/or legal trouble.*

## WHAT A HANDBOOK DOESN'T SAY IS AS IMPORTANT AS WHAT IT DOES

A practice-tailored employee handbook can clarify many of your office policies by addressing such concerns as leaves of absence, overtime pay, parental leave, and salary reviews. However, you must be extremely careful about the subjects you cover in your handbook and how you cover them. Courts increasingly consider personnel handbooks the equivalent of employee-employer contracts in lawsuits filed by disgruntled former employees.

In light of this, your employee handbook should probably *not* cover the following subjects:

- **Salary increases.** While you might briefly describe your salary review procedure, do not specify in your handbook the exact criteria used for raises or list minimum or maximum raise or salary levels.

---

> A handbook may help you reduce your staff turnover rate and improve morale.

- **Termination.** Do not list every possible reason for employee dismissal. If you do, a former employee might sue and win on the grounds that you fired him or her for a reason not listed in your employee handbook.
- **Extended disability.** Most employers don't want to commit themselves to a written policy on this subject. Although you would undoubtedly grant a leave or absence to (or might even continue the salary of) a valued employee who becomes seriously ill, most employers prefer not to lock themselves in by formalizing such a policy in writing.
- **Mandatory retirement.** In the past, many employers were within their rights to require retirement of their employees at a stated age, often 65 or 70. However, the Age Discrimination in Employment Act and its subsequent amendments removed the legality of the age provision. Do not list a mandatory or even suggested age for retirement in your personnel handbook.

## GLOSSARY A USEFUL ADDITION TO EMPLOYEE HANDBOOK

Every medical practice uses certain words, phrases, and abbreviations that are probably going to be unfamiliar to the layman. As a training tool for new employees, especially those who've never worked in a medical practice before, it is helpful prepare a glossary of your most commonly-used technical or practice-specific terms.

Include a glossary in your employee handbook, complete with a definition for each term, and when needed, a phonetic spelling. Require new employees to study the glossary and demonstrate a clear understanding of each word.

> **TIP:** *Create and administer a written test to assess whether new employees have mastered your glossary. Make the successful completion of your test mandatory. Document test results in the employee's personnel file.*

Below is a partial list of words and phrases that might be unfamiliar or unclear to a new employees working in the business office of a medical practice. Add your own words and phrases to this list to create your practice's glossary. Ask for your staff's input for both terms and definitions:

- AMA
- Associate
- Call list
- Cancellation
- Case conference
- Claim
- Collections
- Co-payment
- Corporation
- Courtesy
- Daysheet
- EOB
- HMO
- Informed consent
- No-show
- Post-treatment conference
- PPO
- Production
- Recall

**Do not list every possible reason for employee dismissal.**

## THE LANGUAGE AND MECHANICS OF YOUR HANDBOOK

The information in your employee handbook should be in everyday easy-to-read language. Very often, both users and writers of employee handbooks complain that the major problem with handbooks is difficult, legalistic language. Don't intimidate your employees with a litany of "the party of the first parts." Your handbook won't be effective it your employees won't or can't read and understand it.

Along the same lines, stress the positive in our employee handbook whenever you can. Emphasize employee benefits rather than only rules and regulations. Be warm by using personal pronouns (you, we), rather than more impersonal terms like "the employer" and "the employee."

For example, instead of writing, "The employer will issue a uniform to each employee," you might write, "We will provide you with a uniform." Or, instead of writing, "The practice provides seven paid holidays every year," you might write, "Our employees enjoy seven paid holidays every year."

An employee handbook need not be fancy but it should be functional. However you design it, plan to give each employee a personal copy. Review your handbook at least once a year and budget for changes. Once outdated, a handbook is no longer useful.

> **TIP:** *Don't bind your handbook into a booklet. Rather, use a ring binder with chapter dividers so you can easily add or subtract material as policy changes occur.*

## DISTRIBUTING YOUR HANDBOOK

When your employee handbook is finished, hold a meeting to introduce it and explain its purpose to your staff. Have your office manager give a copy to each employee.

Most importantly, be sure to have all employees sign a statement within a week of receiving the handbook that says that they have read the handbook and understand it. If you must ever dismiss an employee, such a statement serves as concrete proof that you do have office rules and the employee was aware of them. This will protect you from unfair charges by disgruntled former employees.

When distributing changes that are meant to go into the handbook, it is important that everyone receive a copy and know what to do with it. Number the new pages with a number and letter (for example, 64-A, 64-B, 64-C) to indicate where new material is supposed to go in the handbook.

Include a glossary in your employee handbook.

# A Blueprint for Creating Your Own Employee Handbook

| Policy: | What Employees Need to Know: |
| --- | --- |
| Introduction | This manual is for the staff's benefit. Staff members should refer to it whenever they have a question. However, state clearly that the handbook does not supplant any legal documents or certificates. |
| Short History of the practice | Provide a profile of each doctor and a short description of the kinds of services you provide and the patients you serve. |
| Practice philosophy and mission statement | Explain your goals and what you expect from your staff in the way of professional conduct, discretion regarding patient records, and dress. However, avoid requirements that are not job-related. |
| Basic truths | See Appendix 3-A: Giving your Staff the Proper Perspective: The 25 Truths. |
| Work hours | Describe your normal work week including coffee and lunch breaks. However, give yourself the option of changing your practice's hours (or an employee's hours) during any week at your discretion. |
| Pay period | Describe when the period begins and ends and when paychecks are distributed. |
| Probationary period | State the length of our probationary period and when an employee starts to receive fringe benefits. Avoid a gap between the end of probation and the time an employee is eligible for benefits. |
| Employee status | Define what a full-time, part-time, flex-time, or job-sharing employee is and your expectations of each. (See Chapter 3–8: How to Handle Part-Time, Flex-Time, and Job-Sharing Employees.) |
| Overtime | Overtime is to be avoided whenever possible. Describe your overtime payment policy. (See Chapter 3-6: Reducing and Managing Overtime.) |
| Telephone policy | Describe your policies for placing and receiving personal phone calls at work, either on your office phone or the employee's cell phone. State that it is your intention always to put through emergency personal calls right away. |
| Tardiness | Employees are expected to arrive to work on time and ready to work. (See Chapter 3-3: Cracking Down on Absenteeism and Tardiness.) |
| Time clock or sign-in procedure | Describe the procedure for recording work hours. Some employers consider signing in punching a time clock for an absent or late employee as grounds for immediate dismissal. |
| Group insurance | Describe your plan briefly. Refer employees to the separate booklet provided by the insurance company. |
| Other fringe benefits | See Chapter 2-6: Developing a Competitive Benefits Program. |
| Performance review and merit increases | See Chapter 3-11: Reviewing Staff Performance and Salaries. |
| Holidays | List practice holidays and your policy for how holidays are to be counted if they fall during a vacation. See Chapter 3-2: Firm but Fair Policies for Staff Vacations and Holidays. |
| Vacations | See Chapter 3-2: Firm but Fair Policies for Staff Vacations and Holidays. |
| Sick leave and personal time | See Chapter 3-4: Setting Trouble-Free Policies for Parental and Sick Leave. |
| Extended leaves of absence | oSee Chapter 3-4: Setting Trouble-Free Policies for Parental and Sick Leave. |
| Taboos | State taboos clearly. For example, you might make it taboo to talk about salaries with co-workers or to gossip. Explain your patient confidentiality policy. See Appendix 3-B: Staff Guidelines for Confidentiality and Privacy. |
| Additional topics | These may include: pension and profit-sharing plan, exit interviews, hiring or relatives, safety, parking, housekeeping rules, tuition assistance, smoking policy, moonlighting, grievance procedure, gifts, jury duty, funeral leave, personnel records, severance pay, and termination. |

Don't intimidate your employees with a litany of "the party of the first parts."

**TIP:** *Give handbook changes to each member of your staff with a cover letter that explains all of the reasons and background for the policy changes. Have each employee sign and date a statement indicating that they have received the changes, read and understood them, and added them to their own handbook.*

## INFORMATION TO INCLUDE IN YOUR HANDBOOK

To have the most complete personnel handbook possible, you'll want to include as much detailed information as you possibly can and cover a broad range of subjects. The chart on page 179 (A Blueprint for Creating Your Own Employee Handbook) contains many suggestions that draw upon various chapters in this book.

**TIP:** *You might separate personnel policies such as those suggested in the blueprint chart from your personnel procedures (how to answer the phone, make appointments, greet patients, etc.). Consider having two sections to your handbook or creating two handbooks, one on policies and the other on office procedures.* ▲

# Firm But Fair Policies for Staff Vacations and Holidays

*Paid holidays and vacations are a wonderful employee benefit for your staff. However, without some firm policies in place that anticipate and avoid problems, holidays and vacations can backfire in a medical practice and become a source of problems both for the practice and for the staff. This chapter provides concrete tips for reducing vacation and holiday conflicts and particularly for structuring a firm-but-fair vacation policy for new employees. It provides guidance for solo practitioners' vacation scheduling and offers a list of the most common paid holidays in professional practices today.*

*In addition, this chapter offers answers to common holiday and vacation scheduling questions such as how to handle holidays that fall during a vacation and weekend holidays. Finally, this chapter offers specific advice for making the December holiday season a pleasant and trouble-free one for your staff.*

Most employees need time away from their jobs and want it to be time off with pay. However, vacations and holidays, if not properly planned for, can wreak havoc in your office and create disputes between employees. In short, problems with holiday and vacations can defeat the original intent of the time off.

Although you might like to give everyone the time off they'd most like, it is not always possible. You must be firm about your vacation and holiday policies in order to be fair to everyone in your office.

> Vacations and holidays, if not properly planned for, can wreak havoc in your office and create disputes between employees.

It is wise to establish a policy that states that vacation days can't be taken until they're earned. Period.

## RULES THAT REDUCE VACATION CONFLICTS

Most practices give full-time employees two weeks (10 working days) of time off for vacation each year. Some offer only one week of paid vacation for employees who have been working in the practice only one year, providing the second week at the completion of the second year of employment. As well, some offer additional vacation time upon achievement of certain employment anniversaries. Examples: Three weeks for five years, four weeks for ten years.

There are several rules you may find helpful to keep peace in your practice and to simplify scheduling:

- Vacation must be taken in minimum increments—typically three to five days. Otherwise, employees may choose to take a day here or there and won't get needed rest. And, you'll have constant workflow disturbance. As well, running your practice without the employee for a straight week is a terrific opportunity to learn a great deal about him or her and to deter or discover an embezzler.
- Employees can't receive payment in lieu of vacation.
- Vacation can't be accumulated from year to year. This leads to scheduling problem later. And, everyone needs a vacation on a regular basis to gain perspective and freshness. Moreover, requiring annual vacations deters embezzlement.
- Employees should request their vacation time at least three months in advance.
- Vacation scheduling conflicts between staff members will be resolved on the basis of seniority.

## "NO WORK, NO VACATION" A STRICT BUT FAIR POLICY

One of the most common and expensive problems involving staff vacation time occurs during the first year of employment. Typically, a new employee asks to take one or two weeks of vacation time before he or she has accrued this time. This seems rather harmless, so many practice administrators allow it. However, if the employee leaves the practice before the first year of employment is up, the practice may have difficulty recovering the money paid for unearned vacation.

Because this happens so frequently, it is wise to establish a policy that states that vacation days can't be taken until they are earned. Period. If an employee insists on taking time off during the first year, allow him or her to do so. However, pay him or her only for the vacation time that has actually been accrued, NOT for time that hasn't been accrued. This strict policy is the best and fairest way to ensure that your employees don't leave your practice having taken unearned vacation time.

**TIP:** *Some practices try to get around this problem by paying salaries two weeks in arrears. They then offset the last pay period against unwarranted vacation time taken, the cost of damage to or replacement of practice property, etc. Although such a policy protects the employer, it is generally very unpopular with staff. As well, staff may successfully argue that they are entitled to interest on the money held for them. For these reasons, I recommend against this policy.*

## WHAT TO DO WHEN THE SOLO PHYSICIAN TAKES VACATION

In offices with only one doctor, most practices try to have the majority of staffers take vacations at the same time as the doctor. However, a skeleton crew can remain in the closed office to make appointments, deposit payments, bring collections up-to-date, weed through old patient files, reorganize the filing system, look into new equipment purchases, have equipment serviced, have the office deep-cleaned, or take inventory. You might even have remaining staff bring reception area magazine subscriptions up to date or forge ahead on back-burner practice building activities.

Try to keep at least one trustworthy person in the office when it's closed for vacation to do these tasks and also to:

- make or change appointments for patients who call;
- handle billing matters in the regular time allotted; and/or
- refer patients needing immediate care.

**TIP:** *If the employee must schedule vacations for when the office will be closed, state this clearly to prospective employees at the job interview. Have new hires sign a form (in your personnel manual) that states that they have been informed of this policy. Then, give your staff a minimum of three months notice of when you plan to take a vacation or attend a seminar. Six months notice would be better.*

## WHICH HOLIDAYS SHOULD YOU OBSERVE?

Most practices grant at least seven days off with pay each year (for full-time employees). The most popular office holidays are:

- New Year's Day
- Memorial Day
- Independence Day
- Labor Day
- Thanksgiving Day
- The Friday following Thanksgiving
- Christmas Day

> Try to keep at least one trustworthy person in the office when it's closed for vacation.

Holidays should
be fun and
trouble-free,
but that's not
always the case.

In addition, many practices also provide one or more of the following paid holidays:

- The day (or half-day) before Christmas
- The day (or last half of the day) before New Year's Day
- The last half of the day before Thanksgiving
- The employee's birthday
- Religious days, such as Good Friday and Yom Kippur
- Martin Luther King, Jr. Day

## LET STAFF MEMBERS HAVE A SAY IN THEIR HOLIDAYS

Many employees would choose different holidays beyond the basics you provide for them. Therefore, why not establish a "master list" of eight or nine holidays and then let staffers choose two or three of their own? This approach has many benefits:

- Staff members will get time off when they most want or need it.
- Employees of varying religious and ethnic backgrounds may be able to celebrate their holidays without having to use vacation time.
- You will probably reduce the number of days your practice will be understaffed.

> **TIP:** *In large practices, you might have staff members make their selections in a written survey. However, be clear that staff requests are subject to your approval.*

## ESTABLISH ADDITIONAL HOLIDAY POLICIES TO MINIMIZE PROBLEMS

Holidays should be fun and trouble-free, but that's not always the case. There are a few precautions many practices consider worth taking:

- Require staff to work the business day prior to and following holidays in order to be paid for the holidays. *Exception:* Pay absent employees who have a doctor's excuse, have had a death in the family, etc.
- Reward employees who end up having to work on a holiday. Compensate them at time and one-half on those days.
- Decide how you will handle a holiday that falls during a staff member's vacation. Typically, the holiday is *not* counted as a vacation day. For example, if you provide Christmas as a paid holiday and the staff member takes off the whole five-day week, he or she would be using only four vacation days.
- Decide how you will handle a holiday that falls on a weekend. Typically, most practices take off the Friday or Monday adjoining that weekend, usually abiding by the local public school schedule.

**TIP:** *Circulate to your staff your annual holiday and vacation schedule as early as possible, well in advance of the New Year.*

## CONSIDERATIONS ABOUT YOUR STAFF AND DECEMBER HOLIDAYS

The December holiday season is an exciting time. However, it is probably also a time that will require a little bit of extra planning for your office:

- It's a good idea to establish some policies about holiday giving among employees. Many offices use a holiday grab bag and put a strict dollar limit on the gift. Others organize a one-on-one gift exchange by drawing names. In these ways, each employee needs to buy only one gift with a restricted price. This puts less financial and emotional stress on your staff, reduces competition and minimizes the potential for hurt feelings.
- Plan one holiday celebration exclusively for your staff. Don't lump their celebration into an open house for patients or another large party. Invite their families, if possible.
- Do not give a cash holiday bonus only. This becomes expected, and therefore, is almost always taken for granted. It's much better to give a more personalized gift instead of or in addition to money. Some great ideas:
  - Membership to a health, tennis, or exercise club.
  - Season tickets to a local sports team or theater company. This can be divided among your staff. You might buy a block of two or four seats and then let each staff member go to a few events. If so, decide who goes when by lottery.
  - A night on the town for the employee and a guest. Example: Dinner for two at a nice restaurant or dinner theater.
  - A gift certificate to a nice local department store or shopping mall or for a luxury service you know the employee would enjoy.
  - A discount coupon book good throughout the year for stores and restaurants in your community. (These are available in many cities.)
  - A magazine subscription related to the employee's interests. This is a great gift because it keeps on giving with every issue the employee receives.

**TIP:** *Don't give the same exact gift every year. That's too predictable and therefore, more easily undervalued. Show your thoughtfulness by varying what you give, even if that only means a gift certificate to a different restaurant or store each year.* ▲

Many offices use a holiday grab bag and put a strict dollar limit on the gift.

# Cracking Down on Absenteeism and Tardiness

*Employees who have poor attendance can wreak havoc on your practice. Their behavior must be stopped. The effective practice manager must establish clear policies about employee absenteeism and tardiness, and crack down on chronic abusers.*

*This chapter offers practical suggestions for establishing concrete attendance expectations, deterring unnecessary tardiness, and dealing with chronic offenders. It also offers practical advice about some of the stickier attendance issues, such as employee time off for bereavement, civic responsibilities, continuing education, and personal problems. It also suggests a method of tracking attendance and positive ways to stimulate better attendance.*

There are plenty of employees who seek as much personal time off from work as possible, and there are probably just as many who are habitually late. As we all know, poor employee attendance creates problems for everyone else in the practice, from co-workers to patients. Therefore, it is essential to limit unnecessary staff absenteeism and tardiness. Below are some practical and effective tips to improve employee attendance and still allow employees who need time off for legitimate illness or personal business to take it without penalty, fear, or guilt.

## DO YOUR EMPLOYEES KNOW YOUR ATTENDANCE EXPECTATIONS?

To begin, you must make sure that your employees know for certain what kind of attendance you expect from them. Do not assume anything here; rather, spell it out clearly with written policy:

> Poor employee attendance creates problems for everyone else in the practice, from co-workers to patients.

> It may seem harsh to dock a valued employee who is late because of weather or traffic. But in the long run, it is the best way to keep peace and harmony in your practice.

1. All employees are expected to report ready for work on time each day. That means that employees should be dressed and groomed for work, freshened up, finished eating, stowed personal gear, etc., and that they should punch in on the time clock after all that is done, and should be on time.

2. Employees should keep their absences and tardiness at an absolute minimum. Employees are expected to miss work only when it is absolutely unavoidable, and then for as little time as possible. That means that employees should schedule personal appointments on their own time. If the employee must make an appointment during working hours, he or she should try to do so over lunch, and return to work as soon as possible. It is always better to miss one hour of work than two, a half day rather than a whole day, etc.

3. Notify our office immediately when you know you are going to be absent or late.

## HOW TO DETER UNNECESSARY TARDINESS

This simple policy will do the trick:

*"All employees will be docked for any time they miss from work due to traffic, bad weather, or any other outside circumstances that delay their arrival to the office."*

Without question, this is an extremely strict policy, and many practice managers are reluctant to use it. It is, after all, sometimes impossible to arrive on time for work. In fact, you yourself may be held up by traffic or a storm some day. However, there will always be some employees who make a greater effort to get to work in bad weather or traffic than others. Some live close to your office, some live farther away. Who gets paid and who doesn't in such a situation?

The strict policy is the fairest. It may seem harsh to dock a valued employee who is late because of weather or traffic. But in the long run, it is the best way to keep peace and harmony in your practice.

## HOW TO DEAL WITH THE EMPLOYEE WHO IS HABITUALLY LATE

For the employee who is frequently late (or absent), docking his or her paycheck may not be enough of a deterrent. If you've tried everything else, your next step will be to suspend the employee from work.

Example: Anne is late for the eleventh time in the past 2 months, because of "problems at home." What you might say: "Anne, take tomorrow and the rest of the week, without pay, to get your affairs in order. We'll see you back on time next Monday." This tells Anne that you're displeased with her tardiness and that you want her to stop.

## Save On Payroll Taxes During Employee Absences

Keep careful records of wage payments for periods when employees have paid absences. Payroll taxes are levied only on payments for actual services, NOT payments made when the employee is unable to work.

You may be eligible for refunds of payroll taxes, such as Social Security, paid during an employee's paid extended absence. Check with your accountant

If an employee's tardiness gets out of hand, you may have to fire him or her. If so:

1. Document your case by keeping precise records: the date, the time the employee arrived, the reason for lateness, what you said and did about it.
2. Tell the employee that his or her job is on the line. Then explain specifically what he or she has to do to save it, and issue at least three warnings. (Example of a final warning: "Anne, your lateness is hurting the entire staff, and our patients, and I can't allow it. If you're late one more time this month, you will lose your job. And if you begin this pattern of lateness again anytime after this month, you'll lose your job.")
3. Give your last three warnings both verbally and in writing.
4. Follow through and fire the employee as promised if attendance doesn't improve.

## POSITIVE WAYS TO GET EMPLOYEES TO WORK ON TIME

So far, we've discussed negative incentives for employees to come to work on time. However, you could use a positive approach, by rewarding good attendance.

For example, attendance should be one of the components of the employee's performance review. If it is good, you should note it in your semiannual evaluation (and again refer to it in your salary review). You might promise your staff some treat if, as a group, they keep up perfect attendance for a stated length of time—say, a bagel breakfast in your office for two weeks of perfect attendance. Or try this innovative "poker" plan:

1. Have each employee who arrives on time choose a card from a deck of playing cards.
2. At the end of the week, those with perfect attendance and punctuality will have five cards.
3. The best poker hand wins a cash bonus or prize.

> If an employee's tardiness gets out of hand, you may have to fire him or her.

For the employee who is frequently late (or absent), docking his or her paycheck may not be enough of a deterrent.

## HANDLING EMPLOYEE TIME OFF FOR CONTINUING EDUCATION

When a staff member attends a meeting, seminar, or workshop that relates to his or her job or develops professional skills, this is usually not considered time away from work Ordinarily, expenses and an eight-hour day are paid for a full-day conference, whether it is eight hours or not.

However, you should decide whether there is a maximum number of days per year that any staff member can be away from the office to attend courses. As well, you should retain the authority to veto an employee's request for time off for a course, based upon which course it is and when it is scheduled to take place. You do not want to be in a situation in which an employee can take time off to attend a frivolous or irrelevant course during a particularly busy time in your practice, such as when you are short-staffed.

## HANDLING EMPLOYEE TIME OFF FOR CIVIC RESPONSIBILTIIES

Employees should arrange to vote on Election Day before or after working hours. If this is impossible, most practices allow time off to vote at the beginning or end of the work day.

If you compensate an employee for jury duty, you may wish to put a cap on this benefit. Forty hours per year is typical. Furthermore, employees should be required to return to your office for the remainder of the work day whenever they're dismissed or not chosen for jury service.

## HANDLING EMPLOYEE TIME OFF FOR PERSONAL BUSINESS

Unavoidable personal business comes up from time to time that requires an employee to miss work. For example, one of your employees may be:

- summoned to appear in court;
- giving a blood transfusion to an ailing friend;
- taking an important test that's offered only during work hours, such as a driving test or college entrance exam; or
- attending a funeral.

It's essential that the reason for the absence be compelling and unavoidable. A haircut or matinee tickets don't qualify. Employees should understand that they should schedule such personal business during their own time.

Many practices allow employees 1-2 days of time off with pay each year for compelling, unavoidable personal business. Doing so makes for a more honest employer-employee relationship, and deters lying and sick leave abuse. Require a written request for personal time off in advance, as soon as the employee learns of the need for it.

## HANDLING EMPLOYEE TIME OFF FOR BEREAVEMENT

Most practices pay for anywhere from 1-5 days off in the event of the death of an employee's spouse, child, parent, sibling, grandparent, or other very close relative. The employee can then take vacation days for additional needed time off, or elect to take the time without pay.

Dealing tactfully and sensitively with another person's grief can be a challenge. Moreover, you may have conflicting feelings. Although you recognize the necessity for a period of mourning, you may fear the employee's work will suffer. Will he or she be irritable or solemn with patients? Will he or she need additional time off?

Your best strategy is to approach the employee. Often, bereaved people feel like pariahs—that the people they've known for years want to avoid them. Don't avoid them. Meet with the returning employee right away and express how sorry you are about his or her loss. Open the lines of communication.

## WHAT TO DO WHEN THE ABSENT EMPLOYEE RETURNS TO WORK

When an employee returns to work after an absence, take a few minutes to welcome the person back. Then, inquire about the reason for the absence. If the employee says he or she was "sick," "didn't feel well," "had personal business," "a civic responsibility," etc., seek a more definitive explanation. Your records should show a specific reason for every absence.

When appropriate, express concern about the employee. If he or she was sick, ask, "How are you feeling?" If he or she took a test, ask, "How did it go?" If he or she attended a funeral, ask, "Are you all right?" There are two reasons to ask these questions:

1. To show genuine concern for the employee.
2. To let him or her know that you believe him or her, and that you take these matters very seriously.

## DOCUMENT EVERY ABSENCE OR TARDINESS

You'll need a simple documentation system to measure each employee's absentee rate. To begin, establish an individual absentee report for each

> Attendance should be one of the components of the employee's performance review.

Ordinarily,
expenses and
an eight-hour
day are paid
for a full-day
conference,
whether it is
eight hours
or not.

| TABLE 1. Attendance Report for: Susan Rigby | | |
|---|---|---|
| Date: | Absent/Tardy: | Reason |
| 1/13/98 | 1 day | Migraine headache |
| 9/5/98 through 9/9/98 | 5 days | Vacation |
| 10/18/98 | 55 minutes late | Traffic |
| 1/26-28/99 | 3 days | Flu |

staff member. Record the days (or hours) absent for vacation and illness and also days tardy. It might look something like Table 1.

Next, have your business assistant collect individual absentee reports and prepare a cumulative attendance report every month or quarter. This report should document the rate of absenteeism in your practice and identify when and where absentee problems are occurring. To keep it simple, this report need only include the number of absentee hours and the percentage rate for the practice. If you have a large practice, conduct a cumulative absentee analysis by job category as well (business assistants, clinical assistants, etc.).

When your records indicate than an employee might be abusing your paid time off policies, it's time for a formal interview. In such a meeting, express concern and note the frequency of absences. Take disciplinary action if necessary.

Be sure your employees know you are keeping these attendance records. The mere fact that you do indicates that you feel reliability is an essential part of each person's job. Thus, employees will know you consider their attendance to be very important and that you're keeping score.

## RESCHEDULED PAYDAY A FINAL TRICK
Attendance is usually very good on payday. If you have high absenteeism on Monday or on Friday, a common problem, schedule payday for one of those days. ▲

# Setting Trouble-Free Policies for Parental and Sick Leave

*Parental and sick leave are medical staff benefits that can lead to all kinds of problems. This chapter offers specific guidance for heading off the most common and difficult problems, focusing particularly on ways to provide fair benefits to employees who need them without inviting unnecessary absences and policy abuse. It reviews typical medical practice sick leave policies as well as four creative strategies for encouraging and rewarding excellent attendance and deterring abuse. In addition, this chapter suggests ways to structure a parental leave policy that will not only be fair to employees but also help the practice fulfill its legal obligations.*

The smooth operation of your medical practice depends upon the presence of your entire staff.

With rare exception, every person in the workforce will be too sick to come to work at one time or another. In addition, chances are, at least one person in your practice will ask for an extended leave of absence because of a new addition to his or her family.

The forward-thinking medical practice needs to have humane parental and sick leave policies. These should enable sick employees and those with new babies to take time off without worry, guilt, or financial hardship.

Unfortunately, a poorly thought-out or vague parental leave can lead to misinterpretation and resentment. On the other hand, a very liberal or overly simplistic sick leave policy is an open invitation for abuse. Simply paying employees for a given number of sick days without offering an alternative incentive may actually encourage them to play hooky.

The smooth operation of your medical practice depends upon the presence of your entire staff. The unplanned absence of just one team member can lower your efficiency and productivity for the entire day. Thus, although you want your sick employees to stay home without penalty, you can't afford to have a staff member fake illness and call in "sick" because he or she didn't feel like coming to work on a beautiful Friday or a rainy Monday morning.

## WHY IT MAKES SENSE TO PAY FOR UNUSED SICK DAYS

Paying for unused sick days creates an incentive for the well employee to come to work rather than an incentive *not* to. This makes good practice management sense because:

- Paying for unused sick days leads to fewer unnecessary absences.
- Staff members who don't take all of their sick days will feel no resentment towards staff members who do.
- Paying for unused sick days boosts morale, especially when it is paid in a fun way or at year-end.
- Truly sick employees will still have the benefits of paid sick days.
- Paying for unused sick days makes turnover easier. A staff member who gives notice will be likely to work until the last day and help train his or her replacement without using up sick days. And if you have to fire an employee, the extra pay may make the parting hurt a little less.

## TYPICAL SICK LEAVE POLICIES

Most practices simply allot a given number of paid sick days to employees each year. Typically, they pay for up to six days off to be used in the event of the employee's illness. Some additional policies:

> With rare exception, every person in the workforce will be too sick to come to work at one time or another.

- Employees are not granted extra pay or time off for illness that falls during a vacation or holiday.
- Sick leave exceeding the allotted time is time off without pay. However, staff members can use earned vacation time after sick leave is used up.
- Sick leave cannot be accrued beyond one year.
- Sick leave is to be used for illness only. All personal business should be conducted on the employee's own time, whenever possible.
- Any employee taking more than three days of sick leave in a row must bring a note from a physician indicating both the cause of the illness and when the employee is fit enough to return to work.
- The practice pays employees their regular hourly wage or a portion of it for all unused sick days at the end of each year.

## WHY YOU SHOULD HAVE A FAMILY SICK LEAVE POLICY

Most practices state that sick leave is to be used only for the employee's own illness. However, as we all know, many employees must take time off from work when their children are ill. Because single-parent and two-career households are extremely common today, we can expect this trend to continue or increase.

Pretending that sick leave is used for personal illness only creates stress for employees. It forces them to lie, because they must pretend to be sick when they're not. That's why many practices acknowledge the reality of family sick leave and permit sick leave policies to cover the employee's children, spouse, and parents. This type of flexibility reduces stress, increases morale, and leads to more honest employee-employer relationships.

## CREATIVE STRATEGY #1: REWARD PERFECT ATTENDANCE ONLY

If you'd like to be somewhat restrictive with your sick leave pay benefits, here is a payback system that rewards perfect attendance only:

1. Divide the calendar year into quarters.
2. For each consecutive quarter of perfect attendance, employees will earn a progressive amount of time off or extra pay as follows:
   - 1st. quarter: ½ day off or 4 hours pay
   - 2nd. quarter: 1 day off or 8 hours pay
   - 3rd. quarter: 1½ days off or 12 hours pay
   - 4th. quarter: 2 days off or 16 hours pay
3. If the employee receives a full year of the perfect attendance benefit, he or she will start over with a new benefit year.

Pretending that sick leave is used for personal illness only creates stress for employees.

Paying for unused sick days leads to fewer unnecessary absences.

4. If sick time is taken in any quarter, it will be a zero-benefit quarter. The employee then reverts to previous-quarter benefits.

5. New employees become eligible for the first full payroll quarter worked. Employees must work at least 35 hours per week to be eligible.

6. Employees have the option of taking either the time off or the pay. They receive a statement of current status and benefits earned at the end of each quarter in which they have earned benefits. Time off must be arranged the same way as vacation time off, with specified notice and restrictions.

7. Employees may accumulate time off for one year and take it in conjunction with other vacation or holidays.

8. If an employee elects to take pay, payment can't be accumulated and will be made in the next payroll period.

## CREATIVE STRATEGY #2: THE MONTHLY ATTENDANCE LOTTERY

Another way to reward perfect attendance is with a monthly lottery. Here's how:

1. Employees with perfect attendance records qualify for a monthly drawing.

2. On the last working day of the month, one winner is selected at random from the list of eligible employees.

3. The winner receives an attractive cash bonus or prize.

4. The other employees with perfect attendance are rewarded with smaller prizes.

## CREATIVE STRATEGY #3: EARN BONUS DAYS OR PAY

Here's a novel sick leave policy from a large Maryland practice. The program works like a "charm" according to the office manager who says that all five of their offices are fully staffed "99% of the time."

1. Employees earn one "bonus" day for every absence-free month, for a potential total earning of 12 days per year.

2. Employees will not be paid for absences of one or two days as they occur, but will have the opportunity to make up missed days in bonus days in future months.

3. Bonus days for each employee will accumulate every six months (December until June, June until December), at which time the number of accumulated bonus days will be divided in half. The practice pays to employees, in June and December, one-half of unused bonus days at the employee's hourly rate and holds the remaining half in reserve time. These absences will be paid and

deducted from reserve time and/or bonus days as necessary. It is understood that an employee's workday may consist of more or less than eight hours. However, for fairness and simplicity, bonus days are charged and credited on the basis of an eight-hour day.

## CREATIVE STRATEGY #4: SAY IT WITH FLOWERS

If you're looking for an offbeat way to curb sick leave abuse, send a get-well card and flowers or a plant to the staff member's home the day he or she calls in sick. Similarly, if the employee asks to miss work because his or her child is sick, send someone from the office to the employee's home at lunchtime to deliver a helium balloon bouquet, toy, or a package of coloring books and crayons. Pick out gifts that would help to cheer and amuse an ailing, bedridden child.

If the employee (or his or her child) truly is sick, he or she will appreciate your thoughtfulness and generosity. However, if the employee or child is NOT sick, he or she will realize that you take absences seriously and that you believed the story. With any conscience at all, the dishonest employee will feel sorry, foolish, and guilty about lying and abusing your sick leave privileges. More importantly, the employee will be less likely to do it again.

## TIPS FOR GRANTING PARENTAL LEAVE

Parental leave is a common personnel management problem for medical practices. As one doctor told me recently, "I'm starting to think there's something in our drinking water. EVERYONE here is pregnant!"

Most employers provide six or more weeks of unpaid leave after childbirth so parents can stay home and care for their new children. However, there are several things you should know:

- Many states require employers to grant special "parental" leave benefits. See what you must do before you decide what you want to do.
- If you offer short-term disability benefits, make them available to pregnant employees just as you would to anyone who's temporarily disabled. This is sometimes called the "broken leg" rule. (That means that you will treat the pregnant employee just as you'd treat an employee who has a broken leg.)
- You can request pregnant employees to submit a statement as to the probable duration of their absence, *IF* you require similar information from all others requesting short-term disability leave (such as for elective surgery).
- It's worthwhile to request the following information in writing for all short-term disability leaves: the cause of the disability, starting date and duration of leave requested, the physician's verification of the

The unplanned absence of just one team member can lower your efficiency and productivity for the entire day.

To avoid claims of discrimination, offer "parental" or "personal" leave and apply your policies equally to men and women, whether they give birth to or adopt children.

above information, listing by physician of any temporary or permanent restrictions on the employees job functions both before and after his/her leave, and written confirmation from the physician that the employee is fit to return to work.

- If you grant unpaid or paid extended leave for education, travel, or any other non-work related reason, then generally, you can grant parental leave on the same basis.

- Some practices have an explicit unpaid "maternity" leave policy, although requests for other types of unpaid leaves are not routinely granted. To avoid claims of sex discrimination, rename such policies "parental" or "personal" leave and apply them equally to men and women, whether they give birth to or adopt children.

- One way some practices handle parental leave is to permit a combination of sick, personal, and vacation leaves, resulting in several weeks of paid leave. Example: One practice's employees can combine 10 days of accrued sick leave and two weeks of vacation at full play, plus 20 days of temporary disability leave at 2/3 pay. That equals six weeks of fully paid leave.  ▲

# Establishing Guidelines for Employee Dress and Hygiene

*Can you tell your medical practice staff how you want them to look? Where in your office they can eat? Can they chew gum at work? Can they wear red nail polish or a charm bracelet? In the pages that follow, you will see not only that you can establish rules for employee dress and hygiene, but why you should.*

*This chapter suggests several good ways to structure staff rules for wearing uniforms and street clothing. It also covers possible rules for wearing practice nametags, cosmetics, jewelry, hair styles, neatness, stowing of personal possessions, personal hygiene, drinking, eating, smoking, and gum chewing. Finally, this chapter offers practical suggestions for establishing your practice's dress and hygiene "first aid" kit as well as guidance for making your practice's dress and hygiene codes non-discriminatory.*

Each person on your medical practice's staff is an important member of a professional team. Patients, colleagues, potential referral sources, and your community at large may meet members of your support staff long before they meet your doctors. From even the briefest encounters with your staff, they may form opinions of your practice overall and even of your doctors' clinical abilities. How each member your staff speaks, acts, and looks is therefore extremely important.

> Appropriate dress and hygiene are absolute musts in any medical practice.

Your employees may not share your ideas about what constitutes a professional appearance.

Professional, neat clothing worn by those who work in your medical practice will speak volumes about you and your staff. So will a fastidiously clean appearance. Few people would argue that appropriate dress and hygiene are absolute musts in any medical practice. But what, exactly, is appropriate? What does it mean, specifically, to wear "professional, neat clothing" or to have a "fastidiously clean appearance"?

Unfortunately, your employees may not share your ideas about what constitutes a professional appearance. Their standards may differ from your own. Staff input, of course, can be very helpful and important when you establish new dress and hygiene rules. In addition, there is usually room for some degree of individuality in the appearance of your employees. Nonetheless, it is usually necessary to establish, share, and implement basic guidelines for employee dress and hygiene. Often, these rules have to come from the practice's management.

Clear, fair rules for dress and hygiene will ensure that your existing staff, as well as prospective employees, knows what kind of appearance and professional manner is expected of them. In addition, dress and hygiene rules will help you ensure that you treat each member of your staff fairly and consistently. Rules can also serve as invaluable support if you must ever confront a staff member because of problems with his or her appearance.

> **TIP:** *It is essential to establish clear and reasonable rules that do not in any way discriminate against any individual because of race, handicap, gender, ethnicity, etc. (see the Sidebar, Making Dress Codes Non-Discriminatory). In addition, it is wise to have your attorney review any rules you establish before you present them to your staff.*

## HOW TO ESTABLISH A PRACTICE DRESS CODE

A professional practice dress code usually includes descriptions of the uniform(s) and specific types of shoes that can be worn. For non-clinical staff, it may prohibit certain types of street clothing in the practice for reason of safety or appearance.

There are many good ways to establish rules about the way your staff dresses. You *may:*

- Choose one uniform style to be worn by everyone. Many practices choose a uniform style and color that is coordinated with the office décor and logo. In addition, many practices specify the type of shoes, a sweater or jacket, and accessories that may or may not be worn with the practice uniform.

## Making Dress Codes Non-Discriminatory

Employee dress codes are unlawful if they can't be applied equally to both sexes. Thus, if you have a dress and hygiene code, it is very important that you make identical or at least equivalent requirements for both male and female employees in comparable positions.

In addition, it is best to avoid dress and hygiene codes that are targeted to specific racial or ethnic groups. It can be deemed discriminatory in some cases to prohibit hairstyles or garments particular to certain groups of people, if these do not interfere with job performance.

- Allow staff members to choose their own uniforms in any style they like. You might let them choose the style they like but only within limited choices or in a designated color(s) or pattern(s).
- Require staff to have five uniforms in five different colors. Then, you can designate that a different color be worn each day (i.e. yellow on Monday, green on Tuesday, etc.).
- Choose one uniform style but designate that a different color be worn by each member of your staff, for a rainbow effect. In a busy practice, uniform color can help patients remember who helped them. Larger-staffed practices can specify a different uniform color for each department. In addition, staff members may appreciate the chance to choose the color of their uniform and to stand out.
- Require staff to sew a practice emblem or patch onto a plain uniform on the sleeve or breast pocket. An embroidered patch, usually of the practice name and logo, can also be sewn onto lab coats, cardigan sweaters, and jackets.

If some employees in your practice are permitted to wear street clothing to work, it is still important that they look neat, clean, and appropriate. They should wear clothing that won't get in the way of their work and that is consistent with your professional atmosphere. Thus, many practices establish rules for non-uniformed employees. For example, you *might*:

- Prohibit the wearing of very high heels, open-backed or open-toed shoes.
- Provide a jacket or sweater.
- Require a tie and jacket.
- Prohibit backless, low-cut, midriff, or see-through dresses and blouses.
- Prohibit excessively long or flowing sleeves that could get caught in equipment.

**Many practices establish rules for non-uniformed employees.**

A sloppy desk
or workstation
does not reflect
positively or
project the right
image.

## NAMETAGS

All members of your staff, including doctors, should wear a nametag regardless of their position and whether they are wearing a uniform. Nametags are the simplest and best way to ensure that patients and co-workers know to whom they are talking.

To keep things simple, it is best if you provide all of the nametags for your staff. That way you have control over what the nametags look like and can give your tags a consistent, professional look.

> **TIP:** *Have a nametag ready for a new staff member's first day. The nametag will help him or her get acquainted with co-workers and patients more easily and make the "new kid" in your practice feel immediately part of your professional team.*

Almost any office supply or specialty company can engrave nametags inexpensively and quickly. Choose a large, easy-to-read nametag in a color that coordinates with staff uniforms and your décor. When possible, put your practice name and logo (and perhaps motto, if you have one) on the tag as well as the staff member's name and title. That way, patients looking at the nametag will associate the excellent impression they are getting of your staff with you and your practice. This is a very subtle but effective form of internal marketing.

Designate where on the uniform or clothing the nametag is to be worn each day. Also, you may wish to establish rules about embellishing nametags. Decide whether you will allow your staff to add their own stickers or pins to your practice's nametags.

## COSMETICS, HAIR STYLES, AND JEWELRY

If you establish rules about cosmetics, hair styles, and jewelry, be certain to do so consistently for all members of your staff regardless of the person's gender, race, ethnicity, and position in the practice. For example, the following is often discouraged in medical practices for all staff members:

- Loose styles for long hair.
- Brightly colored nail polish.
- Very long fingernails.
- Excessive use of cosmetics and perfume.
- Large or noisy jewelry, especially on the hand or arm.

## HYGIENE

A fastidiously clean personal appearance is a must for the staff of a professional practice. Patients will notice if a uniform is stained or ripped, hands and nails are dirty, or shoes are soiled and scuffed.

Many practices therefore establish personal hygiene rules such as:

- Wash hands each time you use the restroom.
- Wash hands between patients and whenever you sneeze.
- Shoes should be polished and clean and have no torn or dirty laces.
- Uniforms should be sparkling clean, pressed, and show no signs of wear or stains.
- Scrapes and cuts should be covered and dressed with clean bandages.
- Nails should be clean and smooth-edged.

> TIP: *If you permit colored nail polish, you may insist that the employee have a perfect manicure or remove the polish. If so, keep a bottle of nail polish remover on hand in your office.*

## OFFICE NEATNESS

In addition to personal hygiene rules, you may wish to establish rules for the neatness and good order of each employee's work area. A sloppy desk or workstation does not reflect positively or project the right image to patients.

Employees should make it a habit to put their work area in good order before they leave the office at the end of each day. That way, they'll always return to a clean, organized desk or workstation in the morning.

## DRINKING, EATING, SMOKING, AND GUM CHEWING

Some practices allow employees to eat and drink only in specific areas such as an employee break room or kitchen. If employees may eat or drink at their discretion, doing so should not interfere with the task at hand or be done in front of patients. In addition, the employee should clean up food and drink containers, wrappers, and crumbs immediately.

In addition, most practices don't allow smoking on their premises. Those that do allow smoking may still restrict staff smoking to certain times and to areas outside of the office and far away from patients.

Chewing gum is usually prohibited in the professional office, as it is generally thought to project the wrong image. In addition, chewing gum can interfere with the staff member's ability to speak clearly. Along similar lines, most employers prohibit the use of chewing tobacco at the workplace.

> TIP: *Most employers also establish a policy that prohibits the consumption of alcohol and drugs at the workplace and make such behavior grounds for immediate dismissal.*

> By thinking and planning ahead, members of your staff will always be ready to handle a mishap that spoils their appearance.

> Staff handbags and other personal items should be locked safely out of sight in a desk drawer or cabinet while the staff member is working.

## KEEPING SUPPLIES ON HAND FOR EMERGENCIES

Sometimes things happen beyond anyone's control. That's why it's a good idea for you and your staff to keep some emergency dress and hygiene supplies in your office. By thinking and planning ahead, members of your staff will always be ready to handle a mishap that spoils their appearance.

For example, many employees appreciate a medical practice that keeps the following supplies on hand tucked away discreetly in a closet or drawer:

- Extra pantyhose
- Spot remover.
- A nail file
- Comb or brush
- Cosmetics
- Hair clips, barrettes, bands
- Shoe laces
- Safety pins
- Sewing kit
- A spare uniform
- Dental floss, toothbrush, toothpaste, mouthwash
- Folding umbrella
- Cardigan sweater or jacket.

> **TIP:** *Staff members who use these emergency supplies should be responsible for their return or replacement.*

## PERSONAL POSSESSIONS

Staff handbags and other personal items should be locked safely out of sight in a desk drawer or cabinet while the staff member is working. Leaving a handbag or other items in plain view is inappropriate and risky.

In addition, you will need to designate a place in your office for staff coats, umbrellas, boots, and other outerwear. Staff should be told where they should place their belongings neatly at the start of each day. ▲

# Reducing and Managing Overtime

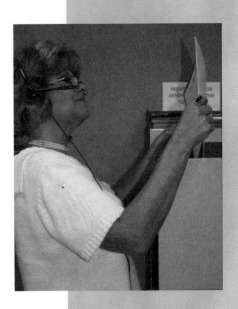

*Overtime is undesirable for many reasons. It can deteriorate staff morale, reinforce and reward inefficiency, and reach deep into your practice's pockets, often without improving your bottom line. Many employers overuse overtime and hold many misconceptions about their legal obligations.*

*This chapter explores specific practice management methods for reducing or eliminating the need for overtime. It dispels three popular misconceptions about employers' legal obligations when paying overtime. Finally, it summarizes the basic rules for paying overtime, including how to calculate an employee's regular rate of pay, how to structure a legitimate workweek, and when and how overtime payments should be made.*

D o you frequently find it necessary to pay your staff overtime? If so, do you know why? In my experience consulting with professional practices, I've found that with rare exception, the most inefficient offices use the most overtime. In many of these practices, paying overtime actually reinforces and rewards staff for their inefficiency. In addition, despite all the overtime paid, offices using the most overtime are almost always less productive than others.

Overtime is undesirable for several reasons. First, members of your staff deserve to complete their day's work and leave for home on time. Making them work late routinely can erode morale. Second, except for the occasional unforeseen emergency, every office should be able to get all their tasks done by the end of the workday. If you can't, something is wrong; either you're understaffed or you're managing the work poorly. Finally, overtime is expensive. Money spent on overtime is almost always better spent on additional staff, incentive bonus programs, and other positive staff management projects.

**Paying overtime actually reinforces and rewards staff for their inefficiency.**

## GET TO THE ROOT OF THE PROBLEM

Before getting into the specifics of managing overtime, it is very important to do all you can to eliminate it. To begin, analyze the overtime patterns in your office. Try to find out what created the need for the overtime in each case and how much overtime was needed. Once you begin to see a pattern emerging, make the changes necessary to correct whatever inefficiencies exist.

For example, suppose you find that your staff works overtime to close and balance out the day whenever you have a particularly long day. Rather than continuing to do things the same inefficient ways, you might adopt a "bank" policy; simply choose an earlier close-out time, roughly one hour before the end of the day, as banks do. The new day can then be started for all transactions after that time. That way, the finished records can be pulled and totaled earlier, leaving plenty of time for your bookkeeper or business assistant to close out the day, check the bank deposit, and have the deposit all made, all by your regular closing time, without working any overtime.

Or, suppose you observe that your staff must frequently work overtime to accommodate the day's patient load. If so, then you are routinely running behind schedule. When this is the problem, it is much better to tackle it head-on rather than to allow it to continue—not only for your staff's sake, and the sake of keeping overtime expenses down, but for the sake of your patients as well. You may need to evaluate your appointment time estimates, or bring in additional staff to accommodate your busy load. Or, if you find that the problem occurs more often on particular days, such as Mondays or days following holidays, you may need to shift your schedule around so you can offer your patients extended hours on those days.

## THREE COMMON MISCONCEPTIONS ABOUT OVERTIME

For the occasional unavoidable overtime, it is important that you handle payments correctly, according to the law. Unfortunately, many employers don't understand the law and hold misconceptions about it.

### Misconception #1

If an employee works too many hours in one week, she can take "comp time" the next week and you won't owe her any overtime. *The Truth:* Overtime is always calculated by the single workweek. If a staff member works 55 hours one week, you can't cut her hours to 25 the next week so they average out to 40. You owe her 15 hours of overtime pay.

### Misconception #2

As long as the employee eats during lunch, she is not working and can't count that time as overtime. *The Truth:* An employee who eats at his/her

> Money spent on overtime is almost always better spent on additional staff, incentive bonus programs, and other positive staff management projects.

desk can easily accumulate overtime during lunch hours. If she so much as opens the mail or answers the phone, the law says she is working. It doesn't matter that you didn't ask her to.

### Misconception #3

If a current or former employee says she is due overtime pay, and it's her word against yours with no records to back her up, the verdict is likely to go with you. *The Truth:* The law requires you to keep complete payroll and time records. Without them, you won't have much chance if the former employee insists she's been underpaid. If it's her word against yours, most juries find in favor of the employee.

## WHY YOU MUST INCLUDE BONUSES IN OVERTIME

Many employers don't pay their staff enough for overtime and in so doing invite federal wage-and-hour investigations. Among the primary offenders are those who provide productivity bonuses for employees but don't include these bonuses when calculating overtime.

Bonuses and commissions paid as incentives must be included in the regular rate of pay when computing overtime. For example, if you pay your receptionist a bonus for successful collection calls, this extra money must be included in her regular hourly pay rate when you compute her overtime.

By law, you are required to include all compensation for employment in the regular hourly rate of pay, except for these specific payments:

1. Gifts
2. Special occasion bonuses
3. Payments to profit-sharing plans
4. Payments to thrift plans
5. Payments to savings plans
6. Irrevocable contributions to bona fide trusts

All other bonuses and commissions must be added to employee's other earnings to determine their regular hourly rate—on which overtime pay is based.

A common error is to assume your bonuses are "discretionary" and therefore needn't be used when computing overtime. The Department of Labor specifically states that for a bonus or commission to qualify for exclusion as discretionary, the employer must offer the discretionary bonus only after the exemplary work has been performed. You abandon this discretion once you promise employees extra money to induce them to work more efficiently.

> Overtime is always calculated by the single workweek.

Bonuses that must be included in the regular rate of pay are those given for exemplary attendance, individual or group production, quality of work, and bonuses contingent upon employment until payment is made.

> **TIP:** *Bonuses based on a percentage of total earnings—both straight and overtime—do not fit into this category. For example, suppose you give employees a 5% year-end bonus based on their yearly wages. A staff member who works 2,000 straight-time hours at $6 per hour and 190 overtime hours at $9 per hour earns a total of $13,710. His bonus, 5% of that figure, is $685.50. Because the bonus itself is already based on overtime earned, you won't need to pay any additional overtime.*

### Nine More Rules about Overtime

There are many more rules governing overtime, in addition to those described above. Your attorney or accountant can advise you about the specifics in your state. However, the following rules generally apply everywhere:

1. The federal Fair Labor Standards Act of 1938 (FLSA), as amended, requires that covered employees receive pay equal to time-and-a-half their normal hourly wage for any hours worked above 40 in a workweek. Employers in every state must obey this law.
2. In addition to FLSA, some states have their own laws regarding overtime pay. These laws frequently cover more employees and are stricter than the federal law. For example, some states require employers to pay overtime compensation for more than eight hours of work in one day, as well as the usual weekly requirements.
3. FLSA exempts administrative, executive, and professional workers from its overtime pay provisions. However, title alone won't exempt workers. Exempt status depends upon duties, responsibilities, and sometimes, salary.
4. The U.S. Labor Department defines an employee's "regular rate" of pay as all pay for employment, with certain exceptions. In general, you can subtract these sums from an employee's compensation to figure his or her regular hourly rate of pay.
   - Reimbursements for expenses incurred on the employer's behalf.
   - Gifts and discretionary bonuses, as described above.
   - Extra payments for occasional periods when no work is performed due to vacation, holidays, or illness.
   - Extra pay received for foregoing holidays or vacation.
   - Employer payments on behalf of an employee to a bona fide savings and profit-sharing plan, as described above.
   - Premiums already paid for overtime.

An employee who eats at his/her desk can easily accumulate overtime during lunch hours.

5. If you've agreed to pay an employee a lump sum for overtime hours—a sum that's independent of how many overtime hours actually worked (for instance, a lump sum to complete a particular job)—this sum MUST be considered part of the employee's regular rate. This is true even if the sum is equal to or greater than the time-and-a-half sum that would be owed on a per-hour basis for the overtime. These lump sum payments can't be credited against overtime compensation due under FLSA.

6. If an employee performs two or more different tasks at different hourly rates, his regular rate for the workweek is the weighted average of such rates.

   **TIP:** *You can make an agreement with the employee to pay overtime for certain work based on the regular rate the employee normally receives for that work only.*

7. Your workweek must be a fixed and regularly recurring period of 168 hours—seven consecutive 24-hour periods. It may begin on any day, but it must remain fixed, except for a permanent change that's not intended to evade FLSA overtime requirements.

8. Overtime should be paid on the regular payday for the period in which the workweek ends. However, if you can't calculate overtime until later, you may pay overtime compensation as soon as is practical, after your regular pay period.

## Where to Get More Information

Because laws change, you should have your attorney review and update the guidelines offered in this chapter. As well, contact your attorney if you ever have a specific question or dispute about paying overtime in your practice.

In addition, you may contact your local wage and hour office for more information on federal overtime laws. Look in the phone book under U.S. Government, Department of Labor, Employment Standards Administration, Wage and Hour Division. In addition, for information on state regulations, contact your state department of labor. ▲

The law requires you to keep complete payroll and time records.

# Preventing Employee Theft

*Medical practices are unfortunately the target of embezzlement more often than you might think. This chapter offers practical suggestions for keeping your employees honest and thwarting a would-be embezzler. It describes the common symptoms of an embezzler at work and offers 15 practical techniques for preventing bookkeeping embezzlement.*

*This chapter also suggests a simple method for conducting mini audits from time to time and precautions to take to ensure the reliability of computer passwords. As well, this chapter advocates keeping tighter control of office supplies and a method for spotting telephone abuse. Finally, this chapter offers suggestions for dealing with employees who steal time on the job.*

Embezzlement is a particularly unpleasant practice management problem that almost always evokes a strong emotional response. Most of us like to trust people and we believe that people are basically honest. We are almost always surprised, disappointed, and hurt when they are not.

The embezzler is in an excellent position to take advantage of you because he or she has inside knowledge of your practice management systems. The embezzler knows the ins and outs of your bookkeeping, check writing, and petty cash methods. He or she usually has almost unlimited opportunities to steal. Great sums go into and out of the typical medical practice every day. It is therefore surprisingly easy for a trusted member of your staff to take a little here and there without being detected or even suspected.

Clearly, the astute practice manager needs to take steps to protect the practice's interests. In this chapter, we will explore some very simple techniques that decrease the opportunity and temptation for

> Most of us like to trust people and we believe that people are basically honest.

embezzlement. As well, you will learn how to detect employee theft early on and nip the problem in the bud. As well, we will consider the different kinds of theft—not only of money, but of other valuable practice resources as well.

## KEEPING YOUR EMPLOYEES HONEST

The best way to prevent embezzlement is to hire the right employees and to treat them well. Some practical tips:

- Check all references a job applicant gives you. Learn to spot resume fraud and uncover signs of embezzlement in former employment. (See Chapter 1-6: Verifying the Job Applicant's Factual Credentials and Chapter 1-7: Gathering Useful Opinions of the Job Applicant.)
- Set a good example. For instance, don't take cash from the petty cash fund to cover your own personal expenses. As well, don't help yourself to practice supplies and products. Doing so sends a dangerous signal to your staff. Before long, they'll follow your lead and help themselves, too.
- Offer generous employee discounts. This makes your services and products accessible and affordable to your staff so they'll be less apt to steal to get what they want or need. As well, a discount will demonstrate to your staff that you care about them, which cuts the temptation to steal to "get even" or because "they deserve it."
- For similar reasons, pay employees a fair wage. Poorly paid employees may feel justified in cheating you.
- Obtain fidelity bond insurance coverage on all employees. The bond can be a relatively inexpensive rider to your general office insurance policy. There are two basic types of bonds. The first, called a *position-schedule* bond, covers whoever fills a specific position. The second, called a *blanket bond*, covers all employees, whatever the job title or duties performed. Most medical practices feel protected by a blanket bond equal to half their annual gross. Those who find this amount requires too high a premium opt instead for a set amount, such as $10,000 or $25,000.

  **TIP:** *Insurance companies won't bond individuals who aren't considered trustworthy. However, once an employee is bonded and steals, the insurer must reimburse you.*

  **TIP:** *Let your employees know they're bonded. That tells them they're not above suspicion. And, they'll know that if they're caught embezzling that they'll definitely be prosecuted.*

## SYMPTOMS OF EMBEZZLEMENT

In many cases of embezzlement, the embezzler's behavior could have tipped off the practice manager. It's important to detect the problem early and put an end to it before the damage becomes severe.

> The embezzler is in an excellent position to take advantage of you.

Below is a list of the most common symptoms to check for in your medical practice. While none of them proves embezzlement, you will want to be on guard if you have an employee who:

- Never wants to take a vacation.
- Refuses to share bookkeeping chores with co-workers.
- Seems to be living far beyond his or her means.
- Shows an unusual amount of enthusiasm for writing accounts off as bad debts. (An embezzler may have already collected the sum for himself or herself.)
- Repeatedly leaves IOUs in the petty cash drawer.
- Receives phone calls from creditors.
- Shows signs of drinking or gambling problems.

## 15 TECHNIQUES FOR PREVENTING BOOKKEEPING EMBEZZLEMENT

It is extremely hard to embezzle from a sound, well-managed bookkeeping system. These techniques make it very difficult to juggle your books:

1. Daily bookkeeping is a must. Delays encourage forgetfulness and dishonesty. Record all transactions at the end of the day or the first thing the next morning. Balance cash receipts daily and prepare a duplicate deposit slip with the names listed.
2. Make bank deposits daily, too.
3. Send statements monthly and be sure that all accounts are billed. When you're ready to give up on an account that hasn't been paid, turn it over to a collection agency. It's a tempting starting point for an embezzler.
4. Bill patients as you provide your services. If treatment occurs over long time, send periodic statements. Account delays give the embezzler valuable time to tamper.
5. Write all checks in permanent ink. If corrections are necessary, void the check or draw a line through the incorrect bookkeeping entry and initial the correct one.

   TIP: *Don't use erasable pens in your office. An embezzler can change the face amount of a check after it's cleared the bank to cover a previous theft or forgery. Or, he or she can change the name of the payee to his or her name, cash the check, and change the name back after it clears the bank.*

6. If you have a facsimile signature stamp, keep it under lock and key. An embezzler can use a signature stamp on unauthorized checks, credit card charge slips, or even prescriptions.

   TIP: *The best precaution is to have no facsimile signature stamp at all.*

The best way to prevent embezzlement is to hire the right employees and to treat them well.

## Obtain fidelity bond insurance coverage on all employees.

7. Review your financial reports at least monthly. Keep a check on your practice performance and be critical and suspicious of changes.

8. Segregate job duties. For example:

| *Have One Employee:* | *Have Another Employee:* |
|---|---|
| Open mail, list, endorse, and total incoming checks. | Make accounts-receivable entries. |
| Reconcile bank statements. | Be in charge of receipts and disbursements. |
| Be responsible for cash receipting. | Be responsible for depositing. |
| Clear your payables. | Write your checks. |

Separating bookkeeping functions in this way means that two or more employees act as a check on one another. It also means that employees could defraud you only by working together, which is far less likely than one embezzler working alone.

9. Write pre-numbered receipts for all money received.

10. Make all disbursements by check except those from petty cash. Always require that petty cash disbursements be supported by vouchers.

11. Always sign checks made payable to yourself for any cash you take out for personal needs.

12. Tell patients to make all payments to your financial secretary so he or she is responsible for all incoming funds.

13. Assure that employees have sufficient time to balance accounts. Rushing causes errors and lapses in security precautions.

14. Insist that all employees take a vacation each year and that vacation days are taken in multiple-day or one-week blocks (not a single day here or there).

15. Insist that all records be kept in the office. Do not allow employees to take bookkeeping chores home to catch up.

## HOW TO CONDUCT A SURPRISE MINI AUDIT

You can further shield yourself from cash embezzlement with this simple weekly audit that takes only a few minutes:

- Pick one day at random to record the name and amount charged to each patient. Be discreet. Jot your notes on an index card as you go through your day. If you don't know the exact charges for an appointment, record it and look it up in your fee schedule later.
- At the end of the day, check each entry on your index card against your office records. If you find a discrepancy, look for what went wrong. It may be an honest error.

- If you can't account for the discrepancy, have your accountant review your financial records.

   **TIP:** *Tell no one you're conducting the audit. Do audits on different days of the week so there's no pattern to them.*

## PASSWORDS PREVENT COMPUTER EMBEZZLEMENT

Computer access passwords given to employees are an excellent safeguard against embezzlement. Passwords restrict staff members' access solely to those areas of the system in which they have responsibilities. For example, an employee who collects cash from patients can be stopped from changing the charge listed in the computer.

Limited access via passwords also prevents staff members from learning confidential financial data about your practice such as salaries. Some tips about using passwords:

- Make passwords easy to remember so they don't have to be written anywhere. However, make them unusual enough so they're hard to guess.
- Change passwords periodically. Staff members tend to learn one another's passwords even if not intentionally.
- Deactivate the password of any employee who leaves your practice, even if the leaving is voluntary. Deactivate the password of any employee you discharge prior to the dismissal. This prevents an angry employee from getting revenge by altering files.
- Restrict access to sensitive files only to staff members who have direct responsibilities in those areas. A good program will allow you to delete sensitive file names from the master menu. This is a desirable feature. The fewer people who know about the sensitive files, the better.

## PREVENTING THEFT OF SMALL OFFICE SUPPLIES

A roll of tape, a file folder, a pen or scissor here or there—many employees will see nothing wrong with taking office supplies home with them. But such theft is wrong, not to mention expensive. Here's a great way to establish a snitchproof inventory system for your office supplies:

- Set aside one centralized location for inventory receipt, storage, and distribution. Supplies all over the office have a way of walking.
- Assign your office manager responsibility for maintaining the supply inventory.
- Store the supplies in a locked cabinet or closet. Give your office manager the key.

> In many cases, the embezzler's behavior could have tipped off the practice manager.

> ## Don't use erasable pens in your office.

- Track who takes what by having everyone—even you—sign for items they take. A "Request for Supplies" form can be circulated regularly, perhaps on a monthly basis.
- When employees see that supply requests are kept on record, pilferage and waste will go down.

  **TIP:** *If staff members ask you why the new system is being introduced, explain that you're trying to determine patterns of supply usage over time so you can take advantage of quantity discounts and other special offers.*

  **TIP:** *Also centralize and track the use of practice postage so employees cannot easily take stamps or run personal letters through your postage meter.*

## CHECK BILLS CLOSELY FOR TELEPHONE ABUSE

Check your monthly telephone bills for these signs of abuse or unwarranted telephone usage:

- Repeated calls to "time" and "weather" or "900" numbers.
- Extra-long calls or frequent calls to the same long-distance number. It's easy to spot calls over nine minutes or more than $9.99. If you suspect abuse, make a one-minute call to the number to see who answers. This can provide a clue as to who made the call and tell you whether the call was legitimately related to practice business.
- Excessive evening or night calls. Or, calls on days your office was closed.

  **TIP:** *Any of these signs may indicate the honest efforts of a hard-working employee and not telephone abuse. Don't accuse anyone of foul play unless you have solid evidence.*

## PREVENTING TIME THEFT

Stealing time on the job is a costly and often overlooked from of employee theft. You have every right to expect that your employees will work for you and only you during the time you pay them to do so.

To begin, check to see that your employees are arriving for work on time and staying until the end of the day. See that they take only the appropriate amount of time off for lunch and breaks. If necessary, install a time clock.

Next, make your expectations clear. Establish rules against personal phone calls, guests, and other personal business during the workday. Tell employees that they are not to use work time to do their taxes, run a side business, entertain a friend, or do anything else of a personal nature that is not directly related to their job duties.

If you catch an employee using work time for personal business, tell him or her that such behavior cannot be tolerated. Note the incident in the employee's personnel file and if the situation warrants it, issue a letter of warning. Discuss the event at the performance review as well as what you will do if the behavior continues. It is reasonable to dock the employee's salary or even to dismiss him or her if he or she continues to use work time for personal business. Just be sure you can substantiate your claim and have adequate documentation.

TIP: *If a pattern of time theft develops, check whether the employee is accomplishing all assigned tasks. Assess the employee's attitude about work. A responsible, hard-working employee will usually not steal time unless he or she is bored and/or able to get all assigned work done first. The best remedy in this case may be to give the employee more challenging work to do.* ▲

Don't accuse anyone of foul play unless you have solid evidence.

# How to Handle Part-Time, Flex-Time, and Job-Sharing Employees

*Offering employment structures other than traditional full-time positions in your practice can help you draw excellent job applicants and also can enable you to increase morale, job satisfaction, and productivity. However, there are many decisions you must make when offering a part-time, flex-time, or job-sharing position. This chapter explores the pros and cons of offering alternative job structures. It suggests ways to make part-time, flex-time, or job-sharing positions work most effectively, both for the employee and for your practice. In addition, this chapter suggests which positions are best suited to alternative structures.*

Some people can't work regular full-time hours.

> Many excellent workers are looking for alternatives to regular full-time employment.

Some people can't work regular full-time hours and balance the responsibilities of their work and personal lives. We now have many more single-parent homes. Many parents of young children are part of the workforce. In addition, many older people today want to or need to continue to work to some extent beyond the usual age of retirement. In addition, many individuals attend school or have health problems and other obligations that limit the number of hours they can work.

Because of the changing nature of today's workforce, there is new demand for good jobs that offer flexible hours and more time off. In short, many excellent workers are looking for alternatives to regular full-time employment, such as:

- Job sharing: A part-time arrangement whereby two or more employees share one full-time position.
- Flex-time: The ability to schedule work hours at times other than usual office hours, and,
- Part-time: A regular staff position requiring fewer hours than full-time.

## HOW ALTERNATIVE ARRANGEMENTS CAN BENEFIT YOU

If you scan the classified employment ads, you'll probably find that there are very few part-time, flex-time, or job-sharing positions advertised. Many employers don't want to be bothered with them or don't even see any benefits to them. Thus, good alternative jobs are scarce and in high demand.

This scarcity can provide a great opportunity for you. By offering attractive alternative employment structures, you can draw from a much broader pool of talented job applicants. In addition, you may be able to retain a valued full-time member of your staff when his or her personal circumstances change.

For example, suppose one of your best employees:

- has a baby and decides to discontinue working full time,
- becomes ill and requires frequent medical treatments or rest,
- has her sick parent move in with her so she can take care of him or her, or
- decides to go back to school to earn a degree.

In these cases, a full-time employee might have to quit. However, you might be able to retain the employee if you allow him or her to work part-time, flexible hours, or if he or she can share the job with another person who has similar time constraints.

Employment alternatives may help you find and keep a staff of very loyal, hard-working individuals. People who work part-time or who share a job or who have flexible hours generally appreciate that fact and are highly motivated to keep their bosses happy. Employers who offer alternative structures to the 40-hour work week report:

- increased office morale
- increased job satisfaction
- increased productivity, and
- decreased absenteeism

In addition, employees who work fewer hours than a full-time schedule are usually not entitled to the full complement of employee benefits offered to full-timers. This can add up to substantial savings for the employer.

## POTENTIAL DRAWBACKS OF ALTERNATIVE ARRANGEMENTS

Of course, there are some potential problems with non–full-time employment arrangements. The most obvious is that you'll probably have more employees in total than you would if everyone worked full time. Thus, there is more need for performance evaluations, tax records, social security payments, benefits, mediation of staff conflicts, recruitment, payroll checks, etc.

Another potential drawback is that if employees work different hours or shifts, you may have a tough time scheduling staff meetings so everyone can attend. You also may have a harder time building team spirit. Job sharing should be mutually beneficial for the individuals and for your practice. You will need to spend extra time and energy to keep everyone up to date and included in everything.

> **TIP:** *These potential drawbacks can be overcome with thoughtful planning and follow-up. Initially, plan to spend a little more time than usual to set up and supervise part-time, flex-time, and job-sharing employees. However, after the honeymoon period is over, they should require no more than the usual amount of time and attention.*

## TIPS FOR JOB-SHARING ARRANGEMENTS

There are many good reasons to consider job sharing in your practice. First, it can enable you to find qualified help for difficult-to-staff evening and weekend shifts. Second, having two people trained to do a job will reduce problems with vacations, absenteeism, and turnover. Finally, two people may bring more talent, experience, and special abilities to the job than one person could.

> If employees work different hours or shifts, you may have a tough time scheduling staff meetings so everyone can attend.

Therefore, before forging ahead, decide:

1. What are the specific job requirements for this position? What are the day-to-day, week-to-week, and month-to-month activities? Can they be divided? Or must both members of the team master all the tasks?

2. Will each member of the partnership perform a first-rate job? Are their styles sufficiently similar? Will they respond equally well to tasks, people, and challenges?

3. Who will be ultimately accountable? Is responsibility shared between the two employees? If so, how? How will you know for sure who has done what?

4. How will the two partners work through their total responsibility effectively? Specifically, how will you handle promotions and raises? Who will get credit? When? And for what? How will you handle schedules? How many days and hours per week will each employee work? When is extra coverage needed for absenteeism, vacations, or special projects? How is this to be handled?

5. Will job sharing cost you more or less? What will be your total anticipated costs for salaries, benefits, holidays, vacation and sick days, and overtime? How does this compare with similar costs for a full-time employee? Are the savings or additional expense worthwhile?

6. How will you handle turnover? On the one hand, if one member of the team leaves, you'll have a hole in your practice until you can fill the position. Thus, you're *twice* as likely to need to recruit for a staff opening than if you had one full-timer. On the other hand, however, losing one of the job-sharing employees still leaves you with the other. Downtime needed for training a new employee is greatly reduced, because there's someone experienced to do the training and carry the ball until the replacement is up to speed. In addition, there's a chance that the remaining employee will assume the position full-time, and you won't have to recruit at all.

7. Would you be better off with two part-timers? Job sharing is not the same thing as hiring two part-time employees. Part-timers generally have separate, limited duties and independent schedules. Employees who share one job work cooperatively and see that the job functions are carried out well and without interruption, as though one person were doing them all. Unlike part-timers, job sharers usually have the flexibility to alter their schedules between themselves, as long as the job is always covered without inconvenience to you, other staff members, or your patients.

> **TIP:** *Some jobs in the medical practice are not well suited to job sharing. For example, one practice administrator is best available all the time. On the other hand, receptionists or clinical assistants might more easily share one job, depending upon the type of practice.*

Job sharing should be mutually beneficial for the individuals and for your practice.

## TIPS FOR FLEX-TIME ARRANGEMENTS

Maintaining flexibility in scheduling work hours may not always be practical in a medical office. Except for a very few positions, you'll need your employees to be there for your patients during regular office hours. However, some employees, such as a bookkeeper or marketing coordinator, may find it possible to start working early, or to end a little later. You might allow this as long as it doesn't interfere with the operations of your office.

Some practices stagger working hours so that some team members start early to prepare for the day's patients while others arrive later and stay later. However, scheduling in these cases is very important, as the office needs to be covered when patients are there.

> **TIP:** *Allowing flex-time in larger practices with many employees means you'll have more to keep track of. To simplify things and keep everyone on schedule, install a time clock.*

## TIPS FOR PART-TIME ARRANGEMENTS

If you feel you need another employee but aren't sure if the workload will support one, you might hire a part-timer to start with. That way, you can control additional salary costs while you learn if the available work warrants the addition of another full-time person.

When hiring a part-timer, there are several things to consider:

1. It may make sense to hire a part-timer who will be available to work full-time in the future. That way, you can save on recruitment and training costs and efforts if you expand the position down the road. However, don't hire a part-timer who prefers full-time work right away. He or she may reluctantly take the job, keep looking for another job, or jump ship as soon as he or she lands a full-time job.

2. If the part-timer won't have consistent work hours, make up his or her schedule several months in advance. A big disadvantage of having a part-timer is that he or she may not be available when most needed. This won't be a problem if you both know in advance what his or her hours will be.

3. Consider hiring a student for a part-time position. To begin, you might see if your local high school or college has a work-experience program. These programs usually test the students' skills and match the best applicant for the position. In addition, they often provide ongoing supervision by a teacher or guidance counselor.

> **TIP:** *When possible, hire a high-school student in his or her junior year for a year-round position, with extra hours during summer and school vacations. This prevents rapid turnover, because the student knows he or she has steady work. And, if things work well, he or she may continue through senior year, or even after graduation.* ▲

**Don't hire a part-timer who prefers full-time work right away.**

# Working with Your Spouse, Children, or Other Close Relatives

*Employing someone you're close to in your medical practice can have many advantages. Yet, as many doctors find, employing relatives can also have its pitfalls.*

*This chapter describes the financial benefits of employing a loved one in your medical practice. It suggests the specific steps you will need to take to legitimize your spouse's, significant other's, or relative's employment.*

*We also explore the personal benefits and drawbacks of employing your spouse or significant other. We include advice from other doctors and spouses who work together and establishes 15 ground rules for working with your spouse. Finally, the chapter includes a 10-question self-quiz for you and your spouse or significant other to help you decide if working together in your medical practice will strengthen or strain your relationship.*

Hiring someone you love to work in your office can work. Yet, while there are many potential benefits with this arrangement, there are also a great many potential problems. These, and the employment alternatives, must be carefully considered before making any commitments.

In this chapter, we will explore the pros and cons and the do's and don'ts of employing a loved one in your medical practice. This information will be useful to you if you are thinking about hiring your spouse, significant other, children, siblings, in-laws, other relatives, or even close friends.

> The spouse may feel that he or she is neither fish nor fowl in the office social dynamics, which can be isolating.

## Special Problems when a New Partner Joins a Solo Practice

Consider this common scenario where a physician has employed his wife as nurse or office manager for many years. The practice has grown and the founder needs a partner. The incoming partner may face a difficult transition with a long-employed office manager. The problems are compounded when that manager is the senior's wife. She may view that the practice is "hers" even more than her husband feels it is "his"; inevitably, troubles will ensue. It takes special awareness, skill, and sensitivity to deal with a junior partner who may feel both confident because of his or her mastery of the most recent techniques and yet unsure of his or her position in the practice and the community.

> There are several good financial incentives for employing your spouse.

# FINANCIAL BENEFITS FOR EMPLOYING YOUR SPOUSE

Having the doctor's spouse work in the practice is nothing new, especially in practices where keeping overhead to a minimum is essential. There are several good financial incentives for employing your spouse:

- Your spouse would qualify to be in your pension plan, which may allow you to put aside more money from which you'll both benefit upon retirement.
- Your spouse would qualify for the tax-free employee benefits you provide, such as insurance and disability coverage.
- Your spouse would qualify for Social Security benefits.
- You may be able to deduct your spouse's travel expenses while accompanying you on continuing education and other business-related trips.
- If you have young children, you could qualify for a tax deduction for child-care expenses.

# HOW TO LEGITIMIZE A SPOUSE'S EMPLOYMENT

Some physicians may not wish to employ their spouses or other relatives because they don't accept the strategy's legitimacy. It is perfectly legitimate, however, to employ your spouse or any relative, provided you know and follow the rules.

Most of these rules boil down to one common denominator: Treat your spouse (or other relative) exactly as you treat the rest of your employees on all office records, tax forms, and payroll checks. This means that you must:

- Establish a personnel file for your spouse.
- Have your spouse present his or her Social Security number.
- Have your spouse complete your regular application for employment. At a minimum, require your spouse's education, employment history, experience, and references. Keep the completed form in the personnel file.
- Have your spouse complete required withholding forms for federal and state income taxes.
  **TIP:** *Be sure you and your spouse don't both claim your children as exemptions, a common oversight.*
- Formally agree to employ your spouse. Prepare and sign an "employment letter." Have your spouse sign it and keep a copy in the personnel file.
- Prepare a job title and description for your spouse listing the specific duties your spouse will perform. Keep a copy in the personnel file.

- Establish a reasonable wage. Your accountant can probably help you determine a wage that won't raise eyebrows at the IRS.
- Keep accurate records of the hours your spouse actually works. The best proof is to use a time clock and have a separate time card for each employee, including your spouse. Or, use a daily or weekly time sheet to record hours and wage.
- Pay wages to your spouse exactly as you do the rest of your employees. At the end of the regular pay period, write a standard business payroll check directly to your spouse.
- Have your spouse deposit paychecks into an interest-bearing account in his or her name. Some advisors recommend against depositing the check into a joint checking account or co-mingling the funds in any manner.
- Enter all payments into your practice's regular accounting records. Treat them as you would other business expenses on your tax returns and financial statements.
- Make sure your state and federal payroll and withholding tax reports reflect the wages you paid to your spouse. Also pay appropriate FICA taxes and be sure your spouse's FICA is withheld from paychecks.

> **TIP:** *These are guidelines only. In addition, meet with your accountant to discuss specific benefits, strategies, and tax consequences of employing your spouse or other family member.*

## PERSONAL BENEFITS AND DRAWBACKS OF EMPLOYING YOUR SPOUSE

Since your spouse has an existing personal interest in your practice's success, he or she is apt to be a highly motivated and conscientious employee. Honesty, loyalty, and trustworthiness are givens. (CONTINUED ON PAGE 230)

---

### Self-Quiz: Does Employing Your Spouse Make Sense for You?

You and your spouse both need to do a lot of thinking before embarking on an employment arrangement. You will need to weigh all the potential pros and cons. If you're in a group practice, you'll want to involve your partners in the decision as well. Here are 10 specific questions to answer:

1. Would you be as compatible as doctor and staff member as you are as wife and husband? Are your working styles and temperaments compatible?
2. Would you each be able to relax at the day's end as well as you do now?
3. Would you value your private time together as much if you spent all day in the same office?
4. Is your spouse better suited for another job than the one in your practice? Does he or she lack important skills, training, or other qualities you'd be able to find in another applicant? Or, is your spouse overqualified for the job?
5. Would your spouse be happier and more fulfilled in another job?
6. Or earn more in another job?
7. What would the chain of command be if you hired your spouse? Who would be the boss? Would your spouse have subordinates to supervise? What would be your spouse's relationship with other doctors?
8. How would the other members of your staff react to your spouse joining their team? Do they already know your spouse? How strong is their current relationship?
9. How would your patients react to your spouse? Might they find it awkward to discuss financial arrangements or confidential clinical matters with your spouse?
10. How would your children react? Would they be more likely to interrupt normal office procedure than any other staff member's children?

When at work, the practice must come first.

## 15 Ground Rules for Working with Your Spouse

Here are 15 specific tips for working successfully with your spouse or significant other. These ideas have been gathered from interviews with numerous doctors and their spouses who work with them:

1. To increase the odds of success, the wife and husband should have an equal commitment to the success of the practice. According to one spouse, "Problems arise when one spouse and the practice are allied against the other spouse."

2. When at work, the practice must come first. Even the most happily married couples quarrel occasionally, but you can't let private disagreements come into the office. Too many people are involved. Decide in advance how you'll handle private disagreements while at work. For instance, agree to call a truce until that evening.

3. Develop independent interests outside of work. Since you work together all day, it's all the more important that you each do something on your own—sports, civic activities, take a course, join a club, exercise program, etc.

4. One of the facts of life for a working spouse is that he or she must cease to be a spouse when inside the office. As one spouse put it, "I must give up the thought that the doctor is my husband, and the office is my office." The spouse must work as part of the team in every way possible. He or she must not ask for special privileges, be late to work, or expect other staff members to cover for him or her because of other commitments, any more so than any other employee.

5. The doctor has the same responsibility. He or she must treat the spouse the same as the rest of the staff. Not favoring the spouse is a given, but the doctor must also guard against dumping on the spouse simply because he or she is the spouse.

6. Don't hire your spouse or any family member unless you feel you can terminate the working relationship without major consequences for your personal relationship. You must feel that you can let your spouse go, and your spouse must feel that he or she can quit. Also, don't hire your spouse if you feel you can't criticize his or her work performance or if your spouse feels he or she can't criticize or speak openly with you about office matters, as any employee would.

7. The spouse should refuse to get involved in office secrets or gossip, especially when told, "Don't tell your wife/husband this, but . . . " Holding confidences could put quite a strain on a marriage.

8. Be on guard for undue pressure on your working spouse. It can be an awful burden for your spouse never to be sure if his or her position and rewards are earned by what he or she does or because of whom he or she is. Be sure to praise your spouse as you would any staff member. ➤

## 15 Ground Rules for Working with Your Spouse (continued)

9. Spread the dirty work evenly. One spouse says that her husband used to delegate all the least desirable jobs in the office to her simply because he knew she would do them and he lacked the managerial strength to delegate unpleasant tasks equally among his staff. Likewise, don't give everyone else the undesirable jobs. This will cause resentment among other staff members.

10. Set a policy for how you and your spouse will handle work during nonworking hours. One spouse reports that she and her husband have set a 30-minute time limit for discussing office news and events each evening. After that, they must change the subject. If they didn't, she says, they might never put work behind them at the end of the day, a problem many working couples have. Another spouse adds, "Because of our mutual interest, there's always something to talk about. But it gets tiresome always to talk about the same things."

11. The spouse should refuse to "plead" another staff member's case with the doctor. He or she should refuse to ask for raises, shifts in job responsibilities, time off, etc. on behalf of a co-worker. This is most likely to occur when the staff member is timid or feels the spouse has a better chance of getting the boss's ear and cooperation.

12. In a marriage, it's normal to discuss concerns and ideas for confidential or difficult work-related matters. If you confide in your spouse, especially on a personnel matter, it must be with the understanding that it will go no further. Nothing will demoralize your staff more than discovering that your spouse knows and may be disclosing embarrassing details of a private dispute between one of them and you. Once destroyed, the privacy and trust of the employer-employee relationship is difficult to rebuild.

13. The working spouse should also avoid difficult situations in which patients reveal secrets they don't want the doctor to know. In such situations, the spouse should encourage patients to talk directly with the doctor.

14. Clearly define the spouse's job duties and jurisdiction. The spouse is either a regular employee, definitely under the management of the head of the office in the same way as the rest of the staff, or he or she is the office manager. The well-managed medical practice has no place for the in-between spouse.

15. Be watchful of jealousy. Both you and your spouse will see each other in relationships with members of the opposite sex. If something makes either of you uncomfortable—a touch, a look, a comment—be sure you can talk openly about it. As one spouse put it, "I really do trust my husband, but I can't help but be aware of his physical contact with other women. But because my husband and I have an understanding about this, I can talk with him and share my concern about how this is affecting our relationship."

> Many couples find that seeing one another all day every day puts a strain on their marriage.

Many married couples enjoy working together and find that such arrangements actually strengthen their relationships.

Of course, there are potential problems, too. The most common is resentment by the rest of the staff who may feel that the spouse-employee gets special treatment and privileges. Also, an occasional patient may feel it's awkward or even unprofessional to have the spouse work in the office.

The employed spouse may find himself or herself in uncomfortable situations. While the spouse is not one of the doctors, he or she can't always be exactly like other members of the staff. Thus, the spouse may feel like neither fish nor fowl in the office social dynamics, which can be isolating.

Finally, many couples find that seeing one another all day every day puts a strain on their marriage for several reasons. First, it can be very hard to unwind at the end of the day when it is so easy to take the problems of work home with you. Some couples who work together talk about little else. Second, some marriages do better when the partners spend time apart to develop separate careers and interests. Their happiness depends just as much on the time they spend away from one another as it does on the time they spend together. Third, some people are very well suited for one another personally but find that working together is impossible. (The opposite is also true. Some people work very well together but couldn't be married to one another for five minutes.)

If you're thinking of employing your spouse, the two of you will want to talk about these potential benefits and problems. To aid your discussion, you may find it helpful to use the self-quiz that accompanies this chapter. ▲

> Some people are very well suited for one another personally but find that working together is impossible.

# How to Keep Employees from Taking You to Court

*A lawsuit from a current or former employee, even an unfounded one, can have a devastating effect on a medical practice. This chapter suggests specific strategies for preventing employee lawsuits, specifically those that often result from mistakes in a practice's recruitment materials, employee handbook, job references, and dress code.*

*In addition, this chapter offers guidance for preventing sexual harassment charges, overtime disputes, and hassles with problem employees. Finally, this chapter suggests four must-have business forms that provide important legal protection for any medical practice.*

W ith the prevalence of high awards in employee rights lawsuits, disgruntled staff members can and increasingly do seek restitution for such offenses as wrongful discharge, sexual harassment, and discrimination. To protect yourself from lawsuits from current and former employees, you must establish fair personnel policies and apply them evenly to all employees. In addition, you must carefully document much of what happens in your practice.

## RECRUITMENT

It is very important that you remove bias and unintentional promises from your employment ads, job application, and interview process. For example, referring in your ads to "recent graduates" may suggest that you are seeking a young employee. This implies age discrimination. Likewise, referring to a position as "permanent" may give prospective employees a false sense of security and imply a promise of a long-term job. Be careful.

> Unhappy employees are among the most likely to bring lawsuits against their employers.

It is smart to have your attorney review your employee handbook to be sure you are not inadvertently discriminating or making promises to employees.

On your application form, it is a good idea to have each candidate read and sign a statement such as the following:

*"I understand that this is employment for no fixed term, terminable by the employer at any time, for any reason. This understanding cannot be changed except in writing by the employer."*

In addition, you should have applicants sign a statement that the information contained on the application form is true and that he or she accepts your right to terminate him if any of the information is later found to be false. Also, have each candidate sign a release giving you permission to contact references, former employers, schools, etc.

## EMPLOYEE HANDBOOK

It is smart to have your attorney review your employee handbook to be sure you are not inadvertently discriminating or making promises to employees. Then, have each employee read the handbook and keep on file a signed, dated statement to that effect. This policy prevents an employee from claiming that you did not properly inform him or her of office procedures, including legitimate grounds for dismissal.

**TIP:** *If you have a written job description for each employee, it is a wise precaution to have each of them sign and date a statement that accompanies job descriptions stating that the description is neither all-inclusive nor an implied employment contract.*

## PROBLEM EMPLOYEES

Unhappy or bitter employees are among the most likely to bring lawsuits against their employers. For this reason, it is smart to standardize your discipline, grievance, and complaint procedure. Then, adhere to these policies strictly to establish your impartiality.

Be accessible to your employees, too. Your availability to hear complaints and resolve problems may prevent a court confrontation. Often, it's best and easier to nip personnel problems in the bud.

In addition, install a formal program of frequent employee performance and salary reviews, documenting your findings. In your review, don't be too generous with "good" and "excellent" evaluations. Be critical and share your honest observations. Record problems such as unexplained absences, tardiness, and disputes with other employees. Keep copies of all documentation in the employee's personnel file.

Finally, refrain from taking impulsive action with employees. For example, in the event of heated disputes between employees, you might obtain written, signed statements from each participant. Then, review these statements as part of your investigation. Before disciplining a staff member, review his or her personnel file carefully, giving consideration to former infractions, length of service, and meritorious evaluations.

## GIVING REFERENCES

If someone contacts you to serve as a reference for a former employee, you must be very careful in what you say. Some employers decide that they will simply verify facts such as salary and dates of employment, and say nothing further. Others agree to say more but limit their discussion to the most positive information that will reflect well on the individual.

This is a tricky issue. On the one hand, you don't want to say or write anything that could be deemed slanderous or libelous or that could hurt a good former employee's chances of getting a job. On the other hand, you have a moral obligation (and perhaps a legal obligation as well) to tell the truth and warn a prospective employer of serious potentially harmful problems.

It may not be possible to leave out all negative information about an employee. But when you do want to give a reference that includes any sensitive information, it is important that everything you say is indisputably true and that you can verify what you say. It is always a good precaution to have your attorney review sensitive references. In addition, follow these guidelines:

- Be specific and stick only to the facts when assessing the employee's performance and skills. For example, "Ms. McKenzie typed my letters using our office word processing system. Once she mastered our office word processing system, she turned out neat, attractive letters with almost no mistakes."
- When appraising the individual's personal qualities, again stick to the facts. "Ms. Chen asked for direction and help more than any other employee. I can recall several instances when she asked me to demonstrate how various pieces of equipment worked, such as our photocopier and telephone system. Because she asked questions, she made fewer mistakes than anyone else in the office."
- When you feel you must include damaging or sensitive information about the individual, state the facts plainly and fully. For example, "Ms. Waters had been coming to the office late, averaging three times a week for more than three months. That was the reason for her dismissal." If you wish, you may try to cast a positive light on negative information, but only if you can do so honestly. For example, "Ms. Johnson admitted to me last year that she had a drinking problem. She recently told me that she spent four months in a clinic and that she now attends AA meeting faithfully. I believe her and I am very proud of her for working so hard to get the problem under control."
- If an individual asks you to write a letter of recommendation or to serve as a reference, be honest if you can't heartily recommend him

> You have a moral and legal obligation to tell the truth and warn a prospective employer of serious potentially harmful problems.

or her. It's best to tell the candidate that your letter will have to include some negative information. You may even discuss the specific items you're going to include. That way, the candidate can decide whether or not you should proceed with the letter.

- If you're asked to write a letter by a prospective employer, you might ask the recipient to call you about the letter or you can call him or her yourself. It may be best to put things in perspective on the phone.
- Base your letter or phone conversation on solid facts and carefully reasoned opinions that are backed up by concrete example. For instance, don't say, "She was lazy," but rather, "I was not satisfied with the way she handled our patients on the telephone" and give specifics.
- Do not withhold information that you know to be vital. If you tell only half the truth or omit important negative information about the candidate that would be critical to the recipient, you may leave yourself open to a lawsuit for failure to warn. Provide all the information you'd need if you were on the receiving end.

> **TIP:** *Especially in cases where an employee has compromised or jeopardized the safety of an employee or patient, it is probably best to discuss the matter with your attorney.*

## PREVENTING CHARGES OF SEXUAL HARASSMENT

An employer accused of sexual harassment has a great deal to lose. Even unfounded accusations can affect one's reputation in the community.

It is a good idea to establish a written policy regarding sexual harassment that outlines your grievance procedures step-by-step. Employees should be informed of their rights. Physicians, office managers, and other employees should be made aware of language, attitude, behaviors, and stereotypes that cause complaints. Most people realize that overt sexual advances can be considered harassing, but so, too, can unnecessary touching, suggestive remarks, and even the telling of off-color jokes.

A formal complaint or a threat of a complaint sometimes arises out of a dismissal for an unrelated reason. Therefore, it is especially important to document all circumstances surrounding the dismissal and to consult with your attorney immediately if a sexual harassment complaint is threatened.

> **TIP:** *In addition to providing employees with a harassment-free work environment from co-workers, you are also responsible for protecting them against harassment from patients or colleagues. Take immediate action if they complain to you about being harassed by anyone.*

---

> An employer accused of sexual harassment has a great deal to lose.

## PARENTAL LEAVE

There are several legal issues associated with unfair parental leave benefits. Most notably, you have the following obligations:

- A pregnant employee can't be discharged or forced to resign because she is pregnant. She must be granted a leave of absence if requested. She must be rehired in the same or an equivalent job after the birth of her child if she chooses to return to work.
- There can be no loss of seniority or other benefits because of parental leave.
- Parental leave and return dates must be set by the employee and her personal physician, not the employer—just as they would be set for any disability leave.
- The right to parental leave is not limited to women and birth parents. Fathers and parents who adopt have won court cases.

## DRESS CODE

Employee dress codes are unlawful if they can't be applied equally to both sexes. Therefore, if you have a dress code of any type, be certain that you make similar requirements for both male and female employees in comparable positions.

## OVERTIME

Under the Fair Labor Standards Act, there are several things you should know:

- Any unpaid "lunch break" must be free of all job duties. If a staff member runs errands for you during his or her lunch hour, he or she is working and you must pay for this time. You must also pay a staff member who stays in at lunch to answer the phone or catch up on paperwork. It does not matter whether the employee volunteered to do the activity.
- Watch out if the staff member who works lunch hours pushes his or her hours over 40 per week. By law, if the total workweek is more than 40 hours, you must pay for all extra hours at the rate of time and a half. "Comp" time must be given within that same week so that the number of hours actually worked remains under 40.
- If a staff member asks to cut his unpaid lunch hour to 15 minutes a day to make it a "coffee break," watch out. You could end up paying him or her for an extra 1¼ hours each week. Federal law says that you must pay for any work break from five to 20 minutes.

## BUSINESS FORMS

Several business forms can help protect you from potential legal suits and fines:

**Document all circumstances surrounding the dismissal.**

> Any unpaid
> "lunch break"
> must be free of
> all job duties.

- Employee Application Form: Subtle interpretation of the law often determines what is discriminatory. Business forms manufacturers have created forms that adhere to EEOC regulations and are still flexible enough so you can ask job-related questions.
- Post-Hiring Form: There is some information you must know about your employees that you can't ask on an employment application. For example, you must know whether an employee is married and has dependents for tax purposes. You should use a post-hiring form for gathering this information.
- Employee Evaluation and Warning Forms: Good records on each employee's job performance could be effective protection in the event that an employee files a discrimination suit against you. Your performance evaluation forms should document the employee's strengths, weaknesses, development, and progress. When you give an employee a job warning, document it by recording the date, time, and place of violation and a description of the offense. Also indicate whether the warning was oral or written, what action was taken, and have the employee read and sign what you have written. Provide space for the employee to give his or her version or answer your charge.
- Occupational Illness or Accident Report Form: A good form covers requirements by the Occupational Safety and Health Administration and helps substantiate insurance claims. It should include factual information such as the employee's name, place and time of accident or onset of illness, description, tools or equipment involved, and medical attention received. In addition, record the cause and cost of the accident, including the injured person's expenses, lost time expenses, make-up time, replacement of materials and equipment, etc. In addition, include a follow-up checklist to keep track of insurance reports and claims you should file.

## ADDITIONAL HELP

Of course, your own attorney can advise you about the legal ramifications of an action such as demotion, firing, a new employee handbook, or a letter of recommendation. In addition, you might contact the legal counsel of your county or state professional society. You may be able to learn of specific precedents that have occurred in other practices that may be relevant to your situation.

Various government agencies can answer questions about fair treatment of employees. Your phone book or local librarian can help you find the right offices to contact. However, you would still need to have an attorney interpret laws as they apply to your practice situation and to update you on local ordinances and restrictions. ▲

# Reviewing Staff Performance and Salaries

*Do you feel like you're on shaky ground when it comes time to evaluate your staff's performance or to give them raises? If so, you're not alone. Staff performance and salary reviews are among the most dreaded tasks among medical practice managers. Yet, they are among the most effective techniques you can use to motivate, manage, correct, and reward your staff.*

*This chapter provides an overview of the different kinds of appraisals you will need to conduct with your staff and the order in which to do them. It suggests that you begin the process by establishing concrete goals for your medical practice and then help each member of your staff follow suit by developing their own performance goals for the next six months.*

*This chapter also provides how-to guidance about conducting regular interim progress reviews with your staff to keep abreast of progress, changes, and problems and to issue ongoing assistance and feedback. It explains how to conduct tension-free semi-annual staff performance reviews and semi-annual or annual salary reviews, including a formula for calculating potential raises for each employee in nine increments. Finally, this chapter offers additional tips for evaluating your staff's performance including job description updates and staff surveys.*

Performance appraisals and salary reviews are an extremely important part of staff management that many medical practices overlook. Evaluations of staff performance and salaries are often dreaded by the practice manager and staff alike. In too many medical practices, staff evaluations are done sporadically, without careful preparation, or not at all. However, scheduled and carefully prepared

> Prompt feedback is far more important in changing staff behavior than the intensity of the feedback.

> The overall objectives you establish for your practice for the coming years will determine the performance objectives for yourself and for each member of your staff.

performance and salary appraisals are among the very best techniques you can use to motivate, manage, correct, and reward your staff.

The key to successful performance evaluations is that they must be based upon achievement of goals and contain no surprises for anyone. If a staff member failed to meet one of his or her objectives or if a staff member handled some situation poorly and you never mentioned it, the formal review will contain many unpleasant and painful surprises. Therefore, it is best not to hold criticism until review time. If you do, not only will you be unlikely to change staff performance as you would like, but you'll possibly make your staff feel angry, guilty, or afraid of you. Worse yet, you might trigger an inappropriate change or behavior in your staff that you can't predict and that you don't want.

Prompt feedback is far more important in changing staff behavior than the intensity of the feedback. For this reason, you'll want to do three types of performance reviews with your staff. Two of them are probably familiar to you already: semi-annual performance and salary reviews. These will be discussed at length in this chapter. The third kind of review, called an *interim* review, is also an extremely important part of the evaluation process because it is the best opportunity to give prompt feedback. As well, a goal-setting meeting is the cornerstone to effective staff performance appraisal.

## PERFORMANCE APPRAISALS BEGIN WITH GOAL SETTING

Do you want your medical practice to open a satellite office? Might you rather prepare your office for needed renovation and/or expansion? Would you like to give your patients a better experience of your practice? How do you feel about taking on a new associate? Offering new services? Changing your hours? Obtaining new equipment? Attracting a new and different kind of patient to your practice? Or is it time for you to prepare your practice for your own retirement?

The overall objectives you establish for your practice for the coming years will determine the performance objectives for yourself and for each member of your staff. That is why establishing practice goals is the first step in staff performance appraisals. If you don't know where you're taking your practice, your staff will have no clue about the kinds of performance they need to improve. Ask your staff for their input in establishing specific and measurable goals for your practice.

TIP: *The most useful goals for your medical practice will be specific, measurable, realistic, ambitious (but attainable), and well-balanced, taking into account all of your responsibilities, your own personality and talents, and how you want your practice to grow.*

Hold a staff meeting to share your overall practice goals with your staff. Explain to them why you want to grow your practice or change in the particular ways that you do. Ask your staff to think about each objective for your practice and what they can do, individually and as a team, to help you meet them. Then set up a meeting to discuss the subject more fully with each staff member. These should be 20–30 minute meetings several days later, when they've had some time to digest what you've said and think about their own objectives.

Ask your staff to prepare for your objective-setting meeting by writing concrete suggestions for their own objectives. Ask them to make their personal objectives as specific as possible. You might give them some examples of good objectives. (Examples: Increase collections by 15%, see 20 more recall patients every month.) However, be sure your staff knows that these are only objectives, not definite assignments.

Tell your staff that you, too, will be thinking about objectives for each of them and writing down your specific suggestions. Then explain that you intend to share this information with them at their meetings.

> **TIP:** *Each employee can't help you meet every one of your practice's goals. For example, your clinical assistant probably won't help you meet goals that have to do with collections or the appointment schedule. These are usually responsibilities of a business assistant. However, each overall practice goal should be covered by at least one person. As well, everyone in your practice should have some overall objectives that do apply specifically to them. Keep this in mind when you create your overall practice objectives and as you suggest individual objectives for each staff member.*

When you meet with each staff member to establish personal goals, the atmosphere of that meeting should not be threatening or tense. Come out from behind your desk and sit beside the staff member. Sometimes, the best meetings occur over a cup of coffee where ideas can be exchanged freely and informally. Tell the staff member what you plan to accomplish in the meeting and how you hope to do this. For example, "As you know, we're meeting today to agree upon your specific objectives for the next six months. I've written down some suggestions and I know you've done the same. Why don't we take out our notes and see what we've come up with?"

Always have your staff tell you about their suggestions first. They may have some of the same ideas that you have and if so, you should give them credit for the ideas. Also, your staff's suggestions will be a good basis for introducing your differing ones.

Summon all your skills in diplomacy when you go through your list with each staff member. In the end, come up with a list of objectives you both

**Always have your staff tell you about their suggestions first.**

Make it clear that each person must not neglect other responsibilities to accomplish new objectives.

want that person to accomplish over the next six months. When it comes down to it, you should retain final veto power about objectives. You can't have people working for your practice who don't do what you want them to do. However, let your staff have as much control in the process as possible. If they have a reasonable way to help you meet your overall objectives, try to let them do it their way, even if it's not exactly what you would have assigned them to do.

Write up a final list of six-month objectives for each staff member with the specific, measurable results you expect and the completion dates. Then have that person sign the list and keep a copy. Put your copy in that employee's personnel file. Tell the staff member that performance reviews will be in six months and that in the meantime, you want to be informed of any problems he or she encounters in reaching the stated objectives. Express your desire to help your staff reach their goals.

Finally, tell your staff that salary reviews will be linked both to performance in the regular areas of job responsibility and to achievement of their new objectives. Make it clear that each person must not neglect other responsibilities to accomplish the new objectives.

## CONDUCTING INTERIM PROGRESS REVIEWS

Interim progress reviews held every four to six weeks will be relatively informal meetings that emphasize your employee's future, not past performance. Frequent meetings of this sort are an excellent chance for you and your staff to correct problems and remove obstacles early on. They also provide a great opportunity for you to recognize unrealistic objectives while there is still time to revise or discard them.

> **TIP:** *It rarely makes sense to wait to eliminate an unrealistic objective until after the employee has been struggling to attain it for six months. Interim progress reviews will alert you to goals that need to be amended or to other problems before the employee gets too far along in the wrong direction and becomes frustrated.*

Interim reviews have other benefits as well. For instance, they help employees learn to budget their time so they are working on their objectives all along. Otherwise, they may not begin on their long-range objectives until right before their six-month performance and salary reviews. Interim reviews also supply you with a chance to provide feedback and data for your six-month reviews. That way, employees won't be blindsided by criticism when you meet with them later.

Finally, interim progress reviews will help you develop a good working relationship with your staff. They will establish you as a source of assistance, support and feedback—not as an aloof judge and critic.

Frequent smaller reviews will make the larger ones you conduct every six months seem less intimidating.

When holding interim progress reviews, it isn't necessary for the employee to prepare anything in advance. Take out your list of the employee's six-month objectives. Go down the list one by one to see how the employee is doing with each personal objective. Also see how you can help the employee meet his or her goals. Ask: "Am I doing everything I can to help you meet Objective #3?" Also ask if you are inadvertently thwarting the employee's efforts and if so, how.

If you have any criticism of the employee's performance or any suggestions for taking a different approach, express them the interim progress review and get the employee to respond. If the employee knows that he or she has made an error, discuss what he or she will do differently in the future to correct or prevent it from happening again. If the employee disagrees with you, try to work out your differences.

After the interim progress review, record what you discussed in brief notes. Keep these along with your list of objectives in the employee's personnel file. They will be useful at your six-month performance and salary reviews.

## SEMI-ANNUAL PERFORMANCE REVIEWS

Six-month performance reviews will be longer and more formal meetings. They will serve as a cumulative summary of all the specific criticisms (positive and negative) and suggestions that you and the employee discussed at the interim progress reports. However, unlike interim reports that focus primarily on future performance, the bulk of the six-month performance review is devoted to reflecting upon the past six months. The employee's effort, personality, and attitude are important in these reviews, but they are not everything. Measurable results count, too. Consider: Did the employee meet the agreed-upon objectives? Two weeks before the scheduled performance review, give a copy of your individual six-month objectives to each employee. (They will have their own copies already but distribute new ones to avoid confusion.) Ask them to report in writing on how well they felt they met each objective, being specific about measurements. For example, if an employee's objective was to make 40 recall calls every week, ask him or her to list how many he or she made every week since you set the objective.

Have each employee submit a copy of his or her self-evaluation to you at least three days before your scheduled performance review. With this in hand, you will be ready to do your own preparation. To begin, prepare a written summary of all your interim progress reviews. If the employee improved in some are¬ that you criticized negatively, say so

**Interim progress reviews will help you develop a good working relationship with your staff.**

## ADDITIONAL TIPS FOR EVALUATING YOUR STAFF

Get more oomph out of your next performance appraisals by trying one or more of the ideas below:

- A few days before your scheduled performance review, give each employee a copy of his or her job description and ask him or her to update it. You do the same, since your perceptions of the job may be different from the employee's. Compare your revisions at the performance review and come up with a final version. That way, you'll always have an updated job description for each employee.

- Conduct a staff survey as part of your performance review procedure. A survey may help you identify widespread problems in your practice management techniques. For more information, see "Staff Surveys Open Lines of Communication," pages 137–138.

- Allow the employee to do as much of the talking, thinking, and concluding as possible. Ask open-ended questions that require more than a *yes* or *no*.

- Don't make these common mistakes when evaluating your staff:
  - Halo Effect: Don't rate all performance based upon your observances of one good trait.
  - Horn Effect: This is the opposite of the halo effect. Don't let one poor rating influence all others and result in a lower evaluation than deserved.
  - Middle Cluster: Don't automatically cluster performance ratings around a middle point on a graded scale. For example, if rating staff members on a scale of 1 to 10 for various tasks and traits, you may be tempted to cluster ratings between 4 and 8. Don't fear high or low ratings when deserved.
  - Latest Behavior: We tend to forget about past problems or accomplishments and to focus instead on what's been happening most recently. This is most likely to be a problem when an employee is evaluated only once every six months or year. Concentrate regular effort on your interim progress reviews.
  - Spillover: Don't allow past evaluations to reflect heavily on the current evaluation.

> There should be no surprises at the six-month review.

in your notes. If he or she still needs work in that area, say that too. Review the employee's self-evaluation and then record whether or not you think he or she met each of his or her objectives, as well as any other relevant comments you have about overall performance.

Remember, there should be no surprises at the six-month review. All of your criticisms and suggestions should have been brought to the employee's attention earlier. Likewise, you should not be surprised to learn that an employee's performance was not what you thought. The interim reviews should keep you up to date.

When you schedule the reviews, be sure you have sufficient uninterrupted private time with each employee. Half an hour is average. Often, holding the meeting in your office will be comfortable for you but not for the employee. If you can, choose some neutral territory. Be sure that the time you reserve for the employee is not disturbed by phone calls, paperwork, etc. Sit beside the employee, not behind a desk or table.

Start the meeting positively so the employee is not put on the defensive. Allow the employee to evaluate himself or herself first. Encourage the employee to open up by showing interest, nodding your head appropriately, asking questions, and avoiding criticism right off the bat. A good place to start is with the employee's self-evaluation which he or she gave to you three days earlier. Give it back to the employee and ask him or her to compare each of his or her objectives with the actual results achieved. This should get the ball rolling.

When you begin to offer your criticism, start by discussing the employee's strengths and accomplishments. Next, swing the evaluation to areas that the employee agrees need improvement. Try to talk about weaknesses in terms of growth and opportunity. Finally, state your position about growth areas the employee did not mention. Refer to your notes to link the criticism to the interim progress reviews. For example, "You'll remember when we talked in January that we had reviewed that encounter with Mrs. Miller when she said you were rude to her on the phone. At that time, we agreed that you would always identify yourself to the caller by name and refrain from saying 'hold on.' I think there's still some room for improvement here because. . . ."

> **TIP:** *You do not have to seek the employee's agreement or engage in an argument. Simply state your opinion and move on until you're done.*

If the notes you prepared for the review do not need to be changed in any way, have the employee read and sign them right away. However, if they do need revision, have him or her read and sign them later. Then give the employee a copy of the review and keep the original in his or her personnel file. Clip together the written objectives for that six-month period, the notes from all the interim reports, the employee's self-evaluation, and the signed performance reviews. Now you're ready to prepare for the next six months.

After all the performance reviews, it's time to formulate your next six month's development plans and to set new individual objectives with each employee. Failure to reach certain objectives may suggest areas in which individuals need more training, effort, or help.

## CONDUCTING SALARY REVIEWS

Schedule salary reviews with your staff once or twice a year. If possible, do not schedule performance and salary reviews close together. Doing so often creates a tremendous flurry of activity a week or two before "raise time" with everyone trying frantically to outdo each other to impress the boss. Then a week or two after the review everyone may become more relaxed and slip back into their old ways.

> Start the meeting positively so the employee is not put on the defensive.

# Employees do not automatically deserve a raise for surviving another six months or year in your practice.

Determine whether or not the employee deserves a raise on the basis of the meeting of objectives and overall performance. Many practice mangers decide the amount of the raise by using this formula:

- Figure out the highest salary you're willing to pay for the highest quality person in each employee's position.
- Determine the minimal salary you must pay in your area to get a quality person with potential.
- Divide the range between the two salary extremes by eight to get nine distinct salary steps.
- Raise the employee's salary one step for good performance or perhaps two steps for outstanding performance.

**TIP:** *Don't raise salary for mediocre or poor performance. Employees do not automatically deserve a raise for surviving another six months or year in your practice (unless that raise is a cost-of-living adjustment, which should be designated as such).* ▲

# Giving Positive Feedback and Constructive Criticism

*Giving effective feedback to your employees, both positive and negative, is essential if they are to improve, grow, and thrive in their jobs. This chapter describes specific strategies for injecting more positive feedback into every work day. It explains why praising your staff is important, offers 10 specific suggestions for giving meaningful and effective praise, and includes a sample letter of commendation that might go into an employee's personnel file. As well, this chapter offers insights into employees' responses to praise. Finally, it describes 15 tried-and-true strategies for giving constructive criticism that will get results.*

Generous helpings of praise and criticism are key ingredients for good staff management and motivation.

Generous helpings of praise and criticism are key ingredients for good staff management and motivation. Unfortunately, most employees muddle along day after day without any clue as to how they're doing. Thus, their bad habits and mistakes continue, and their best efforts and achievements go unrewarded.

Many employers feel uncomfortable facing their staff with comments about their performance, either positive or negative. They assume, incorrectly, that employees already knows how they're doing. They take good work for granted and curse the bad work silently, to themselves.

Clearly, anyone supervising others needs to learn how to give feedback sensitively, at the right time, and in the right way. With practice and guidance, praise and constructive criticism will become second nature and a great tool for boosting morale and performance.

## WHY PRAISE IS IMPORTANT

A few well-chosen, well-timed words from you can sometimes do more for an employee's morale than money, promotions, or other tangible rewards. But in most cases, the little feedback employees receive from their supervisors concentrates on their weaknesses and mistakes.

Although criticism is important, the boss who never seems to remember good work may be his or her own worst enemy. Over time, employees will feel unappreciated, defensive, and angry and will reduce their efforts.

## 10 TIPS FOR GIVING MORE POSITIVE FEEDBACK

Praise should not be limited to formal performance reviews but doled out generously on a regular basis. Listed below are ten specific ways to give positive feedback:

1. Keep a written record of each employee's good work, such as meeting deadlines, developing good relationships with patients or mastering new skills. Keep these lists in your personnel files and refer to them at performance reviews.
2. Praise good work publicly when you can. For example, you might congratulate successful efforts at staff meetings.
3. At the performance review, ask the employee what he or she has done right since the last review. This is your chance to catch up and reward good performance you haven't noticed.
4. Catch your staff doing something right and commend them for it. Don't look only for monumental efforts or results. Each of us is proud of our accomplishments, whether large or small, and values recognition.

> Most employees muddle along day after day without any clue as to how they're doing.

5. Be specific with praise. Use the same approach you'd use if they'd made a mistake, only tell them the good things they've done. For example, instead of saying, vaguely, "You're very good with kids," you might say, "I'm very impressed with the way you handled Alicia Hills this morning. She was very frightened but you turned her around in no time. Great going!"

6. Praise promptly. If too much time elapses, you may avoid saying anything because you're embarrassed. Or, you do say something and the employee wonders why you're just now getting around to it.

7. Don't overdo it. Too much praise seems insincere and is just as ineffective as too little.

8. Praise employees for specific things they've done, but from time to time, let them know that you also appreciate them for who they are. Tell each person how important he or she is to you and your practice overall, and why. For example, write a personal note of thanks to each employee at Thanksgiving or a Thanksgiving poem, enumerating the many reasons you are thankful to have him or her in your practice (see below).

9. When the employee accomplishes something important, put your praise in writing. A letter of commendation or thank you card sent to the employee's home (with a copy in the personnel file) can be extremely effective (See sample letter, Appendix 2-D).

10. Praise your staff as a whole, but also look for chances to praise and reward individuals for their outstanding efforts and achievements.

> Anyone supervising others needs to learn how to give feedback sensitively.

---

### Thanksgiving Poem Tells Staff You Care

*Try writing and distributing to your staff a Thanksgiving poem like the one below to let them know how much you appreciate them:*

This Thanksgiving, I am especially grateful for:

Rosemary's infectious giggle and smile,
Supriya's attention to detail and eagle-eyes for finding mistakes,
Ramone's limericks (even though they make us groan),
Nkeng's quick thinking and creative solutions to problems,
Rosa's special way of calming even the most frazzled nerves,
Carol's ability to handle seventeen things at once without
    getting ruffled,
Petra's can-do attitude especially when the chips are down,
Sandy's knack of keeping us all in line even when we get the sillies,
Dr. G's offbeat sense of humor and oh-so-tasteful ties.

This Thanksgiving, I am especially grateful for my amazing staff.

> The next time you praise a member of your staff, study the reactions you receive.

## RESPONSE TO PRAISE CAN HELP YOU INCREASE PRODUCTIVITY

The next time you praise a member of your staff, study the reactions you receive. Praise triggers reactions from the deepest parts of the personality. Knowing what makes people tick, based upon their reactions to praise, can be a great help in unlocking their potential.

The important thing to look for is not so much the response to an isolated incident, but rather, the pattern of reactions to praise. Although there are of course exceptions, the following is often true:

- People who respond to praise with disbelief often try hard to be accepted by those around them. They're often willing workers who are eager to please.
- People who turn praise into a joke are usually trying to keep a certain distance from you and others around them. They value privacy and make it hard to others to form close relationships with them on the job. Similarly, employees who make light of or belittle their own good work may want to avoid the spotlight.
- People who pass on a share of the credit to others generally enjoy teamwork and work well with others.
- People who respond with embarrassment are usually sensitive, hard-working, and trustworthy employees. However, you may find it hard to supervise them without hurting their feelings or embarrassing them from time to time.
- People who react by changing the subject and continuing with the business at hand are often no-nonsense achievers, independent thinkers, and potentially, well-organized managers.
- People who accept praise graciously and easily are generally assertive, independent, and well-satisfied with their own performance. Such people may have the potential to take on more responsibility.

## GIVING CRITICISM THAT GETS RESULTS

Few people like to be criticized. However, you'll find that your staff will accept criticism more willingly if you offer it in a constructive, rather than a destructive manner.

The following guidelines will help you obtain the results you want without making employees feel "put down," angry, or alienated:

1. **Choose a good time to discuss employee problems.** Never criticize a staff member in a chance encounter or in front of other employees or patients. Avoid coming down on employees when you or they are in the middle of major work or a personal crisis. And, don't have a talk at the end of the work week, when the employee is likely to go home and stew over your criticisms all weekend.

2. **Pinpoint the specific behavior(s) you want to criticize.** Be precise and use a concrete example. For instance, don't give general criticism like, "You always misplace things." Rather, say, "You misplaced Mrs. Brown's file. That's the fourth file you've misplaced this week."

3. **Criticize the act, not the person.** For instance, say, "The file drawer is very disorganized," not, "You're a slob." Or say, "You've refused to work overtime three times this month," not, "You're lazy."

4. **Be certain the change you seek is possible.** Don't ask for results the employee is unable or unwilling to make. For example, don't say, "Would you please stop blowing your nose? That allergy of yours is driving us nuts." Rather, you might suggest, "Might you be able to blow your nose away from patients? They may not know you have allergies and assume you're sick—and contagious."

5. **Offer the person motivation to improve.** Will your criticism help that individual grow personally, achieve greater success, make the job run more smoothly, improve his or her relationship with you or others, or offer some other benefit? If so, focus on this positive aspect. For example, you might say, "Re-filing patient's files promptly and correctly will make it much easier for all of us to find the files when we need them."

6. **State clearly what you want the person to do, and when possible, establish deadlines for results.** Again, be as specific as you can. Spell out the precise changes you'd like to see. For example, don't say, "Please be more considerate." Instead, say, "Please wait to take your lunch break until you know the phone and reception desk are covered."

7. **Make sure you are understood.** If in doubt, ask the person to repeat your criticism in his or her own words.

8. **When appropriate, state your criticism as opinion, not proven fact.** That will make it easier to take. For example, don't state as fact, "You don't try hard enough." Instead, offer the opinion, "It seems to me that you could try harder when . . ."

9. **Indicate your willingness to work with the individual to improve.** When appropriate, admit some responsibility for management failure, and try to find joint solutions.

10. **Curb your anger.** Body language and voice tone convey your attitude as much as what you say. Even the most constructive criticism loses its effectiveness when delivered through clenched teeth.

11. **Don't criticize with humor or sarcasm.** It only weakens the impact of your criticism and can backfire by making the employee think the criticism isn't serious.

> Never criticize a staff member in a chance encounter or in front of other employees or patients.

## Criticize the act, not the person.

12. Avoid comparing the employee to other staff members, or to his or her "infallible" predecessor. Each person is unique. Comparisons almost always cause hurt, and make co-workers competitive and resentful of one another.

13. Don't exaggerate. Telling an assistant she "never" fills out forms correctly, when of course she does sometimes, may result in your total message being ignored.

14. Don't assume you know all the facts. Before you criticize an employee, make sure you know why he or she behaves the way he or she did. You may find that your employee's behavior was caused by factors outside his or her control, such as office policy, other employees—even you.

15. Don't save criticism. Storing up complaints and dumping them all at once can be devastating. ▲

# Managing the Employee in Crisis

*People have problems—sometimes, serious ones. As long as people work in your practice, you can expect that from time to time, their problems will find their way into your office. Although any practice manager with a heart will want to be sensitive to problems that employees face, we cannot allow their problems to interfere with the well-being of the patients or with the smooth operation of the practice.*

*This chapter offers practical suggestions for identifying and handling employees in crisis. It suggests specific techniques for dealing with employees who have problems at home, are angry, rely too heavily on excuses, have outside business interests interfere with the practice, and those who are job-shoppers. It offers guidance on what to say and not say in face-to-face meetings with employees in crisis and provides examples when documentation and termination may be necessary.*

No matter how well you recruit, motivate, and manage your employees, you will still have to deal with personnel problems from time to time. As you do, keep in mind that you can't let a problem employee drag down your practice. At some point, you must draw the line and see that employees don't cross it.

## MANAGING THE TROUBLED EMPLOYEE

Suppose you've just called your business assistant, Jennifer Curtis, into your office. Although she's usually a good employee, both her work quantity and quality have deteriorated in recent weeks, and her attitude has been poor. You don't know why.

This morning, you overheard her on the phone with a patient who wanted to reschedule an appointment. She seemed annoyed by the

> Troubled staff members may need more help than you are able or willing to give.

## Avoid sharing personal experiences that diminish the importance of their problems.

call and barely civil. Citing the incident, you say, "Your work hasn't been up to your usual high standards, Jennifer. Is there something I can do to help?"

"I've really been under pressure at home lately," Jennifer begins. "My mother's in the hospital, and the kids are driving me crazy. I think Jason, our oldest, is taking drugs. Alan has been passed over for a promotion and is taking it out on me. We have knock-down, drag-out fights every night. I can't sleep. I have a constant headache. And I just can't seem to concentrate on what I'm doing."

What do you say? That you know how she feels? That things could be worse? That she should leave her problems at home?

You may be tempted to hand Jennifer a tissue, give her a shoulder to cry on, and say, "There, there, everything's going to be all right." Unfortunately, this isn't likely to help matters very much. Troubled staff members may need more help than you are able or willing to give. In the meantime, they can damage the quality of professional care or hurt your relationship with patients, if you let them.

Of course, you should try your best to be understanding of employees' personal problems. Empathize with them, even if you haven't experienced similar problems or don't believe their situations are "that bad." In addition:

1. Don't accuse the employee of wrongdoing or guess at his or her problems. Rather, try to get him or her to tell you what's wrong. For example, you might say, "I'm becoming quite concerned about the number of accidents you are having in the office." Use open-ended questions to draw the employee out and listen. For example, "Tell me about these accidents."

2. Acknowledge what the employee says, but don't judge.

3. Avoid sharing personal experiences that diminish the importance of their problems.

4. Know your limitations. Some domestic problems are minor and temporary, others complex and long-term. Remember that you are not a marriage counselor, cheerleader, or magician. Suggest where troubled employees might turn for help.

> **TIP:** *Explain that seeking counseling will be a positive step toward feeling better and improving work performance. Emphasize other benefits of counseling, such as that the employee will set the goals, pace, and tone for the sessions, and that he or she will be able to keep the content of the sessions confidential. Help the employee by compiling a list of referral sources. Suggest that he or she use the nearest phone to schedule the first appointment with a counselor.*

5. No matter what, stick to your agenda. Job productivity must not suffer. Let employees know that although you care about them, you can't afford to let their personal problems damage your practice. Explain calmly that you have a responsibility to provide your patients with quality care.

6. Determine how the troubled employee's performance must change and set a deadline. If his or her poor performance might lead to dismissal, explain this. Although the employee is already troubled, you will do him or her no favor by hiding the fact that his or her job is in jeopardy. Moreover, should you have to dismiss the employee, you can't do so out of the blue. You'll need to have warned the employee formally—and more than once. To follow up, schedule another meeting with the troubled employee to review whether these performance changes have been made.

7. Document everything. Follow up each meeting with a letter to the employee, in which you review what you discussed. Keep a written record of your observations, evaluations, and discussions. This documentation may be valuable if it becomes necessary to dismiss the employee. Reviewing your documentation will also reassure you that you did all you could to help.

## MANAGING THE ANGRY EMPLOYEE

An employee's anger should be his or her problem, not yours. Don't get caught up and respond in kind. Doing so will only worsen an already bad situation. Instead:

1. React calmly and professionally. Do not raise your voice or lose control.

2. Avoid bringing personalities or your personal likes and dislikes into the discussion.

3. Concentrate on the problem at hand and concrete solutions.

4. Slow things down. Take as much time as you need to look for an objective and productive response. See that the problem is resolved based on reason, not emotional appeasement or punishment. For example, you might say, "We need to get this vacation schedule worked out. Let's each think about it and meet again tomorrow morning."

## MANAGING THE EXCUSEAHOLIC

Do you have an employee who relies too heavily on making excuses for not getting work done? If you've got an excuseaholic on your staff, take action:

1. Don't get lost in the details. For instance, don't let the employee go into long, blow-by-blow accounts about the car trouble or alarm clock failure that kept him or her from doing what he or she was

> Take as much time as you need to look for an objective and productive response.

supposed to do. Although cutting off lengthy excuses may seem rude or cold, do it. The details won't change things.

2. Explain what needs to be done, thoroughly. Once you've heard the excuse, be absolutely clear about what you expect next. List deadlines, repeat instructions, and ask, "Do I make myself clear?" Don't give the employee the opportunity to disappoint you any further.

3. Keep track of the excuses. Record:
   - What you asked for.
   - When you expected to receive it.
   - What happened.
   - The employee's excuse, and
   - The results.

   If the employee has legitimate excuses, your written record may help you identify and solve problems in your practice. But, if the employee's excuses are inadequate, false, or at least, suspicious, a written record will help you realize that. As well, documentation may be valuable legal protection if you end up terminating the employee.

4. Warn the employee. When excuses are excessive, meet to review your excuse record. Express your concern and dissatisfaction. Give fair warning if the employee's job is in jeopardy. Outline specifically how his or her performance must change. If appropriate, suggest sources of counseling. (See "Managing the Troubled Employee" section above.)

5. Follow through. Meet with the employee again after he or she has had time to improve. If you've seen some progress, say so, and outline again the kinds of performance you expect. If he or she has made no attempt or has been unable to curb excuses, give one last warning, and follow through.

## MANAGING THE ENTREPRENEUR

Today you're likely to find more and more full-time employees with part-time side businesses. They may sell cosmetics, educational toys, kitchen storage containers, vitamins, or various other products and services. A staff entrepreneur shouldn't pose a problem for you, unless his or her side business spills into your office.

You know you've got a problem if the staff entrepreneur is using your time and contacts to sell something or to work on a personal project. You also have a problem if he or she uses your supplies, copy machine, fax, e-mail, word processor, or phones to make sales/business calls from work. The problem is most serious if co-workers and patients

> Some practices make it policy that no outside entrepreneurial activities can be pursued during work hours.

feel that the staff entrepreneur is pressuring them to buy something, host a party, give them sales leads, etc.

If you have a staff entrepreneur, here are some steps you can take to keep things under control:

1. Explain that the staff entrepreneur's activities should not take the time of co-workers, not just while at work, but during breaks. Scheduled breaks give staff a chance to relax, which will be harder if they are being targeted for sales pitches.

2. Some entrepreneur's activities can also erode office morale. Being pushed to buy products may be offensive to some and may deteriorate an otherwise good working relationship.

3. If the office entrepreneur's work is affected by his or her outside interests, meet immediately and explain specifically how he or she must change. Documentation and follow-up should be the same as for any personnel problem.

4. Even if the individual's own performance is not affected, document and discuss instances where group productivity or morale has declined, or if someone has complained.

5. Some practices make it policy that no outside entrepreneurial activities can be pursued during work hours.

## MANAGING THE JOB-SHOPPING EMPLOYEE

Here are the telltale signs that an employee is shopping for another job:

1. He or she takes longer-than-usual lunch breaks. Or, he or she turns down invitations from co-workers he or she usually eats with. (The employee may be going on lunch-hour job interviews.)

2. He or she dresses up more frequently and is better groomed than usual. Perhaps he or she wears professional business suits and accessories all of a sudden.

3. He or she may seem anxious to use up vacation time and personal days.

4. He or she spends more time than usual on the phone or behind closed office doors.

5. His or her attitude changes. He or she becomes less caring, taking a "why bother" approach. Or, he or she may start complaining or voicing negative opinions more than in the past.

If you suspect that an employee is job shopping, there are several things you might do:

1. Act fast. You may be able to turn things around before it's too late. Discuss specific points of job dissatisfaction, and when possible, take steps to improve things.

> Don't be afraid to ask the employee outright if he or she is job hunting.

> ### Ultimatums and counter-offers usually don't work.

2. Don't be afraid to ask the employee outright if he or she is job hunting. If it turns out that he or she is not, the employee will get a motivational kick knowing you obviously care.

   **TIP:** *Don't accuse the employee of job shopping. Rather, ask about it thoughtfully, and tell the employee why you think it is possible if he or she asks. If the employee is not job shopping, there may be something else going on that he or she wants to discuss with you.*

3. Don't drag things out if the employee is determined to take another position. Ultimatums and counteroffers usually don't work. Even if the employee accepts, he or she will probably end up leaving after a short time anyway.

## MANAGING FEUDING EMPLOYEES

Have you ever had to resolve a conflict among members of your staff? When you must step into a conflict, you should try to settle it quickly and fairly.

1. Interview the disputants in each other's presence. Ask each person to tell you how he or she sees the problem.

2. Focus attention and discussion on the current problem.

3. Don't support either viewpoint.

4. Make the disputants come up with their own proposed solution.

5. Schedule follow-up meetings to review progress.

Once again, if the problem begins to interfere with the smooth running of your office, confront the employees directly and explain precisely how their performance must change. Document everything, and take whatever steps are necessary to protect the well-being of your practice. ▲

# How to Steer Clear of Legal Problems When You Fire

*Recent court decisions and the publicity they've gotten may explain why lawsuits from ex-employees are on the rise. However, you can keep firing from coming back to haunt you by taking several precautionary steps.*

*This chapter suggests what you need to do before, during, and after you fire an employee to help prevent wrongful discharge suits. As well, this chapter explores steps you can take to keep unemployment benefits to a minimum.*

These days, an employee who believes he's been wrongfully discharged may bring his grievance to court. And, more than ever, he has a good shot at winning. This trend has led to a new, increasingly common breed of lawsuits, and to go with them, new personnel management worries.

Recent court decisions and the resultant publicity they've gotten may explain why lawsuits from ex-employers are on the rise. Recent cases have broken new ground in limiting the right to discharge employees *at will*. (These judgments view employees' jobs as "property rights," of which they may not be deprived without just cause.) Other court decisions have read implied agreements of "good faith" or "fair dealing" into informal employment relationships. Some courts have even viewed abusive discharges as *torts* (personal wrongs) and awarded substantial judgments. (Tort remedies can be quite large because they may include damages for mental anguish and punitive awards.)

How can you make sure that when you fire an employee, it's truly over? How can you keep your action from coming back to haunt you as an

> When interviewing, avoid words like *job security*, *lifelong relationship* with the practice, and *regular advancement.*

abusive discharge suit? Fortunately, employees suing for wrongful discharge must *prove* you fired wrongly. You can take steps to ensure that such proof is difficult or impossible to produce.

## WHAT YOU CAN DO TO PREVENT LAWSUITS BEFORE YOU FIRE

Below are ten tactics to help you prevent discharged employees from taking you to court that you can take before you fire them:

1. Overhaul your practice documents. Review employment ads, application forms, personnel policies, handbooks, manuals, job descriptions, etc., preferably with your attorney. Remove statements that can be interpreted as "discriminatory" or "biased". Also make sure documents don't make or imply promises about how long or how safe an employee's job will be.

   For example, don't advertise a job as *permanent*. The courts may interpret that word literally. Instead, say the position is *regular*, as in, "This is a regular, full-time position". Also, avoid the word *career* in recruitment ads. The courts may interpret that word to mean that you offered a guaranteed, long-term position in your practice.

2. When interviewing, avoid words like *job security, lifelong relationship with the practice,* and *regular advancement.* Statements like these may persuade qualified applicants to accept your position, but they can backfire later if you decide to terminate the employee.

   **TIP:** *Don't imply job security, either. For example, don't say things like, "Do good work and you'll always have a job here." Smart: Express salaries on a weekly or monthly basis only. "Annual" salary may be interpreted to imply employment for at least one year's duration.*

3. Print a disclaimer statement on employment applications for candidates to read and sign. State clearly that you retain the right to terminate the employee at any time. Position the disclaimer directly above the line where the applicant signs and dates the form. Print it in boldface type for emphasis.

4. Have employees sign a receipt for their copy of your personnel handbook. That way, you can prove later that they were indeed informed of all your office policies. For example, here's a sample statement to sign and date:

   *"I have received and reviewed the policies and procedures in (name of handbook) and agree to abide by them during the term of my employment with the practice, realizing that changes can occur at any time. I understand that this personnel guide is not a contract and that*

### Standardize your grievance procedure.

*nothing in this guide constitutes an offer or contract between (practice name) and myself."*

5. Use probation carefully. Some practices hire staff with a specified probationary period. (They become regular employees only after completing probation satisfactorily.) The danger is that passing probation might be interpreted as guaranteed employment, "tenure," or a contract. Therefore, if you specify probation, add a disclaimer to the probationary agreement, stating that you retain the right to terminate at any time, even *after* probation.

6. Use standardized, progressive discipline. Establish a consistent procedure for dealing with infractions of rules, policies, and misbehavior on the job. For example, you might start with a verbal warning. For the second offense, you might issue a written warning, have the employee sign it, and place it in his personnel file. Subsequent offenses should bring increasingly sterner warnings threatening suspension or termination.

> **TIP:** *Be consistent by treating every employee the same every time. Keep records of all steps in the procedure in the employee's personnel file. Do what you say you will do.*

7. Standardize your grievance procedure. Employees who are treated fairly are unlikely to bring lawsuits. Try to solve little problems before they grow into big ones. Make yourself accessible to your staff.

8. Document everything. When a staff problem arises, note it in your personnel files. For example, note all absences, poor work, fighting with other staff, insubordination—in essence, all acts that might induce or contribute to dismissal.

9. Evaluate employees periodically and honestly. Don't write satisfactory or favorable evaluations for unsatisfactory performance to make employees feel good or to be well-liked. Evaluations that don't accurately express the employee's job performance may be used against you in court by an employee trying to prove unjust dismissal.

> **TIP:** *Give at least three reprimands before you discharge an employee. Each reprimand should describe how the employee has failed to do what you asked. It should specify precisely how the employee needs to change and impose a deadline for doing so. The third reprimand should warn that the consequence of failure will be termination. Important: Both you and the employee should sign each reprimand.*

10. As a last-ditch effort, try the "Day Off With Pay" technique. After all the reprimands, give the employee a "decision making leave

**Choreograph the exit interview to make it as graceful and easy as possible.**

day" with pay. Instruct him to use the time to think about his situation and the importance of the job. Afterward, ask the employee if he wants to keep his job. If he does, have him agree to specific changes and deadlines. Explain that if he doesn't shape up as described, he will be fired. Document the entire process.

> **TIP:** *Called "positive discipline," this radical technique elicits laughs from many people. However, many companies, including some very big and successful ones, currently use it with positive results.*

## WHAT YOU CAN DO WHEN YOU FIRE

It is essential to make the actual firing process as airtight as possible. Here are some suggestions:

1. In a few instances, an employee might do something so terrible that it warrants immediate, unanticipated dismissal. However, in all other cases, the employee should know that his performance has been unsatisfactory and that the dismissal is coming. Review your performance appraisals and written reprimands before meeting with the employee to be sure he is aware of his performance shortcomings, and so you can refer to them.

2. Choreograph the exit to make it as graceful and easy as possible. Show departing employees respect and consideration. Specifically:

   - Do the firing at the end of the day on Friday. That way, an angry ex-employee will have the weekend to cool off before deciding upon a course of action or retaliation. As well, being fired on Friday is generally less embarrassing, since the ex-employee won't have to face co-workers or patients while cleaning out his desk after the termination. He'll also have less opportunity to try to get others involved and poison them against you. Even though an ex-employee may be completely wrong or even irrational, it won't help your reputation if he tells your patients how unreasonable or unfair you are.

   - Hold the termination meeting in your private office or another place where you will have complete privacy and no interruptions. Don't conduct the termination in the employee's office or workstation.

   - Don't stand when you're doing the termination. Sit beside the employee, in front of your desk, or at a conference table.

   - Get to the point quickly. Do the termination within the first five minutes. Take the rest of the recommended half hour to put the person back together, listening and offering support. However, don't meet for longer than 30 minutes. Spending hours discussing what's wrong with an individual is of little value.

If the terminated employee has signatory power over your practice bank accounts, withdraw this power immediately.

- Don't use platitudes like "I know how you feel" or make promises you won't or can't keep.
- Don't become defensive or try too hard to justify your decision. State facts, refer to performance reviews and written reprimands, and listen.
- Don't change your stance during the termination meeting. If you feel that you might like to change your opinion, end the meeting and get back to the individual later. Take time to think through the decision.

3. Make sure the employee gets everything due to him. Include:
   - pay for unused vacation time,
   - any vested portion of fringe benefits plans,
   - severance pay according to established policy, and
   - any other already-scheduled benefit.

Tell the fired employee about all the insurance you have provided (health, life, disability) and when his coverage is discontinued (automatically, in 30, 60, or 90 days, etc.). Also tell the employee whether and how he can pick up the coverage himself.

> TIP: *Give the employee all pertinent information about his insurance on a prepared form. Ask him to read it at the termination meeting and sign it. Keep a copy in the employee's personnel file. Even if you've informed employees of their benefits when you hired them, it's a good idea to protect yourself and inform them about their coverage again as they leave. (Also true if they resign.) Courts have held that employers must tell employees about the possibility of converting their insurance plan to individual coverage.*

Have checks and the statement of insurance benefits ready so the ex-employee can leave with them with a minimum of fuss.

4. Collect all office equipment, supplies, patient files and lists, financial papers, and keys from the terminated employee before he leaves your building. Then escort him out (or have your office manager do this). In anger or humiliation, some people try to get revenge when they've been terminated and sabotage files, steal, or vandalize the office.

> TIP: *If the terminated employee has signatory power over your practice bank accounts, withdraw this power immediately. Remove his or her computer password from your system.*

5. Don't discuss the reason for the employee's dismissal with others. Seemingly harmless remarks can come back to plague you in the form of a slander suit.

6. Later, give factual, supportable employment references. Unfavorable or unsupported references can lead to claims for libel, slander, or emotional distress.

> In the long run, it is best for everyone if you terminate the employee who can't or won't improve.

7. With all of this in mind, do everything you can to assist the terminated employee with re-employment. Employees who find new jobs quickly are less likely to sue for wrongful discharge. You might advise ex-employees about counseling and job placement services in your community, or you might give them a book about job hunting.

> **TIP:** *Don't promise to help the ex-employee get a new job. If you don't come through, the individual may feel like he's been terminated twice. As well, don't give the ex-employee office space, secretarial services, or use of your office equipment for the job search.*

## HOW TO KEEP UNEMPLOYMENT BENEFITS TO A MINIMUM

Not all terminated employees are eligible for unemployment insurance benefits. For example, the following types of employees are ineligible for benefits:

- Unavailable for work.
- Fired for misconduct.
- Refused to accept suitable work.
- Quit without good cause.
- Misrepresented facts to receive benefits.
- Receives some form of "wages."

To minimize benefits, ask for a written resignation from all staff members who leave your practice of their own choosing. This documentation provides positive proof that they did, in fact, quit of their own volition and are not eligible for unemployment benefits.

> **TIP:** *If you think an ex-employee is no longer eligible for unemployment benefits, or if your account is otherwise being charged unjustly, be sure to contact your state unemployment office immediately.*

## DON'T CRY TOO HARD OVER FIRED EMPLOYEES

Firing is difficult for most people to do, and you will probably feel badly about having to do it. However, don't brood too long. Very often, employees who quit or are fired are usually replaced by someone better.

It is unrealistic to think that you can be successful with employees 100% of the time. Sometimes, no matter how hard we try, we will hire the wrong person. Other times, the person we hired was right at the time

---

Keep records of all steps in the procedure in the employee's personnel file.

but changes. We can't look into a crystal ball and know for certain how each employee will develop over time.

In the long run, it is best for everyone if you terminate the employee who can't or won't improve. Not only are you likely to find someone better to replace him, but you have an obligation to protect your reputation, quality of care, and the team spirit in your practice. In addition, it is unlikely that you are doing the employee a favor by letting him stay. Chances are, he is not happy in the job, either.

Remember, it is the rare employer who never needs to fire. When you've got a problem employee who won't change:

1. Admit it.
2. End it well, protecting yourself against wrongful discharge suits.
3. Learn what you can from the experience.
4. Most importantly, move on. ▲

> We can't look into a crystal ball and know for certain how each employee will develop over time.

# Administering an Employee Exit Survey to Pinpoint Practice Management Problems

*Valued employees may leave your practice but still serve as valuable sources of practice management support. This chapter suggests administering an exit survey to departing employees, both on their last day of work and months later. Through such a survey, the former employee has a structured method for offering constructive feedback about your practice management systems and techniques.*

*This chapter also offers sample exit survey questions and discusses the benefits and how-to's for implementing a former employees' alumni relations program for your practice.*

Try to spend a little time with the departing employee to uncover the hidden strengths and weaknesses in your practice management skills.

> A voluntary exit survey conducted on an employee's last day of work (and another conducted months later) can be a fabulous way to help you identify and address problem areas.

When an employee tells you that he or she is quitting, you will probably turn your attention immediately to the tasks of finding a suitable replacement. Of course, recruiting for new staff is vitally important, because that is where your future lies. You will need a new employee on the double to fill the opening and to keep your practice running as smoothly as possible. However, before jumping ahead to Help Wanted ads, screening job applicants, interviewing, checking references, etc., it also makes good sense to spend a little time with the departing employee to uncover the hidden strengths and weaknesses in your practice management skills.

When the employee's last day of work is a cordial one, it can be very beneficial to meet with him or her one last time to provide closure and also to discuss the employee's observations and ideas for improving your practice. As part of (or instead of) such a one-on-one interview, a voluntary exit survey conducted on an employee's last day of work (and another conducted months later) can be a fabulous way to help you identify and address problem areas. The exit survey can help you improve working conditions for your remaining and future staff and also your patients' experiences of your practice.

The exit survey can also be an excellent public relations tool. If your departing employee has harbored misconceptions about past events in your practice, the exit survey can give you one last chance to uncover them and set the record straight. Leaving things on the best terms possible with departing employees will mean that they will be more likely to speak highly of your practice to others and may even become a strong referral source.

## SAMPLE QUESTIONS FOR YOUR EXIT SURVEY

Of course, the survey questions you develop to ask your departing employees should be based upon your practice's particular circumstances and goals. However, a sample list of survey questions to get you started appears in the Sidebar.

## CONDUCT A SECOND SURVEY MONTHS LATER

An exit survey administered on the employee's last day is a good beginning. However, you may not get the whole story at that time. The employee may believe that saying negative things about you or other employees will result in bad references in the future and that these in turn will hinder him or her from getting another job. Or, he or she may be upset, confused, or angry and blurt out things he or she doesn't mean.

# Sample Employee Exit Survey

1. Was your decision to leave our practice influenced by any of the following (can check more than one)?:

    ___ Type of work

    ___ Pay

    ___ Hours

    ___ Benefits

    ___ Better job opportunity

    ___ Relocation to another geographic area

    ___ Commuting distance

    ___ Supervision

    ___ Family/personal circumstances

    ___ Illness or physical condition

    ___ Co-workers

    ___ Office conditions/atmosphere

    Other:_____

    _____

2. Will you be working in or looking for work in another medical practice?

    ___ Yes

    ___ No

    ___ Not Sure

    If yes, what does the new practice offer you that your job with our practice did not?_____

3. Please evaluate the doctor/practice administrator by ranking each of the following practice management skills as either "Almost Always," "Usually," "Sometimes," or "Never." My doctor/practice administrator:

    a. Demonstrated fair and equal treatment of staff.

    b. Provided recognition and feedback.

    c. Encouraged cooperation.

    d. Resolved complaints, grievances, and problems.

    e. Gave clear instructions.

    f. Made expectations clear.

    g. Rewarded good performance.

4. Please rate the following as "Excellent," "Good," "Fair," "Poor," or "Unable to Tell":

    a. Quality of professional services received by patients.

    b. Office appearance.

    c. Office equipment.

    d. Professional competence of doctor(s).

5. How would you describe your typical workload? Was it (check one):

    ___ Too heavy?

    ___ Just right?

    ___ Too light?

6. How would you describe your chances for advancement? Were they (check one):

    ___ Excellent?

    ___ Good?

    ___ Fair?

    ___ Poor?

7. How did you feel about the rate of pay and the employee benefits provided by our practice? (Rate the following as "Excellent," "Good," "Fair," "Poor," or "No Opinion":

    a. Rate of pay for your job.

    b. Paid holidays.

    c. Paid vacations.

    d. Bonus programs.

    e. Life insurance.

    f. Medical and dental insurance.

    g. Retirement plan.

    h. Uniform allowance.

    i. Continuing education tuition reimbursement.

8. What did you like most about your job?

9. What did you like most about the practice?

10. What did you like least about your job?

11. What did you like least about the practice?

12. Would you recommend our practice to a friend as a place to work? Why or why not?

13. Would you recommend a friend to our practice as a patient? Why or why not?

Please provide any additional comments about your job or the practice.

Stay in touch with former employees to continue to find ways to improve your practice.

You can learn more accurate reasons for employee turnover best by sending a second follow-up questionnaire to employees three to six months after they have left your practice. By then, most former employees will be enjoying the security of their new jobs. They will have had enough time to get over any initial upset or confusion that they felt at the time of their departure. Months later, they will be more likely to reveal their true attitudes about your practice, office policies, and other employees.

> **TIP:** *Provide a self-addressed stamped envelope for the employee's survey response. Mark the envelope "Confidential" or address it to your home, not office. The former employee may not want to mail a completed survey to your office for fear that it will be opened and read by the wrong people. In addition, you may send a letter to the former employee with the survey suggesting that he or she can call you personally to answer the survey by phone, thus ensuring confidentiality.*

## "ALUMNI" RELATIONS PROGRAM ANOTHER WAY TO PINPOINT PROBLEMS

Many practices go the extra mile to stay in touch with former employees to continue to find ways to improve their practices. Among these, some have created successful staff "alumni" relations programs. You might begin such a program simply by placing the names and addresses of all ex-employees on your mailing list to receive your patient newsletter and other general practice announcements. In addition, you might invite former employees to attend your open houses, health fairs, speeches in the community—even an annual staff social event such as a December holiday party or summer picnic.

Although you can't expect everyone you've employed over the years to respond to such mailings and invitations, many will. Those who do will be more likely to suggest ideas for improving your practice and may become an active referral source or even a patient. You may even be able to fill a temporary or permanent staff opening down the road with a former employee *if* you've maintained a good relationship with him or her.

> **TIP:** *Of course, if an employee's departure is unpleasant and future contact is undesirable, it's best to leave well enough alone. Omit such names from your active staff alumni list.* ▲

# A-Z Treasury
# of Quick-Reference
# Staff Management
# Checklists

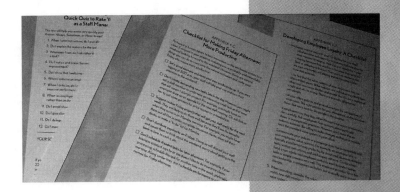

### APPENDIX 1-A
## Checklist for Retaining Personnel Records

Personnel records can be your best defense if an employee ever sues you. Yet many medical practices discard employees' records too soon after they have stopped working in the practice. While precise time frames vary (and there's no single statue of limitations), you should keep personnel records at least several years:

1. Retain ex-employees' records (earnings, reviews, letters of resignation, etc.) for six years or longer.

2. Retain job applications and resumes for at least two years.

3. To guarantee that your practice is meeting the Fair Labor Standard Act's (FLSA) requirements, retain the following payroll records for each employee:

   ☐ Full name as used in Social Security records

   ☐ Home address including zip code

   ☐ Date of birth if under 19 years of age

   ☐ Gender

   ☐ Job title

   ☐ Time and day of week on which employee's workweek begins

   ☐ Total wages paid each period

   ☐ Date of each payment and pay period it covers

   ☐ Hours worked each workday and workweek

   ☐ Total daily or weekly straight-time earnings or wages due, including amount due for overtime work but excluding overtime premiums

   ☐ Total additions to or deductions from wages paid each pay period, along with a record of dates, amounts, and nature of such additions and deductions

> Personnel records can be your best defense if an employee ever sues you.

APPENDIX 1-B

# Quick Quiz to Rate Yourself as a Staff Manager

This test will help you assess very quickly your staff management skills. Answer *Always*, *Sometimes*, or *Never* to each question below:

1. When I give instructions, do I give all the necessary information?

2. Do I explain the reasons for the tasks I assign?

3. Whenever I can, do I ask rather than order an employee to perform a task?

4. Do I notice and praise the employee who shows even small improvement?

5. Do I show that I welcome criticism and suggestions for change?

6. When I criticize an employee, do I keep it private?

7. When I criticize, do I give the employee specific face-saving ways to improve performance?

8. When an employee makes a mistake, do I focus on how to correct it rather than on the blame?

9. Do I avoid showing favoritism to employees I like?

10. Do I give slow learners a chance?

11. Do I delegate authority?

12. Do I maintain control of my staff?

---

YOUR SCORE:  4 points for each   Always

2 points for each   Sometimes

0 points for each   Never

If you score 36 or more, you're an excellent supervisor. A score of 22–34 indicates you're moderately effective that that some of your staff management skills could be sharpened. A score of 20 or less suggests that you need to improve your staff management methods and attitudes.

> Do you notice and praise the employee who shows even small improvement?

APPENDIX 1-C
# Checklist for Making Friday Afternoon More Productive

Perhaps it is human nature to lose momentum as the workweek comes to a close. Everyone in your practice, including you, is probably understandably tired and looking forward to the weekend. However, there are several things you can do to overcome this natural inclination and make your Friday afternoons more productive:

☐ Set a good example and keep your own productivity up. If you start lagging at 3:00 p.m., your staff will take your cue and turn their attention to the weekend.

☐ Don't initiate demanding new tasks late in the day. However, you might ask a staff member to undertake an interesting small task at that time that will support a larger project. For example, you might have an employee draw up an agenda for the next staff meeting. Or, ask him or her to call some printers for price quotes on a needed job.

☐ Suggest routine Friday projects that will get your staff ready for the next week. They are likely to do them well because they'll see the benefits when they come in on Monday morning. For example, you might have them put all files in order, complete insurance claims, clean off their desks, or make a "to do" list for Monday.

☐ Don't distribute paychecks on Fridays. Doing so will distract your staff and cause them to think about the weekend, worry about getting to the bank in time to cash it, etc.

☐ Don't schedule dreaded tasks for later afternoon. For example, if your business assistant says he or she doesn't like to do insurance claims processing, schedule this task for another time in the week, preferably a morning. Along similar lines, don't schedule performance or salary reviews for Friday afternoon.

> It is human nature to lose momentum as the workweek comes to a close.

Employees
typically spend
several hours
each year at
office birthday
parties.

APPENDIX 1-D
## Action Steps for Handling Staff Birthday Parties

Did you know that employees typically spend several hours each year at office birthday parties? Thirty minutes per celebration is pretty average for most medical practices. Some offices devote even more time to birthday celebrations.

You will probably need to set a policy about how staff birthdays are to be celebrated in your medical practice, especially if you have more than a few employees. For example, you might:

☐ Suggest that the person celebrating the birthday bring in a cake, cookies, or similar treat that morning for everyone to share at your morning staff meeting. Have everyone sing "Happy Birthday" and give presents then, so they staff doesn't spent time gathering together to do so later in the day.

☐ If co-workers wish to take the birthday man or woman out to celebrate, ask that the do so after hours, not during lunch time, breaks, or business hours.

☐ Limit the amount co-workers can spend on birthday presents. For example, you might make it policy that each person contributes no more than a few dollars for a joint gift.

   **TIP:** *Setting a dollar limit for staff birthday presents helps your staff know to handle your birthday, too. They may feel awkward or confused and not know what's appropriate.*

☐ Consider giving each staff member his or her birthday off. Many employers offer this benefit because employees like it and it helps keep office routine more normal.

APPENDIX 1-E

# Factors that Influence Recruitment Success: A Checklist

Why do job applicants say *yes* when offered a job? In addition to obvious components such as wages and benefits offered, applicants may base their decision to accept or reject employment based upon their reaction to the recruitment process itself. The following factors influence recruitment success the most:

1. How you come across. Job applicants will judge you on:

   ☐ Your knowledge of him or her from the application and resume.

   ☐ Your knowledge of the job.

   ☐ Your personality and appearance.

   ☐ The nature and timing of your contacts with him or her. For example, the applicant will be influenced by how quickly you followed up after the interview and whether it was by phone or letter. (Phone calls are preferred.)

   ☐ The job-relatedness of the recruitment process. Asking questions the applicant feels aren't related to the job causes resentment and in some cases may be illegal.

2. How the applicant learned about you. New employees attracted through inside means (referral) may be more likely to say yes than those who become aware of the position through outside means (such as classified ads).

3. How you sell the job and your practice. Applicants who feel "oversold" may become suspicious of you and decline your offer. So, too, may applicants who have received a lukewarm description or impression of the opportunity.

> **TIP:** *Let your job applicants discuss the job offer honestly with your current employees (as long as they don't discuss salary and your employees are basically happy.) Doing so will give job candidates a positive yet realistic picture of the job and your practice. Because of this, they will be more inclined to say yes to your job offer. Applicants who have had a positive experience talking with your staff are also more likely to acclimate to the new position quickly. As well, they typically experience greater satisfaction once on the job and are less inclined to leave.*

> Applicants who feel "oversold" may become suspicious of you and decline your offer.

APPENDIX 1-F
# Quick-Action Checklist for Motivating Staff

What strategies can you use to light a fire under your staff? Here are eight great ideas:

1. Participative goal setting. Employees should ideally participate in setting their own goals so they feel they have a personal stake in them. Everyone in your practice can set four kinds of goals for themselves: routine, problem-solving, innovative, and individual career/personal development.

2. Develop two-way communication. Staff members will be motivated if they feel you care about them. Frequent feedback and reinforcement is essential.

3. Employee personal development. Help your staff to develop themselves by asking them where they would like to be in five or ten years. Then discuss the specific ways you can help them get there. Establish concrete goals for education and job development to help them achieve their long-term goals.

4. Conduct effective performance appraisals. Ask employees to evaluate you and suggest ways you can be a better supervisor and motivator.

5. Provide rewards, tangible and intangible. Ask employees what they truly want and then find ways to give it to them. The paycheck is not always the best motivator since it's generally based upon time and is regular and predictable. Paying "piecework" or by the task is also not a strong motivator since it, too, is predictable. The most motivating rewards tend to be those that are based upon performance and are intermittent. Therefore, don't give rewards according to time (such as regular annual raises). Rather, base them upon performance and goal achievement.

    TIP: *When a reward is predictable, it loses its value quickly. Don't be predictable about your rewards. Rather, pick what's significant and establish a variety of incentives and rewards for those accomplishments.*

6. Involvement in decision making. Find ways to let your staff make decisions. Or better yet, help them work up to making big decisions by practicing on smaller ones. Increased responsibility can be extremely motivating.

7. Meaningful delegation. Delegation should ideally lead to job enrichment, not simply job enlargement. When delegating, try to give your staff higher levels of responsibility, not simply more work at the same level of responsibility.

8. Build trust. Motivation is next to impossible if your staff believes you're trying to take advantage of them. Share your successes and give your staff opportunities to earn more money and responsibility. Be quick with rewards when they're due.

> The most motivating rewards tend to be those that are based upon performance and are intermittent.

## APPENDIX 1-G
# Resolving Anger without Blowing Up: A Checklist

When you're really mad at a staff member, do you vent your anger by blowing your stack? Does someone on your staff really know how to press your buttons? If so, here are a few ideas for developing a healthy control of your anger. Try them the next time one or more members of your staff makes you see red:

☐ Make a list of things you're angry about. Next to each cause, list who's at fault and why. Then, in a third column, write down your part in the problem. This process helps you get a handle on the kind of general anger you can feel against someone else. It helps separate legitimate gripes against others from problems you've helped create.

☐ Stop and try to consider the staff member's point of view. Is he or she under a lot of stress or having a bad day? Sensitivity may dissipate your anger and prevent you from lashing out and making a small problem into a bigger one.

☐ Stop and consider your environment. Are you hot, cold, tired, hungry, sick, just off the crowded freeway or surrounded by shrieking children or other unpleasantness? If so, you're far more susceptible to explosions of anger and may take your frustration out on innocent others. Here, counting to 10 really does help.

☐ Don't "should" yourself. Much of our anger is based upon what we think we or others should be doing. Try not to apply your value system to others.

☐ Laugh more. Laughter really does help. Try to see the humor in the situation.

☐ Remain courteous. It's tempting to be rude or sarcastic when you're angry at your staff. However, courtesy helps you feel in control and prevents provoking greater anger in others.

☐ Take time out. If need be, put your anger aside until you can act more calmly.

> Sensitivity may dissipate your anger and prevent you from lashing out.

## Action Steps for Managing Latchkey Parents

> Responsible working parents are concerned about the safety and well-being of their latchkey children.

Social and economic conditions have increased the number of latchkey children in this country—children who go home from school each day to an empty house or apartment because the parent or parents are at work. Responsible working parents are concerned about the safety and well-being of their latchkey children. Unfortunately, their concerns can sometimes interfere with their motivation, productivity, and behavior on the job.

If you have latchkey parents on your staff, consider how you might prevent their natural parental concerns from becoming a costly problem for your medical practice:

- The latchkey parent may spend time on the job in contact with the child. A check-in phone call is most common, but some parents actually make a quick trip home or have the child stop in at the office before going to the empty house or apartment. If a staff member feels he or she must take time away from work to be involved with the child, be understanding and supportive. However, try to rearrange your schedule so his or her late-afternoon coffee break coincides with the time that is needed for the phone call or visit.

- Offer child care as a fringe benefit.

- Don't ignore a problem if one exists with latchkey parents. However, avoid ultimatums that insist that they separate family concerns from their jobs. When possible, look for positive solutions. For example, you may offer to change or reduce a latchkey parent's hours so he or she can be home for his or her children at least a few days each week. That may require additional part-time staff and/or rescheduling of other staff members. However, it may be worth doing this when the problem is serious and the employee is truly valuable to your medical practice.

APPENDIX 1-I

# Holiday Extras Your Staff Will Remember All Year: A Checklist

Here are a few little extras you can do for or give to your employees during the holiday season to show how much you appreciate them all year long:

- [ ] Close the office at noon on your last workday and take your staff out for a long, leisurely lunch.

- [ ] Give each employee an afternoon off with pay to do some last-minute shopping.

- [ ] Plan an evening get-together so spouses can attend. Gather everyone at your home for appetizers and then go out for dinner at a favorite restaurant.

- [ ] Give each employee a night on the town. Tickets to a play or dinner theater will make the evening memorable.

- [ ] Give a year's membership to a health or exercise club, to a discount warehouse store, or to the Automobile Club of America (AAA).

- [ ] Give season tickets to your local football, basketball, baseball, or hockey games. Or, buy one block of four season tickets and have staff draw lots to see who gets the block for which games.

- [ ] Send employees to a professional development conference in a destination they've always wanted to visit.

- [ ] Give employees subscriptions to magazines they want. A well-chosen subscription keeps giving throughout the year as the employee receives another issue of the magazine in the mail.

- [ ] Give employees a gift certificate to take a course from your local recreation department. Perhaps they've always wanted to study Chinese cooking, watercolor painting, or computer graphics. Let them pick.

- [ ] Give employees a consultation with a color and image consultant.

> A well-chosen magazine subscription keeps giving throughout the year.

APPENDIX 1-J

# Checklist for Selling Your Staff on Change

Change can almost always be viewed as threatening because the effects of a particular change are ultimately unknown and unpredictable. It is a characteristic of human nature to need certainty and predictability. We generally prefer the known to the unknown. Often, an employee will be reluctant to let go of an old behavior or set of rules, not because he or she can't see the problem of it, but because he or she is afraid of what a new, untried alternative will feel like.

There is almost always resistance to change. Understanding and overcoming this resistance is the key to instituting changes in your practice:

☐ Remember that all behavior makes sense to the person engaging in it. The experience of one person is never exactly like that of another. As long as the person's behavior doesn't make sense to us, we can assume that it is because we don't understand enough about the person's point of view. For example, if a staff member refuses to use your new computer system to schedule appointments, you may simply think he or she is lazy. However, your employee may have good reasons for avoiding the computer (good reasons to him or her, that is). For instance, your employee may genuinely believe that using the new computer system will take longer than the way you used to schedule appointments. Your employee may fear that the new system will lead to more mistakes or that the computer will garble the information. Perhaps your employee has had a bad experience using a new computer system before and is averse to technology changes.

☐ When introducing change, begin by selling the benefits. Explain in specific and personal terms all the advantages and benefits your staff will enjoy from the new changes (saves time, prevents headaches, less overtime, etc.).

☐ Involve everyone on your staff as much as possible. For example, call a staff meeting to announce a major change so everyone learns about it at the same time. Hold a staff brainstorming session to come up with new policies and procedures for handling problems.

☐ Give reasons for the change. Provide all the background and the logical steps you took to come to the new conclusion.

☐ Provide ample time. Don't expect overnight miracles.

☐ Anticipate complaints and questions and head them off whenever you can. However, be prepared to take a firm stance if you come up against resistance.

☐ Provide explicit instructions for change—who will do what, by when, how, etc.

☐ Provide generous feedback and support. When you know a change is difficult, say so and compliment your staff for their good efforts. Make sure each person on your staff knows what's expected of them, how they're doing, and how much you appreciate their efforts.

**We generally prefer the known to the unknown.**

APPENDIX 1-K

# Action Checklist for Using a Payroll Service

Is your business assistant, bookkeeper, or office manager overburdened at times? If so, you might consider freeing him or her up by using an outside payroll service. Here's what you need to know:

☐ In medical practices with five or six employees, it can take your business assistant up to two hours to perform all of the payroll tasks each pay period. Practices with more employees naturally require more time.

☐ By using a payroll service, your employee could use the time and energy he or she would spend on payroll more profitably, for example, on collections, insurance processing, recall, and practice building activities. These tasks can bring dollars into your practice and should often take precedence over a function (such as payroll) that can be handled satisfactorily outside the practice.

☐ An outside payroll service may not cost as much as you think. Look in your telephone directory under "Payroll Services" or "Business Services for more information and to request a price estimate.

> An outside payroll service may not cost as much as you think.

> Termination is usually the final step, after at least three reprimands and warnings.

APPENDIX 1-L

# Valid Reasons to Fire: A Checklist

There are many reasons to fire an employee. For openers:

☐ Excessive absenteeism or tardiness. Unless a serious illness occurs and the employee provides needed documentation/proof, more than 10–12 sick days per year is generally considered to be excessive.

☐ Not reporting to work without phoning (three or more times).

☐ Drunkenness/drug use that interfered with job performance.

☐ Gross inattention to business.

☐ Repeated and documented discourtesy to patients, co-workers, or supervisors.

☐ Dishonesty: Falsifying records, embezzling money, etc.

☐ Refusing to carry out orders without satisfactory reason.

☐ Breech of confidentiality.

☐ Gross antisocial or harmful behavior.

> **TIP:** *Except in cases when an employee causes serious harm to others and discharge is immediate, termination is usually the final step, after at least three written reprimands and warnings.*

APPENDIX 1-M

# 10 Steps for Gaining and Keeping Your Staff's Respect

Here are 10 excellent ways to gain and keep your staff's respect:

1. Give honest answers to your employees' questions. If you don't know the answer or can't answer a delicate question, say so.

2. Keep professional matters on a professional level. However, when the discussing a topic is appropriate but not of a professional nature, don't be afraid to join in and show your lighter side. Do not take part in inappropriate conversations.

3. Control your temper in difficult situations. Your staff respect will falter if you lose control when things go wrong.

4. Show your staff that you value their time. Effective employees lose respect for a boss who wastes time and will take their cue from him or her.

5. Listen to what your staff is saying even when you disagree. Attention shows respect for another person's ideas.

6. Keep your promises to your staff. Don't make promises you don't intend to keep or that you know you can't.

7. Playing favorites within your staff is a sure way to lose respect, even from the person being favored.

8. Make a point of remembering each employee's ideas, special talents, and capabilities.

9. Support your staff as much as possible in difficult situations, especially ones where other people are involved.

10. Ask your staff for their suggestions and ideas. They'll appreciate your interest in them and in turn, show more interest in yours.

> Playing favorites within your staff is a sure way to lose respect, even from the person being favored.

APPENDIX 1-N

# Checklist for Recognizing Fear of Failure in Your Employees

Excessive fear of failure causes stress, errors, and poor decisions. As well, it can thwart your efforts to develop team spirit and high productivity in your practice.

A new employee or one who has just been promoted is a most likely victim. However, any staff member is vulnerable. For his reason, look for these symptoms of excessive fear in your staff:

☐ Frequent absences. (This may indicate the employee's desire to escape the cause of his or her anxiety.)

☐ Unexplained resistance to change.

☐ Frequent confusion. Excessive fear interferes with our ability to listen and understand.

☐ Frequent poor decisions or inability to make decisions.

☐ Unexpected personality changes.

☐ Excessive overtime. The employee may be trying to show you that he or she is a hard worker. He or she may be afraid to delegate responsibility to others. Or, the employee may be spending more time with tasks than is reasonably necessary for fear of mistakes.

☐ Clashes with co-workers.

☐ Inability to meet deadlines.

☐ Denying or concealing mistakes.

☐ Extreme concern or worry about failure.

If you suspect that an employee has an excessive fear of failure, meet with him or her in private. Explain that you expect some mistakes of every employee, that mistakes are an inevitable and normal part of the learning process. Ask the employee if he or she feels more training or instruction is needed.

Make sure new and newly promoted employees have a clear picture of what is expected of them. Clear expectations will help cut fear of the unknown. Provide a concise written job description with the employee's help. Install a program of periodic performance reviews so the employee has regular feedback.

Unfortunately, fear of failure can be a self-fulfilling prophecy. As well, the symptoms listed in the checklist above may indicate a problem of an entirely different nature (illness, personal problems, substance abuse, etc.). The important thing is that you confront the troubled employee in a supportive way, but that you also protect your medical practice's interests.

Give the employee help when you can and then describe specifically how his or her performance must change and by when. Follow up with more performance evaluations, feedback, and support. However, be prepared to draw the line if the employee won't or can't improve.

> Excessive fear of failure causes stress, errors, and poor decisions.

## APPENDIX 1-O
# Quiz: Is Your "Nice" Quotient Too High?

Who doesn't want to have a friendly relationship with staff? But in any medical practice, there are times when you have to be firm. Otherwise, you can undermine the smooth management of your practice. Your staff looks to you for direction and consistency.

Ask yourself these questions to find out if your "nice" quotient is too high:

1. Do you discipline employees and then try to soften the reprimand when they start complaining or get upset? The best course is to discipline firmly and fairly and then move on. If action is warranted and the individual is now aware of the consequences of his or her behavior, you've done your job. But if you reduce the reprimand or consequences, the employee probably won't change. Instead, he or she will learn that you can be manipulated.

2. Do you hesitate to confront a performance problem because you know the employee is sensitive? It is wrong to succumb to emotional blackmail. Remember, you are running the medical practice and each employee must do his or her share of the work.

3. Do you give your employees undeserved high ratings during performance appraisals because they're nice people, they need money, or they've been with you a long time?

4. Do you bend the rules or look the other way for employees you like?

5. Do you want your employees to get along like one big happy family? But then, when conflicts occur, do you avoid responsibility and tell them to work it out themselves when you know you should intervene?

6. Do you find it painfully difficult to say *no*? Or worse, do you hedge by saying *maybe* or *yes* when you shouldn't?

7. Do you bring your personal problems or intimate details of your personal life to the office? Sharing personal matters (money, family, love life) is okay to a degree for others in the office. However, doing so can diminish your authority and create role conflicts for you and your staff.

YOUR SCORE: If you answered yes to several of these questions, you may be everyone's buddy but no one's boss. As a result, your medical practice may not be running as smoothly as it might because you're managing with your heart, not your head.

Remember, your employees look up to you to be in charge, no matter how unpopular some of your decisions may be.

> In any medical practice, there are times when you have to be firm.

## Action Steps for Drawing New Patients from Recruitment

Recruitment can be a practice-building activity if you play your cards right.

Although turnover is costly and time-consuming, don't be so glum the next time you have a staff opening. Recruitment can be a practice-building activity (for some practices) if you play your cards right.

Think about your recruitment efforts not only from the job applicant's viewpoint, but also from those of potential patients. After all, every applicant is a potential patient or referrer. You want his or her experience to be so positive that it will be almost impossible for him or her to resist making an appointment or telling family and friends about your medical practice. Here are some suggestions:

- Invest time and money in your classified ad. A good ad will not only attract more qualified applicants, but will also grab the attention of potential patients.

- In the ad copy, list the features of your practice that would attract both applicants and new patients. For example, you might describe your newly remodeled office, convenient location on public transportation routes, free parking, personal attention given to every patient, caring professionals, continuing education of staff, etc.

- Display your practice name prominently in the ad exactly as you print it elsewhere in your marketing efforts. Besides getting your name across clearly to applicants, featuring your name in this way can jog a reader's memory of seeing the same name on your office sign or phone directory ad.

- In your ad, consider inviting all interested applicants to visit your office to complete an application form. Although telephone screening is simpler, your odds for gaining new patients and referrals increase with every applicant who comes through your door. For crowd control, establish limited drop-in hours. Offer juice or other drinks to applicants.

- Depending upon your area of practice, you might ask applicants to specify the last time they had a routine examination on your application form.

- Prepare a packet of information about your practice for applicants to take with them. In a large envelope or folder, include a photocopied letter from you (addressed "Dear Applicant"—see Appendix 2-K for a sample), your *curriculum vita*, practice brochure, business card, several issues of your patient newsletter, copies of newspaper clippings about you or articles you've written, copies of your print ads, and perhaps even an inexpensive giveaway item such as a refrigerator magnet, keychain, or imprinted pen. For a more aggressive effort (and depending again upon your area of practice), you might include a discount certificate good toward a first examination. Finally, if you're looking for speaking invitations in your community, include a list of talks you can give to community groups. The applicant may belong to an organization that can invite you to speak.

- If possible, give all applicants who visit a short tour and introduction to your practice. Thank each applicant and give him or her the packet you've prepared. Tell applicants the date you plan to make a hiring decision and explain how you will contact them.

- Once you've completed your search, send each rejected applicant a personalized letter and a one-year complimentary subscription to your patient newsletter. If an applicant has not had a recent examination (you'll know from his or her application), recommend one.

- Place all rejected applicants on your mailing list and include them in practice-building mailings. Send them invitations to practice events (such as open houses, office tours, and health fairs), holiday greeting cards, entry blanks to contests you sponsor, survey questionnaires, and news articles about you and your practice.

- To leave a very good impression, especially with candidates you've interviewed, send rejected applicants a small thank-you gift. This keeps the lines of communication open between your medical practice and quality applicants you can't use right away.

> Place all rejected applicants on your mailing list and include them in all practice-building mailings.

> Even staff members who love their jobs may feel listless on Monday morning.

APPENDIX 1-Q

# Checklist for Beating the Monday Blues

Even staff members who love their jobs may feel listless on Monday and wish they had just one more day to be at home. Monday morning depression is perfectly normal and strikes millions of us each week.

To make Monday a bit less depressing, you and your staff can:

☐ Plan ahead and save enjoyable tasks for Monday mornings.

☐ Try getting a good start on a project you enjoy on Friday. Then pick it up again on Monday.

☐ Plan to have something you especially like for lunch on Monday.

☐ Limit alcohol and tobacco consumption over the weekend.

☐ Relax your standards at home on the weekend. If you're easier on yourself about household chores, you're more likely to feel rested on Monday.

☐ Begin a new project at work just for you, such as adding something appealing to your work station.

☐ Try to have something enjoyable planned for the following weekend so you have something to look forward to.

☐ Go to sleep early on Sunday night.

☐ Clean your desk on Friday so you can have a fresh start on Monday.

☐ Institute a fun Monday ritual. For example, you might post a "Joke of the Week" on your staff bulletin board.

☐ Distribute paychecks on Monday.

APPENDIX 1-R

# Action Steps for Respecting Your Staff's Privacy

You know that you have an obligation to keep information about your patients confidential. What you may not realize is that as an employer, you also have a very important responsibility to respect your staff's privacy. Some action steps:

- Don't include information in personnel files that is irrelevant to job-related decisions.

- Assure employees that the information in their personnel files is open only to practice personnel with a "need to know." If necessary, keep separate files for sensitive information such as medical information.

- Tell employees the reasons for any information you collect about them.

- Require an employee's permission for release of any file data to outsiders, except to confirm employment dates or to cooperate with law enforcement officials.

- Allow employees to see information in their personnel files upon request.

- When an employee is not in your office, don't give his or her whereabouts to people who ask, unless you have permission to do so. For example, don't tell inquirers that a vacationing employee is out of town and where he or she is. Doing so could tip off a burglar that his or her home is vacant. As well, don't tell patients who ask that an employee is in the hospital without his or her permission. The employee may not want anyone to know about it.

- Don't share sensitive personal information about an employee with anyone. For example, if you learn that an employee has a broken engagement, a fight with his or her spouse, a son who has been arrested, or even that the employee failed his or her driving test, it is not your place to tell others about it.

- Don't take part in office gossip. As well, discourage gossip among staff members.

- Give constructive criticism in private, not in front of co-workers or patients.

As an employer, you have a very important responsibility to respect your staff's privacy.

> Avoid using double standards or perpetuating insidious gender stereotypes.

# Action Checklist for Managing Men and Women

Here are six things you can do to ensure that you treat the men and women who work for you equally:

1. Buck the stereotypes. Do you think women are "sweet," "sensitive," and "ladylike"? Or do you think they're "bitchy," "castrating," or "aggressive"? Men who fit in the latter category are often thought of as "ambitious," "masculine," and "on their way up." Do you think a man who shows his emotions is weak or "wimpy"? Do you think a woman who shows her emotions is "acting like a typical woman"? Avoid using double standards like these or perpetuating insidious gender stereotypes.

2. Don't assume that women's goals for salary and promotions are different from men's. Meet regularly with each member of your staff to discuss performance and future plans.

3. Don't expect women or men to take on responsibilities for which they are not fairly compensated. Ask yourself if you would offer a person of the opposite gender with the same talents and aspirations a similar position, salary, and job duties.

4. If a member of your staff tells you of sexual harassment from a patient, co-worker, etc., take it seriously and act.

5. Don't refer to the women on your staff as your "girls" or the men on your staff as your "boys."

6. Establish non-discriminatory dress and hygiene codes. Make similar requirements for both men and women employees in comparable positions.

APPENDIX 1-T

# What to Know about Using Graphology in Hiring: A Checklist

Many employers now use graphology (handwriting analysis) in staff selection. Some facts you should know:

☐ Roughly 5,000 U.S. companies have hired professional graphologists.

☐ The law doesn't require employers to tell the individual that handwriting analysis will be done. However, most do anyway.

☐ The handwriting sample should be produced while the writer is in a natural, relaxed state. Knowing they're writing a sample for analysis can make people tense.

> **TIP:** *Have job applicants write a paragraph on the application form describing their experiences or expected contributions. After the sample has been written and you've narrowed your choice of applicants, tell each one the handwriting will be analyzed, unless they object.*

☐ Graphology proponents claim that handwriting analysis can help judge a prospective employee's personality and potential. They contend that the technique is nondiscriminatory because handwriting doesn't reveal physical characteristics.

☐ Graphology opponents argue that factors such as age and illness might be indicated, since graphologists say they can assess health status from handwriting.

☐ Poor handwriting often results when the mind performs faster than the hand. It's not necessarily a sign of poor character.

☐ Graphology is used more often in Europe.

☐ Employers can legally use any method they want to screen job applicants, so long as its use doesn't adversely impact minority, disabled, or female applicants.

☐ Some experts believe that handwriting analysis by a qualified analyst can be more reliable and revealing than psychological testing.

☐ *Graphology* is the generic term of the study of handwriting. *Graphoanalysis* is a specific method of handwriting analysis taught by the International Graphoanalysis Society.

☐ Graphologists say handwriting can tell you whether a person is honest or dishonest; industrious or lazy; mentally alert or sluggish; weak or strong willed; careful or sloppy with details; well- or poorly-organized; able to work independently; able to handle responsibility; able to exercise leadership; analytical; quick-thinking; able to follow through with a project.

> Poor handwriting is not necessarily a sign of poor character.

They also say that handwriting reveals what a person has been, now is, and is likely to be in the future.

☐ To a handwriting analyst, check our telephone directory under "Handwriting Analysis."

☐ A handwriting analysis can cost up to several hundred dollars, depending upon how much detail you want in your report and the qualifications of the analyst.

Graphologists say that handwriting reveals what a person has been, now is, and is likely to be in the future.

APPENDIX 1-U
# Checklist for Issuing Directives

Few people enjoy being told what to do. However, there may be times when you have no choice but to issue directives to your staff. Follow these guidelines whenever you feel you must issue a directive:

☐ Limit the use of directives.

☐ Explain the need for all directives. Include the facts and conditions that have made each directive necessary.

☐ Be sure that staff members have the background and ability to meet the goal of the directive.

☐ Avoid surprise. Prepare employees for the directive.

☐ Show the importance and applicability of the directive to those who receive it.

☐ Leave no doubts about who is to do what, where, when, and how. Issue directives fairly and assign tasks equally.

☐ Don't condescend.

☐ Use the "we" approach whenever you can do so sincerely. The team idea is important even with directives.

☐ Make directives brief and simple. Present directions logically in steps.

☐ Provide feedback and follow-up once the directive has been carried out. Thank employees when appropriate.

## Few people enjoy being told what to do.

APPENDIX 1-V

# Checklist for Incorporating Japanese Management Methods

The productivity of Japanese workers and the quality of their products became hugely interesting to managers in the United States in the latter part of the 20th century, and continues to be a source of study today. Some Japanese methods probably wouldn't work well in the United States. For one thing, Japanese workers are very often employed by the same company for a lifetime. By contrast, most American employees prize their mobility and hold several jobs or even careers over their lives. As well, Japanese companies promote largely on the basis of seniority. In the United States, we place more emphasis on merit increases and individual achievement.

Despite these differences, the following methods used by managers in Japan are well worth consideration for those who manage the staff of a medical practice:

☐ Employees who work in companies in Japan are often made to feel they are part of a family. Emphasis is on harmony within the workplace. Mangers take personal interest in their employees as whole people.

☐ Japanese managers ask their employees how they feel about policy changes. They involve employees at all levels as much as possible in the planning before change is implemented. Because of this, the employees feel a personal investment and stake in each change and the company's success.

☐ When handling errors or poor performance, Japanese managers try to allow employees to save face whenever they can. Entire groups of employees are involved in a search for a solution.

☐ Loyalty to the employer is fostered by group decision-making. Japanese managers try to seek consensus whenever possible before decisions are implemented.

> Japanese managers try to allow employees to save face whenever they can.

APPENDIX 1-W

## Anticipating Problems with High-Morale Employees: A Checklist

It practically goes without saying that every medical practice wants its employees' morale to soar. Enthusiastic, super-charged employees tend to be very creative, hard-working, and productive, and they function well as a team. Much of the material in this book is geared toward keeping your staff morale as high as possible.

However, be warned that with a very high morale group come some new personnel management concerns. Learn to anticipate the following problems with your high-morale employees:

☐ If morale disappears suddenly in a high-morale practice, productivity may fall to lower levels than if the high morale never existed. High morale groups may have very high highs and very low lows.

☐ High morale depends in large part upon the appearance of progress. Thus, there is great temptation among high-morale employees to falsify or exaggerate progress reports and to deny or downplay the importance of problems.

☐ In general, high morale groups tend to resist change. They may be especially prone to problems when the medical practice changes leadership (for example, hires a new office manager), replaces unproductive employees, or offers unsolicited advice or direction.

☐ High-morale groups tend to place little emphasis on routine basics such as office safety, theft prevention, cost considerations, and office and equipment maintenance.

> High morale groups may have very high highs and very low lows.

APPENDIX 1-X

# Checklist for Keeping Office Gossip to a Minimum

Here's what a medical practice manager can do to discourage gossip among employees:

☐ Don't gossip yourself or tolerate gossip from others. Employees are likely to take their lead from you and do as you do.

☐ Good office policy: Any discussion about a patient should be done in the office only, behind closed doors, with appropriate staff members with a "need to know," only when necessary, and about relevant information.

☐ If the doctor's spouse is employed in the practice, he or she should not participate in office gossip. In particular, the doctor's spouse must not allow himself or herself to be put in the position of holding secrets from his or her spouse. As well, the spouse should not share privileged information he or she has learned from the doctor.

☐ Do not share the details of a staff member's leaving especially when you fire for cause. Do not speculate on a staff member's personal problems with others or share information a staff member has told you in confidence.

☐ Head off gossip by announcing important office news early. Call a staff meeting so everyone hears the same information in the same way and at the same time.

☐ Avoid secrets. Give everyone equal access to information when they should have it.

☐ When office gossip is rampant: Call a staff meeting to give a general warning; meet individually with known offenders; explain specifically how you want things to change citing personnel policy (in your handbook) and specific gossip you have heard.

☐ Repeated malicious gossip (and certainly breech of patient confidentiality) can be grounds for dismissal. Give appropriate warnings and written reprimands to known offenders. Follow through with threatened action.

**Head off gossip by announcing important news early.**

## APPENDIX 1-Y

# Checklist for Overcoming Staff Computer Anxiety

*Computerphobia. Cyberphobia. Technophobia. Technostress.* This new jargon describes a very common anxiety about using new automated equipment. You may find that some employees resist learning and using new technologies. If so, here is what you can do to overcome their computer anxiety:

☐ Tell your staff your reasons for using the new system. Communicate a positive attitude and your commitment to the technology. Stress the ways the equipment or new system will help your staff get their jobs done.

☐ When possible, involve staff in the equipment acquisition process. Get their input at vendor meetings and when assessing needs.

☐ Make training accessible to everyone. After intense initial training, make auxiliary programs available for more advanced stages of skill and development.

☐ Provide proper facilities for staff using equipment. Consider rest breaks, lighting, ventilation, air conditioning, furniture, and equipment configuration.

☐ Avoid using computer jargon.

☐ Allow employees to spend time alone with the new equipment. Let them work at their own level and pace to develop their understanding of the equipment capabilities.

Communicate a positive attitude and your commitment to new technology.

Avoid hiring people whose value systems resemble those of employees who didn't work out.

APPENDIX 1-Z

# Developing Employee Loyalty: A Checklist

Do your employees *want* to stay with you? Or do they have to stay? Progressive medical practice managers try to improve staff retention by reinforcing positive reasons for staying. How can you determine if your employees are staying because they want to or because they have to? You'll need to look at attitudes to find out. Then you can reinforce the positive reasons your employees are staying and tackle some of the negatives. The six-step process:

1. Accept the fact that the value systems of your employees may be quite different than yours. What satisfies one individual may likely turn off another, and *vice versa*. Realize and accept that it is not a matter of who is right and who is wrong. There are dramatic differences between people.

2. Look at your office policies and procedures from the perspective of your employees. The right policies for pay, attendance, and promotion are those that work best for the people in the practice.

3. Ask employees why they stay, either through a survey or in interviews. Listen carefully. Ask employees their opinions about particular policies or management practices. However, don't make this an academic exercise. Be willing to make changes so that your policies match the prevalent value system in your office.

4. Communicate your policies in a language style that is compatible with your employees' value systems. For example, an employee who is basically a conformist may prefer highly structured situations, detailed tasks, written instructions, and unchanging patterns. On the other hand, a non-conformist employee probably won't tolerate routine tasks or simple answers very well. This employee provides his or her own leadership, is outspoken on beliefs, but is usually quick to make changes.

5. When recruiting, consider the value systems of those who stay and match new staff members accordingly. Avoid hiring people whose value systems resemble those of employees who didn't work out.

6. Remember, eliminating the negatives and accentuating the positives is a process, not a short-term program. Employee involvement is crucial. People believe in what they help create.

Sample Letters That
Enhance Staff
Recruitment,
Motivation and
Management

## Tips for Composing Effective Letters for Your Staff

The ideal letter to a member of your staff is concise, crisp, and appropriate in appearance. While it's important to avoid misspellings, improper usage, smudges, poorly-aligned margins, and illegible handwriting, such beauty is only skin deep. The heart of any letter to your staff is its message and the words you use to convey it. These tips will help you compose better letters and improve those you currently use with your staff.

1. Send letters to your staff immediately after the event that occasions it. A note of congratulations, welcome to the practice, condolence, or thanks becomes diluted if you don't write it promptly.

2. Make your first sentence work hard. Your employee wants to know at once what your letter is about, so tell him or her.

3. Choose stationery, whether to type or handwrite the letter, and a salutation and closing that expresses the same level of formality as your relationship with the employee and the subject of your letter.

4. Avoid adding a postscript. With word processing, it is not necessary and suggests that the body of the letter was badly organized.

5. Be specific so your employee will know precisely what you mean.

6. Add the personal touch when appropriate. Call the employee by name and use pronouns such as you, your, we, our, and me.

7. End the letter when you've said all you need to say.

8. Use typographic devices for clarity and emphasis. For example, put key ideas into indented or bulleted paragraphs. Use italics and boldface print for emphasis, but not too much.

9. Avoid legal or bureaucratic language.

10. Choose a tone that is appropriate for the message. Friendliness and informality are most appropriate for a note of thanks or congratulations. A written reprimand or directive usually requires a more formal tone.

11. Keep paragraphs short, probably no more than five sentences. Short paragraphs invite reading, add punch, and are clearer.

12. Check the length of your sentences. Sentences with 22 or more words are usually too long and lower readability. Vary sentence length to avoid monotony.

13. Avoid negative language when you can.

14. If your handwriting is illegible, type all your letters and notes, even informal ones.

> The heart of any letter to your staff is its message and the words you use to convey it.

15. Be enthusiastic and lively when you can. Compare these two letters:

Blah: I am pleased to join the staff for lunch on Wednesday for my birthday as requested in your invitation memo of October 14. I will be at Gallagher's Pub promptly at 12:30.

Upbeat: Thank you! With pleasure I accept your invitation to have lunch on October 14 with the staff to celebrate my birthday. Tell everyone that I will be at Gallagher's Pub at 12:30 on Wednesday and that I am planning to be very hungry that day.

A written reprimand or directive usually requires a more formal tone.

APPENDIX 2-A
## Welcoming a New Employee to Your Practice

*Mail this letter to the new employee so it arrives at his or her home before the first day of work.*

Dear _____:

    Monday, February 7 is your first day of work. Let me take this opportunity to welcome you personally to our medical practice. Dr. Fishbaine, Dr. Sullivan, Ms. Browning, and the entire staff at Family Medical are just as pleased as I that you decided to accept our employment offer.

    As you know, we begin our day at 7:30 a.m. Please park your car in the rear of the building in the staff parking lot. As well, would you please keep your calendar clear for lunch on your first day? We like to take all new employees out to get better acquainted.

    Once again, welcome to the Family Medical Center of Springfield. We wish you the best of luck in your new job. May it bring you everything you want.

"Would you please keep your calendar clear for lunch on your first day? We like to take all new employees out to get better acquainted."

APPENDIX 2-B

## Introducing a New Staff Member to Patients

*Send this letter to all patients of record when you make an addition to your staff. If appropriate (and with permission), include some information about the new employee's education, background, interests, and family.*

> "In our continuing effort to offer you the best medical care and service possible, we're proud to announce a new addition to our staff."

Dear Ms. Patient:

In our continuing effort to offer you the best medical care and service possible, we're proud to announce a new addition to our staff. Bonnie McDaniel is our new nurse practitioner. Your support helped made this addition possible.

Bonnie received her training at the (name of school) where she graduated with high distinction. Prior to joining us, she served as a nurse practitioner for the Women's Health Center of Madison, Wisconsin. She is an avid swimmer and quilter and claims to be Pennsylvania's biggest fan of rock-a-billy music.

Bonnie's husband Daryl is responsible for moving the McDaniel family to Altoona. He will begin teaching tenth grade English at Altoona High this fall and will also coach the boys' soccer team. The McDaniels have two boys themselves, James (11) and Brian (7), as well as an enormous St. Bernard they call *Tiny*.

Bonnie looks forward to meeting you personally and we all look forward to seeing you again at your next appointment. Please be sure to give Bonnie your warmest Altoona welcome.

## APPENDIX 2-C
# Rejecting a Job Applicant

*Be as sincere, personal, and encouraging as you can possibly be. Remember, the rejected job applicant may become your next patient or referral source:*

Dear _____:

Thank you for your recent application for employment at the Family Medical Center of Hartford.

We have carefully reviewed your qualifications, skills, and experience and appreciate your thoroughness. Although we have filled the position for which you have applied, we would like very much to retain your application in our active files in the event of future openings.

Again, thank you so much for your interest in our practice and for your time and effort. We wish you much luck in your search for new employment and in everything you do.

"Although we have filled the position for which you have applied, we would like very much to retain your application in our active files."

APPENDIX 2-D
## Thanking an Employee for Good Work on a Special Project

*Handwrite this note and put it in the employee's mailbox the morning after a big event in your practice. When appropriate, include a small gift with the note.*

"Please know that your many weeks of hard work, creativity, and attention to detail have paid off and are appreciated."

Dear _____:

It's hard to believe that the Family Allergy Center of St. Louis's first annual open house has already come and gone. I know that you have worked long and hard to make this program the success it was.

Please know that your many weeks of hard work, creativity, and attention to detail paid off and are appreciated. I am certain that our patients, colleagues, and neighbors in the community are all a little more enriched by your wonderful efforts. The open house was very informative, well-organized, and above all, fun. I am most impressed with the way you were able to generate favorable publicity for our practice, which no doubt brought us such high attendance.

Thank you from the bottom of my heart for going the extra mile. You deserve much credit for a job well done.

## APPENDIX 2-E
# Offering a Get Well Wish

*The following letter might be handwritten inside a get-well card or enclosed with a gift or flowers sent to the ailing employee. Of course, no letter can take the place of a personal visit or phone call. Send a letter only when you can't reach or see the employee or as a follow-up to a visit.*

Dear _____,

    Tamara Turner told me this morning that you had a serious car accident over the weekend. I have tried to reach you at the hospital but they informed me that you cannot have visitors or calls right now.

    Please accept my wishes for a speedy recovery. We all hope that your injuries are not too serious and that you will be well again very soon.

    If there is anything any of us can do for either you or your family, please don't hesitate to call.

    Best wishes from all of us here to you and your family. I'll be by to see you as soon as they let me.

> "We all hope that your injuries are not too serious and that you will be well again very soon."

APPENDIX 2-F
# Offering Sympathy and Condolences

*Handwrite this letter on personal stationery or inside a sympathy card. Send it soon after the death.*

> Dear _____,
>
> I was greatly shocked yesterday to learn of your mother's sudden death. Please accept my sincere condolences.
>
> There is little anyone can do or say at a time like this. I wanted you to know that my thoughts and deepest sympathy are with you during these trying times.
>
> I would like very much to help you and your family in any way I can. Please call me personally if there's something I can do or if you'd like to talk.

"I wanted you to know that my thoughts and deepest sympathy are with you during these trying times."

APPENDIX 2-G

# Thanking the Employee for a Suggestion

*Ideally, every employee suggestion should be acknowledged, even ideas you can't use. Mention the actual suggestion the employee made in your letter and tell him or her what you intend to do about it.*

Dear _____,

    I am most pleased to receive your recent suggestion for revising our collection procedure. Most certainly, collections have been a continuing problem area for us. We need some aggressive new ways to deal with delinquent patients, especially those in the over-90-day category.

    I will be looking into the Small Claims Court as you have suggested. However, I am concerned about the affect taking a patient to court may have on our reputation in the community. Let's put this topic on the agenda for our next staff meeting.

    I'm forwarding a copy of your suggestion to Arlene and to Dr. Nguyen. Your effort and initiative are greatly appreciated. I hope you will continue to submit additional ideas to me when they occur to you. Thank you — keep up the good work.

"Your effort and initiative are greatly appreciated."

APPENDIX 2-H
# Reprimanding Poor Job Performance

*Because of the sensitive nature of this letter, personally hand deliver it to the employee or mail it to him or her in a sealed opaque envelope marked "confidential." As well, you will probably want to type this letter yourself Or, if you must have another employee to type the letter, make him or her aware that the information it contains is confidential. Make two copies of the letter and have the employee sign one, which you'll keep in the personnel file. Give him or her the other. Provide space for rebuttal or comments, signature, and a date.*

"We cannot tolerate tardiness in our office and this is clearly outlined in our personnel manual."

---

Dear _____:

I would like to take this opportunity to review what we discussed at our meeting this morning. To begin, you have arrived at least 20 minutes late for work on four separate mornings this month:

Monday, August 12: 24 minutes

Thursday, August 15: 33 minutes

Monday, August 19: 42 minutes

Tuesday, August 20: 27 minutes

In each of these instances, you did not call our office to inform us of the delay, nor did you offer as an excuse any compelling emergencies or circumstances beyond your control.

We cannot tolerate tardiness in our office and this is clearly outlined in our personnel manual. As well, the importance of punctuality was stressed during our orientation and at your last performance review.

As per our conversation this morning, you have agreed that you will come to work on time from now on, arrive in the office no later than 8:00 sharp and ready to work. In the even of some unforeseen

emergency—and I use that word with great care—
you have agreed that you will call our office as soon
as is practical to inform us of any delays.

Please sign this letter and return it to me. Use
the space below or add additional sheets for any
additional comments you may have. I look forward to
seeing you on time for work from now on.

_____
*(Your Signature)*

Employee's comments:

_____

_____

_____

_____

_____

_____

Attach additional paper as necessary.

Employee's signature: _____

Date:_____

> "I look forward to seeing you on time for work from now on."

## Saying Goodbye to a Valued Employee

*The following letter might be handwritten inside a going-away card and presented with a gift on the employee's last day of work.*

> "I still have trouble believing that you won't be part of our practice anymore."

Dear _____,

    I still have trouble believing that you won't be part of our practice anymore. Everyone here is going to miss you more than you may imagine – especially me.

    It has been a genuine pleasure working with you over the last six years. You have always given 100% to this practice and have done a wonderful job for us. You should be very proud whenever you think of your days at Fair Oaks Skin Care Center.

    I wish you all the best with the birth of your child and look forward to meeting your little one very soon. I am sure you and Tom will enjoy being parents. Children have brought Melinda and me the greatest joy we have ever known.

    Please let's stay in touch. And please, won't you let us know if you are ever of thinking of returning to work somewhere down the road?

    We all wish you an easy, speedy delivery and a healthy baby boy or girl. Best of luck, Mom.

## APPENDIX 2-J
# Recommending a Former Employee

*Stick to documented, provable facts only. Speak about specifics when you can.*

Dear _____:

    It is with much enthusiasm that I write this letter of recommendation for Ms. Meredith Schutz, who served as our practice's receptionist this year. Ms Schutz was an outstanding new employee and made many positive contributions to our practice.

    Ms. Schutz possesses great organizational skills and has a natural ability to get along with people. She worked diligently to handle our incoming calls smoothly and courteously. Ms. Schutz scheduled appointments, greeted patients, called delinquent accounts, filed insurance claims, and performed a myriad of other duties. Everything she did she did well.

    When Ms. Schutz informed me that she was leaving Miami and had to resign her position, I was deeply saddened. She is truly one of the finest new employees I have supervised in my 12 years in practice. She has been well-respected by her co-workers and by our patients and handles her responsibilities very professionally. Ms. Schutz would be an asset to any organization in which she worked. We at the Miami Ophthalmology Center will surely miss her.

> Stick to documented, provable facts only.

APPENDIX 2-K
## Thanking a Job Applicant for Applying

*Duplicate this letter and include it in an information packet you put together for job applicants. Include in the packet your brochure, patient newsletter, copies of articles you wrote, topics of talks you can give, a giveaway (pen, keychain, etc.) and other material that will make a favorable impression on the applicant.*

Dear Applicant:

Thank you so much for your interest in becoming a receptionist for OB-GYN Associates of Tucson. We greatly appreciate the time you have taken to visit us today and complete our application form.

OB-GYN Associates of Tucson is a five-doctor practice that began in 1989. We have two nurse practitioners on staff as well. We are blessed with a wonderful location and the nicest staff and patients in the world. In this information packet, you will find many materials that describe our practice philosophy, services, education and training. As well, we have included an example of our patient newsletter and reprints of some of the articles we have contributed to several publications.

We will be in touch soon about the open receptionist position. In the meantime, we would greatly appreciate it if you would let us know if you have another job offer before accepting a position elsewhere. Please know that we are very glad that you stopped in today and submitted your application. Thank you for your consideration of our practice.

APPENDIX 2-L
## Encouraging Staff during a Tough Time

*Every employee in the practice can receive a typed letter like this one. However, it will be most effective if you handwrite a different personal sentiment on the bottom of each letter.*

Dear _____,

As you know, we have had an extremely difficult two weeks here at Austin Foot Center ever since Dr. Gonzalez had his heart attack. I wanted each of you to know how very much Dr. Gonzalez and I appreciate the hard work you have done to accommodate our patients. Without your efforts, neither one of us knows how we ever could have survived this difficult time.

Dr. Gonzalez is recovering well from his bypass surgery and he is doing everything he can to make sure he returns to us as quickly as possible. He told me today how much he appreciates all of your cards and gifts and that he misses you all a great deal. I know that every one of you has stayed late and/or come in to our office early to do extra work and that we will continue to need that extra support from you until Dr. Gonzales returns. Your dedication to our practice and to our patients is an inspiration. Please accept the enclosed gift card to (name of store or restaurant) as our very small way of saying *thank you* for everything you are doing. You mean the world to us.

> "Your dedication to our practice and to our patients is an inspiration."

APPENDIX 2-M
## Adding New Material to Your Employee Handbook

*Provide space at the bottom of this letter for a signature and date.*

> "Your input during the last several staff meetings has been very helpful."

Dear _____:

At long last we have completed our new and improved policy about staff vacation schedules. Your input on this topic during the last several staff meetings has been very helpful. The fruits of our labors are the two pages attached to this letter entitled Vacation Policy Amendment. They are numbered 14-A and 14-B.

Please read this new vacation policy carefully and insert pages 14-A and 14-B in your employee handbook behind page 14. Then, please read, sign, and date the statement below and return this form to me. Thank you.

_____
*(Your Signature)*

I have read and understand the new policy for staff vacations entitled Vacation Policy Amendment and inserted this new policy as pages 14-A and 14-B in my employee handbook.

Employee's signature: _____

Date:_____

APPENDIX 2-N
## Introducing a Yearly Benefits Statement

*Attach this letter to a yearly benefits statement that you give to your staff early in January. For more information on this topic, see Chapter 2-7: Developing a Competitive Benefits Program.*

---

Dear _____:

Happy New Year! I hope that you had a wonderful holiday and that the coming year brings you good health and great happiness.

As is our custom, I am attaching a summary of the benefits you received as an employee in our pediatric practice in the last calendar year. Many employees have told me that they find this summary very helpful. You will see that your statement includes all of the benefits you received including paid vacation, paid sick leave, paid holidays, uniform allowances, tuition reimbursement, travel allowances, insurance payments, childcare allowances, grooming allowances, and/or discounted professional services and products. Please let me know if you have any questions about the benefits you received last year or about those that you will be receiving in the coming new year.

I want to take this opportunity to tell you what a pleasure it is to work with you and how much you mean to our patients and to our practice. What you do here makes a huge difference. I especially appreciate the positive attitude you bring with you to work every day. I look forward to another wonderful year working side by side with you to provide the best possible medical care for our pediatric patients. Thank you so much for everything you do.

> "I want to take this opportunity to tell you what a pleasure it is to work with you and how much you mean to our patients and to our practice."

# Catching an Employee Doing Something Right

*So much of what an employee hears from a supervisor is negative. Try writing a letter like this when you notice an employee doing something right. Keep a copy of the letter in the employee's personnel file.*

"You have a true gift with people, one that I know comes from deep inside you."

---

Dear _____,

This morning, I happened to overhear you speaking with Mrs. O'Malley in Exam Room #2. I gathered from the gist of the conversation that Mrs. O'Malley was very worried about getting her test results today and that she shared some of this concern with you. I want you to know how very impressed I am with the way you handled this delicate situation. I thought you did a fantastic job of allaying Mrs. O'Malley's fears without giving her a false sense of hope or security. I especially appreciate the kind things you said about my abilities and your faith in me as a doctor. That helped Mrs. O'Malley a lot, I'm sure, but it also meant a great deal to me.

You have a true gift with people, one that I know comes from deep inside you and that cannot be taught in nursing school. This is not the first time I have seen you do this kind of thing with one of our patients. I want you to know that I do not take your talents and your efforts for granted. I appreciate them. Our patients and I are very lucky to have you here to help us.

Thank you so much for the wonderful way you handled Mrs. O'Malley this morning and for everything you do here for all of us every day.

APPENDIX 2-P
## Issuing a Directive in Writing

*Some instructions are best given in writing. Use a memo like this one when giving simple instructions to your staff that will not be likely to elicit confusion or an angry or emotional response.*

Dear _____,

On Monday, November 15, 16, and 17 we will be having our parking lot repaved and repainted. We will need all of our staff and patients to park elsewhere during this time so the new pavement and the new lines can dry properly. Here's what you need to know:

Mount Calvary Baptist Church next door has graciously agreed to allow our staff and patients to use their rear parking lot during these three days. Please park your car in back of the Mt. Calvary. Do not park in the spaces in front of the church or along the driveway. They are reserved for and marked for the church elders and ministers.

If you prefer not to park in Mount Calvary's parking lot, you may be able to find street parking along the north side of Maple Avenue. However, please remember that there is no street parking permitted on the south side of Maple Avenue. You will be very likely to be ticketed if you park anywhere on the south side. Trust me – I know.

Do not use our staff entrance during November 15, 16, and 17, even if it looks to you like the parking lot is ready to use. The new pavement will be tender for a while and easily dented if you try to walk on it.

> Some instructions are best given in writing.

Use a memo when giving simple instructions to your staff that will not be likely to elicit confusion or an angry or emotional response.

Therefore, please enter and exit our building through the main entrance.

Resume parking in our freshly paved lot and using our staff entrance starting on Thursday, November 18th.

Thank you for your cooperation during our parking lot renovation. I know we will all be happy to see those potholes go. As well, you will be pleased to know that we are installing a speed hump near the entrance of our lot to the lot to deter speeding. I know this has been a topic of much concern at our staff meetings. As well, we are installing a sign at the entrance to the lot that instructs drivers to slow down.

Please let me know if you have any questions about parking or entering the building or about the new speed hump and sign. Thanks again.

# Tools for Staff Training

APPENDIX 3-A

# Giving Your Staff the Proper Perspective: The 25 Basic Truths

*In most medical practices, new employees delve into the specifics of their jobs without getting the lay of the land. They do not always know what kind of attitude, conduct, or perspective they will need to succeed in their new jobs. It is up to their new bosses to provide this insight. This appendix presents 25 basic "truths" every medical practice employee should know from the start. These truths could be added to a handbook for new employees. In addition, more seasoned staff members could read them; they are in an excellent position to contribute additional "truths" of their own that are specific to the practice and specialty.*

In most medical practices, new employees delve into the specifics of their jobs without getting the lay of the land.

Staff training, motivation, and management usually center on the specific policies and procedures that make a medical practice run smoothly. This is as it should be, because it is through policies and procedures that you will ensure that your patients are treated fairly, properly, and consistently.

However, before you delve too far into the specifics—for example, the nuts and bolts of appointment scheduling, financial arrangements, collections, insurance claims processing, and clinical procedures—it is a very good idea to try to give your new employees the proper perspective. Doing so will help them be better learners and will ultimately make them more motivated, better-informed employees.

Below are 25 basic underlying truths that are crucial to the success of any medical practice. You might make them part of your employee handbook and require that all new employees read and sign them. In addition, you may wish to review them with your current staff and ask them to help you add additional truths that are specific to your practice or specialty.

## 25 TRUTHS EVERY EMPLOYEE SHOULD KNOW

1. You are part of a team. No one person on our staff can single-handedly be responsible for the practice's success. One of your most important responsibilities in this job is to get along with your co-workers and to welcome new staff members to our practice.

2. The most important person in this practice is NOT:
   - the doctor.
   - the office manager.
   - the receptionist.
   - the bookkeeper.
   - the appointment secretary.
   - the nurse/nurse practitioner.
   - the lab technician.
   - any of your co-workers.
   - you.

   It is the **PATIENT**.

3. Every patient in this practice deserves to be treated with the utmost respect and as a welcomed guest. Be courteous to patients—always—and do your best to make every patient as comfortable as possible.

4. You are part of a top-quality operation. The doctor provides the best possible professional care for our patients. We do not cut corners or skimp. Similarly, you must insist on doing a first-rate job in everything you do, too.

> Before you delve too far into the specifics, it is a very good idea to try to give your new employees the proper perspective.

5. A professional office staff must look and act professional at all times. There is no room for carelessness in your appearance, conduct, manner, speech, or workstation.

6. As an employee in this practice, you must represent the doctor and the profession to the public. This is true both inside and outside the practice.

7. Patients' questions are important. You have an obligation to regard all questions and concerns as serious and valid. Never belittle or ignore a patient's questions or feelings, no matter how obvious or trivial they may seem.

8. Patients' fears and pain are real to them. If a patient is apprehensive about treatment or complains of experiencing pain or fear, those feelings deserve your respect. Never minimize or deny the way a patient feels.

9. What goes on in this practice is confidential. Everything you see and hear should not leave this office and should be discussed appropriately and only when necessary. Be mindful of who is around when you speak.

10. We need your complete loyalty. Do not talk about the doctor or a co-worker negatively either inside the practice to a fellow staff member or patient, or outside the practice. If you do not like something that's happened here, tell the doctor or office manager. That's the only way he or she will ever be able to do something about it.

11. The way you say things can make a tremendous difference in the way people will react. We must be especially careful when we talk to patients. Our language can either calm or aggravate their fears and concerns. Therefore, when you talk to them, try to use the most positive, professional language you possibly can (Table 1).

> "A professional office staff must look and act professonal at all times."

### TABLE 1.
### Using Positive, Professional Language

| Say or write this: | Instead of this: |
| --- | --- |
| Schedule change | Cancellation |
| Established patient | Old patient |
| Substantial investment | Expensive/high fee |
| Injection | Needle, shot |
| Medication | Drug |
| Reception area | Waiting room |
| Fee, investment | Price, cost |
| Interrupted schedule | Running late |
| Inconvenience | Trouble |
| Please help me understand. | What do you mean? |
| He's with a patient. | He's busy. |
| I appreciate how you feel. | You're wrong. |

TIP: *Add to this list your own preferred language for procedures and phrases specific to your practice or specialty. Your staff can help you come up with a list of preferred terminology tailored to your specific needs.*

12. As a member of this staff, your education should never stop. Seek worthwhile educational opportunities such as courses, seminars, conferences, lectures, training programs, and meetings. Read publications and books and listen to audio and videotape programs that will help you grow in your job. Ask your co-workers to teach you new skills.

13. Staff meetings are important, and you are expected to attend and participate in them. They keep us all informed of problems, new policies, and plans that are vital to continuing and expanding the success of the practice.

14. You are responsible for the tasks assigned to you. This is true even if you delegate part of a job to someone else.

15. We need your enthusiasm. If you're positive and confident, our patients and co-workers will pick up on that attitude. But if you're negative, complain, and carry a frown on your face, your attitude will be reflected here as well.

16. You will make mistakes, and that is perfectly understandable. However, you should have two goals. First, do your best to anticipate and prevent mistakes whenever you can. Get help when you're in over your head. And second, when you do make a mistake, admit it, take steps to correct it, and learn from it so you won't repeat it. Then, share what you've learned with your co-workers and the doctor so we don't make the same mistakes again.

17. Medical care may seem costly to you and to the patient. Nonetheless, we put quite a lot of thought into our fee schedule and feel that or our fees are fair and reasonable. They are based on much more than the cost of the materials and the equipment alone. Other variables include:

    - the time, skill, and education needed to perform the procedure,
    - the reputation the doctor has established by performing the procedure, and
    - the length of time the doctor has been in practice.

    If you're ever in doubt about the reasonableness or fairness of a particular fee, ask the doctor or office manager to explain it. You must feel confident about our fees to discuss them confidently with patients and to feel good about what we do.

18. A highly productive day in our practice doesn't happen by accident or luck. It depends upon careful planning and tight control of the appointment schedule. In addition, our productivity relies on our staying focused and on schedule.

19. Avoid negative assumptions about patients. For example, do not assume that a patient has financial difficulties, is not intelligent, is irresponsible,

> "You must feel confident about our fees to discuss them confidently with patients and to feel good about what we do."

---

**TABLE 2.**
## How to Present Information to Patients

| Ask this: | Instead of this: |
|---|---|
| Do you prefer a morning or afternoon appointment? | Would you like to make an appointment at this time? |
| Will that be check, cash, or credit card? | Would you like to pay for this now? |
| Would you like to hold a few moments or should I call you back? | Can you hold? |
| The doctor can see you in half an hour. Would you like to wait here? | The doctor can see you in half an hour. OK? |

---

or is a troublemaker based upon appearance or first impression. Give all patients the benefit of the doubt until they prove to you otherwise.

20. The doctor's time is one of the most valuable assets of this practice. You are here in large part to free the doctor so he or she can spend as much time as possible providing services to patients. Therefore, you should do everything in your power to prevent unnecessary interruptions of his/her work.

21. You must control the tasks you undertake, not the other way around. For example, you should control the appointment schedule, conversations with patients, financial arrangements, our collections system, your time, and your own career development. These will not control you unless you let them.

22. Whenever possible, present information to patients so they will give you the kind of response you truly want. Generally, that means that you'll need to phrase questions to them so they can't be answered with a simple *no* (Table 2).

23. Compliment patients whenever you can do so honestly. Don't lie, but praise or reinforce a patient if you possibly can. It will make him the patient feel terrific and communicate that you care.

24. Tell the doctor when a patient says anything negative about him/her or the practice. For example, a patient might complain about having to wait, difficulty finding a parking space or getting through on the telephone, a painful procedure, not understanding his/her treatment, the temperature in the office, or even the office location. Tell the doctor all of this, even when there's no apparent remedy for the complaint or if it seems to you to be unfounded. In addition, tell the doctor how you responded to the patient's complaint and when and how he or she lodged it.

For one thing, the patient's complaint is right to him/her, even if it is wrong to us. It deserves a response. For another, the doctor needs to know how patients feel, since their attitudes can affect the success of their treatment. But most importantly, telling the doctor about problems that exist in the practice will be the only way he/she can ever solve them.

> "You must control the tasks you undertake, not the other way around."

25. You do make a difference. Do not underestimate the impact you can have on patients, your co-workers, and on the practice as a whole. Put forth your best effort every day, even if it seems no one will notice the difference. Someone inevitably will.  ▲

"Do not underestimate the impact you can have on patients, your co-workers, and on the practice as a whole."

APPENDIX 3-B

# Staff Guidelines for Confidentiality and Privacy

*Every medical practice employee knows that personal information about patients is confidential. But what exactly does patient confidentiality mean? How can a medical practice employee keep from breaking a patient's confidence unintentionally? And how does an employee keep practice information other than that about patients confidential?*

*Certainly, confidentiality begins with a sensitive employee who doesn't gossip and doesn't share sensitive information with the wrong people. But guarding a patient's confidentiality is a bit more complex than that. This chapter suggests 25 of the more subtle points of confidentiality and privacy for employees in a medical practice. You may wish to include these guidelines in your personnel manual and/or distribute them at an upcoming staff meeting.*

"Say only what you must and only then, to the people who must hear it."

"Never talk in front of a patient as though he or she isn't there."

## 25 GUIDELINES FOR GUARDING CONFIDENTIALITY AND PRIVACY

1. **The walls have ears.** Don't talk about our patients or other confidential matters concerning the practice outside the office. Even if it is appropriate and necessary for you and another staff member to discuss a patient or his or her problems, needs, or circumstances, doing so in a restaurant, on a bus, in a store, or in any other public place is dangerous and invites others to listen.

2. **Reduce the risk of a confidence leak.** Don't discuss patients and their circumstances or problems any more than you have to to do your work. Say only what you must and only then, to the people who must hear it. The less you talk about a patient, the less opportunity there is for confidential information to leak out.

3. **Step into my office.** Do you help new patients complete their get-acquainted forms and health histories? If so, conduct your get-acquainted interviews in a quiet, private room away from the reception area. The information you need to complete such a form is confidential. Even simple questions about the patient's age or health history are personal.

4. **What's good for the goose.** The same is true of established patients in the practice. If you have sensitive or confidential questions to ask when they come to the reception desk for their appointments (such as asking them to describe their problems), invite them to meet with you in a private room to give you the needed information.

5. **Respect patient confidentiality on the phone.** Take confidential or sensitive telephone calls in a quiet, private area away fro the reception desk, patients, and other staff members. If the situation warrants it, offer to call back or ask the caller to wait while you transfer the call. He or she will appreciate your discretion and usually not object to waiting.

6. **No invisible patients, please.** Never talk in front of a patient as though he or she isn't there. This is not only rude but one of the best ways to let confidential information leak out.

7. **There's a time and place for everything.** When you do need to discuss confidential information with a fellow staff member, do so in an appropriate place in your office. The hallway or reception desk is generally not a good place. Be sure that the room where you're meeting has a closed door and that sound doesn't travel through the walls to the wrong ears. Keep your voice low.

8. **Even debtors have a right to confidentiality.** Don't share confidential information about patients with collection agencies. Agencies almost always ask you to provide them with a breakdown of a delinquent patient's financial record. When providing this record, don't supply too-

specific information about the patient's treatment. The best approach is a cautious one. Give a list of financial data and dates.

9. **Collection letters are confidential, too.** Don't send collection notices to a patient on postcards. Likewise, don't mail notices in envelopes that are printed with words or symbols denoting *collection*. Both actions are considered an invasion of the patient's right to privacy.

10. **Don't discuss debtors.** Don't discuss a patient's debt or financial arrangement with your practice with the patient's friends, employer, co-workers, or anyone else outside the practice except the patient himself, a collection agency, or an attorney.

11. **Guard your computer access password.** Choose a computer password that's easy to remember but unusual enough so it's hard to guess. Don't write it down. Change your password periodically.

12. **Use code numbers instead of names.** If an employee has access to computerized personnel records, use employee code numbers in place of names. This can deter employees from learning confidential information about one another.

13. **Right this way, please.** Escort all patients everywhere they have to go in the office. If an emergency requires you to leave the patient for a few minutes anywhere but the reception area, do not leave patient records available to that patient. Whenever possible, ask another staff member to cover for you.

14. **Label your own information as confidential.** If you tell a fellow staff member information about yourself that you'd like kept confidential, say so. That way you'll avoid misunderstandings.

15. **Let's not keep this between us.** Do not promise a patient that you'll keep information about him or her from the doctor. A good response: "Mr. Reed, I appreciate the sensitive nature of this situation and I do want to know very much. However, I also want to help you. I'll have to tell Dr. Wong because she'll want to do what is right for you." Pause and let the patient continue. In many instances, the patient will tell you anyway and you will avoid the unpleasant situation of being in the middle.

16. **Be wary of questions.** Don't supply confidential information about your patients or staff to creditors, employers, or other people who ask for it. If you're in doubt, refer such questions to the practice manager.

17. **Protect confidentiality in writing.** If you have a patient newsletter or news bulletin board, be sure you don't violate a patient's privacy or confidentiality in anything you write or post. If you wish to publish news or photographs about patients (birthdays, anniversaries, marriages, births, etc.), check first to get the patient's written permission. The same is true for news about fellow staff members.

> "When an employee is fired, tell inquiring patients that the employee is 'no longer with the practice' and leave it at that."

"Think before
you speak.
Simply, there
is no better
way to guard
confidentiality
and privacy."

18. **Other occasions for permission.** Also get patients' permission for any other practice marketing activities that involve them. For example, you may want to write about patients in press releases or talk about them in a speech. If so, get the permission of anyone involved before you proceed.

19. **Gone but not forgotten.** When an employee is fired, tell inquiring patients that the employee is "no longer with the practice" and leave it at that. Do not go into the circumstances or events that lead up to the dismissal or your own opinion.

20. **Deter snoopers.** Do not allow your computer screen to be viewed, intentionally or unintentionally, by unauthorized personnel. Exit all computer programs that might contain personal health information when leaving a computer workstation.

21. **Leave careful messages.** If you leave messages about your patients on an answering machine or voice mail system, be careful what of what you say. You never know who might hear the message.

22. **Watch what you say on a cell phone.** When you talk on a cell phone, your conversation might be picked up by strangers. Never give a patient's full name or address or other confidential over a cell phone.

23. **Don't call out.** Never call out any information that might be considered to be personal. For example, don't call out a diagnosis, test results, or test requirements.

24. **Know when to break a confidence.** It is important for you to share confidential information with the appropriate people in your practice if it involves a patient's health or well-being. For example, if a patient whispers to you that he or she is having chest pain but doesn't want anyone to know, do not keep that confidence. Tell the appropriate people right away.

25. **Think before you speak.** Simply, there is no better way to guard confidentiality and privacy in your medical practice. ▲

# INDEX